# ASSUME NOTHING

## Encounters with Assassins, Spies, Presidents, and Would-Be Masters of the Universe

Edward Jay Epstein

BOOKS

New York • London

First American edition published in 2023 by Encounter Books,
an activity of Encounter for Culture and Education, Inc.,
a nonprofit, tax-exempt corporation.
Encounter Books website address: www.encounterbooks.com

Manufactured in the United States and printed on
acid-free paper. The paper used in this publication meets
the minimum requirements of ANSI/NISO Z39.48-1992
(R 1997) (*Permanence of Paper*).

FIRST AMERICAN EDITION

Library of Congress Cataloging-in-Publication Data
is available for this title under the ISBN 978-1-64177-294-5


1  2  3  4  5  6  7  8  9  20  23

*For Susana Duncan*

In order to seek truth, it is necessary once in the course of our life to doubt, as far as possible, of all things.

—René Descartes

# CONTENTS

# PART ONE

# ON THE SERENDIPITY TRAIL

# CHAPTER ONE

# THE NABOKOV IMPERATIVE

I was born in Brooklyn, New York, on December 6, 1935, to well-to-do Jewish parents. My father was a financier in the fur trade; my mother, a talented sculptor. By the time I was 12, I was six feet two and 200 pounds. The accident of premature height, though only a temporary advantage that would ebb as I entered adulthood, conferred on me bold social confidence that would remain. A mediocre student, I went to four different schools in Brooklyn. The first was PS 99, whose experimental penmanship program that replaced script with block letters ruined my handwriting forever. After my father died at a very young age, my mother remarried, and I transferred to PS 139. On graduation, I went to Boys High School and transferred to Midwood High School. I attended Boys High School for only a day because of a loophole in New York's mandatory assignment system. I had been assigned to Erasmus, the high school for my Flatbush district, but I wanted to go to Midwood, a newer, less crowded and more highly regarded public school that was out of my district. With some enterprise, I discovered that any male student, if he objected to a coed school, could transfer to the city's aptly named Boys High School and, if he then changed his mind about an all-male education, could instantly transfer to any other school in Brooklyn.

3

Boys High School was in the heart of Bedford-Stuyvesant, which I saw was an unmistakably poor African American area. My walk from the trolley car stop to the high school was my first encounter with the reality of the urban world that lay beyond my protective cocoon in Flatbush. One hour after arriving there, I informed the admission office that I wanted to transfer to a coed school. My ploy worked. The next day I was enrolled in Midwood, located back in the cocoon a block from Brooklyn College. Two years later, my family moved to the suburban town of Rockville Centre on Long Island, which my mother and stepfather thought was a safer environment for children. I transferred to South Side High School. Unlike Midwood, it had extracurricular activities, and I joined the stamp club, which helped stoke my interest in foreign places and my wanderlust. I was able to get a driving license at the age of 16 in Rockville Centre, in contrast to the minimum age of 18 in New York City, and drive around Long Island, an activity that did not help with my grades.

When it came time to choose a college, I decided on Cornell, a university situated on top of a high hill overlooking Lake Cayuga in Upstate New York. Since I applied late, my stepfather turned to a connection at his country club to help me get in. About 60 Jewish businessmen, including my stepfather, had created the Cold Spring Harbor Country Club a few years earlier because many of the country clubs on Long Island did not admit Jews. As a remedy, they bought the Otto Kahn estate, complete with a castle, on the North Shore of Long Island, converted the elaborate stables into a clubhouse, and built an 18-hole golf course. I used to explore the empty castle, a smaller version of San Simeon, while my parents were playing golf before it was sold to a military academy. My stepfather's connection was Morris Ginsburg, another founding member. His son Martin, an ace golfer, was at Cornell and, at his father's request, vouched for me with the dean of admission. Favors like this were not uncommon at the golf club. Indeed, they were the coin of the realm there. Soon after I was admitted, I thanked Martin, whose fiancée at the time, Ruth Bader, went on to become a Supreme Court justice and a friend of my mother's at the country club.

In September 1953, I took the Lehigh Valley Railroad to Ithaca, to go to Cornell. It was the first time I had ever been away from home, and for the first year, I found it a disorienting, if necessary, transition to adulthood. The uniform for male students was dirty white bucks shoes, khaki slacks, button-down shirts, and rep ties. Coeds wore long skirts, cashmere sweaters, and, if they were dating someone, a fraternity pin.

At the beginning of my sophomore year, I wandered into Lit 311. It was not that I had any interest in European literature—or any literature. I was just shopping for a class that met on Monday, Wednesday, and Friday mornings so that I wouldn't have any Saturday classes. "Literature" also filled one of the requirements for graduation. Lit 311 was officially called European Literature of the Nineteenth Century but was unofficially known as "Dirty Lit" by the *Cornell Daily Sun* since it dealt with adultery in *Anna Karenina* and *Madame Bovary*.

The professor was Vladimir Nabokov, an émigré from the ruling class of czarist Russia. He had been born on April 22, 1899, in Saint Petersburg, then the capital of the Russian empire, and after he fled the Bolshevik Revolution in 1917, he moved first to the Ukraine Republic, then to Germany, France, and the United States, where he wound up teaching at Cornell. Not having met any European intellectuals, I was duly impressed. About six feet tall and balding, he stood, with what I took to be an aristocratic bearing, on the stage of the 250-seat lecture hall in Goldwin Smith. Facing him on the stage was his white-haired wife Vera, whom he identified only as "my course assistant." He made it clear from the first lecture that he had little interest in fraternizing with students, who would be known not by their names but by their seat numbers. Mine was 121. His only rule was that we could not leave his lecture, even to use the bathroom, without a doctor's note.

He then described his requisites for reading the assigned books. He said we did not need to know anything about their historical context and that we should under no circumstance identify with any of the characters in them, since novels are works of pure invention. The authors, he continued, had one and only one purpose: to enchant the reader. All we needed to appreciate them, aside from a pocket dictionary and a good memory, were our own spines. He assured us that the authors he had selected—Leo Tolstoy, Nikolai Gogol, Marcel Proust, James Joyce, Jane Austen, Franz Kafka, Gustave Flaubert, and Robert Louis Stevenson—would produce tingling we could detect there.

So began the course. Unfortunately, distracted by the gorges, lakes, movie houses, corridor dates, and other more local enchantments of Ithaca, I did not get around to reading any of *Anna Karenina* before Nabokov sprang a pop quiz. It consisted of an essay question: "Describe the train station in which Anna first met Vronsky."

Initially, I was stymied. Having not yet read the book, I did not know how Tolstoy had portrayed the station. But I did recall the station shown in the 1948 movie starring Vivien Leigh. I was able to visualize a vulnerable-looking Leigh in her black dress, wandering through the station. To fill the exam book, I described in detail everything shown in the movie, from a bearded vendor hawking tea in a potbellied copper samovar to two white doves nesting overhead. Only after the exam did I learn that many of the details I described from the movie were not to be found in the book. Evidently, director Julien Duvivier had had ideas of his own. Consequently, when Nabokov asked "seat 121" to report to his office after class, I fully expected to be failed, or even thrown out of Dirty Lit.

What I had not considered was Nabokov's theory that great novelists create pictures in the minds of their readers that go far beyond what they describe in the words in their books. In any case, since I was presumably the only one taking the exam to confirm his theory by describing images that were not in the book, and since he apparently had no idea of Duvivier's film, he not only gave me the numerical equivalent of an A but also offered me a one-day-a-week job as an "auxiliary course assistant." I was to be paid $10 a week. Oddly enough, it also involved movies.

Every Wednesday, the movies changed at the four theaters in downtown Ithaca. Nabokov referred to these theaters as "the near near," "the near far," "the far near," and "the far far." My task, which used up most of my weekly payment, was to see all four new movies on Wednesday and Thursday and then brief him on them on Friday morning. He said that since he had time to see only one movie, this briefing would help him decide which one of them, if any, to see. It was a perfect job for me: I got paid for seeing movies.

All went well for the next couple of months. I had caught up with the reading and greatly enjoyed my Friday morning chats with Nabokov in his office on the second floor of Goldwin Smith. Even though they rarely lasted more than five minutes, they made me the envy of the other students in Dirty Lit. Vera was usually sitting across the desk from him, making me feel as though I had interrupted their extended study date. My undoing came just after he had lectured on Gogol's *Dead Souls*.

The day before, I had seen *The Queen of Spades*, a 1949 British film based on Alexander Pushkin's 1833 short story. It concerned a Russian officer who, in his desperation to win at cards, murdered an elderly Russian countess while trying to learn her secret method of picking cards in the game of faro. He seemed uninterested in having me recount the plot, which he must have known well, but his head shot up when I said in conclusion that it reminded me of *Dead Souls*. Vera also turned around and stared directly at me. Peering intently at me, Nabokov asked, "Why do you think that?"

I instantly realized my remark apparently connected with a view he had, or was developing, concerning these two Russian writers. At that point, I should have left the office, making some excuse about needing to give the question more thought. Instead, I said pathetically, "They are both Russian."

His face dropped, and Vera turned back to face him. While my gig continued for several more weeks, it was never the same.

When I returned to Cornell the next year, a friend, who was a fledgling cataloger at the Cornell University Library, told me of her recent encounter with Nabokov. She explained that as a matter of practice, the library bought one copy of every trade book published. So it acquired a single copy of Nabokov's *Lolita*, which was just published by the Olympia Press in Paris, and my friend duly cataloged it, which put it in the university-wide system. No sooner had she done so than Nabokov dashed into the library and demanded it be removed. She called the director for backup. But Nabokov was insistent. He said the presence of the book in the library would jeopardize his career. The vehemence of Nabokov's reaction also might have proceeded from insecurity about his job. Despite his eminence, he lacked tenure at Cornell in 1955. In any case, he demanded that the book be instantly pulled from shelves. When the director told him that it had already been entered in the catalog, he shouted that it must be deaccessioned and its catalog card destroyed. But, as the director calmly explained, library rules made expunging of a book into nonexistence impossible. The best he could offer was putting *Lolita* in the so-called "locked press" section in which hard-core pornography was kept. Nabokov asked if students could access it there. The director replied that students would need to get special permission to read it. Not wanting *Lolita* thrown in with real pornography, Nabokov stormed out of the library in a temper tantrum.

Since I was having my own troubles with administration rules, I could sympathize with Nabokov's frustration in unsuccessfully tilting with the library administration. There was a silver lining: *Lolita* would become a number one best seller and be made into a movie by Stanley Kubrick.

I did not see Nabokov after he left Cornell in 1956, but I did read with great interest an extraordinary review he had written in 1950 that he had chosen not to publish. It was of his own memoir, then called *Conclusive Evidence* and later retitled *Speak, Memory*. What particularly spoke to me in that review was his observation, "The unravelling of a riddle is the purest and most basic act of the human mind." I took it as my personal imperative.

# CHAPTER TWO

# ENCOUNTERING THE CIA

On November 10, 1954, a story appeared on the front page of the *Cornell Daily Sun* that began, "The spirit of Prometheus was reincarnated and the campus and the routine of the arts school upset when, yesterday morning, Ed Epstein, '57, made a dramatic horse and buggy appearance for his 10 AM class in Boardman Hall."

As the story explained, the reason I elected this quaint form of transportation was that my driving privileges had been suspended for my sophomore year because I had transgressed the rules by having a car on campus my freshman year. Oddly enough, it was not that difficult finding a buggy in 1954 in Upstate New York. I went to several local farms, and, at the third one, the farmer offered to sell me both the buggy and a horse named Wisconsin for $200. Driving it onto campus had consequences though. I was put on probation and, when I refused to rein in my horse and buggy, double probation. I then gave the buggy and horse to a local farmer, but my probation was not lifted. It was the beginning of a downward spiral. I stopped attending classes, my grades plunged, and the following year I was asked to leave Cornell. I considered it a temporary setback.

Moving back to my parents' home, I was given a membership

to the Museum of Modern Art. I spent my days watching, over and over again, all the movies of Alfred Hitchcock in their chronological order. This peculiar education served me well when I later went to Harvard, where Hitchcock was the rage.

A man of leisure now, I decided to travel to Europe. I had the resources. When I was seven, my father died at the age of 28 while playing sudden-death overtime in a championship handball match in Brighton Beach. His death left me with both a phobia of participating in sports and a substantial sum of money that I would receive when I turned 21. Two years after his death, my mother remarried Louis J. Epstein, a shoe manufacturer. Louis was generous and kind to me, giving me his surname, so, at the age of 10, my name was legally changed from Edward Levinson to Edward Jay Epstein.

After I received my inheritance, I set out in 1957 on the Cunard Line's SS *Vulcania* for Trieste, where I picked up a Mercedes 180 coupe in the tax-free zone, intending to sell it at a profit in America (since I could bring it in duty-free as accompanied baggage on a boat).

In September 1958, I was in Paris attempting, without success, to learn French at the Alliance Française. Bored with my classes, I had my first weeklong glimpse into the postwar intellectual-political complex. It came about because I had a car, which a film producer desperately needed to get to Greece to make a film on the island of Rhodes. The producer was Thomas Rowe, an American expatriate documentarian I had just met at the Café Flore. The film was to be made up of interviews of high-powered politicians, editors, and writers who were coming to an event organized by the Congress for Cultural Freedom. "Who?" I asked.

He reeled off names of a dozen or so of the interviewees. They included Hugh Gaitskell, then leader of the Labour Party in Britain; Walter Reuther, the head of the powerful United Automobile Workers union; Moshe Sharett, the former prime minister of Israel; Prince

Kukrit Pramoj, a book publisher in Thailand; Raymond Aron, the French author of *The Opium of the Intellectuals*; Stephen Spender, the British poet laureate and coeditor of *Encounter*; Richard Rovere, the Washington correspondent of the *New Yorker*; Edward Shils, the editor of *Minerva*; and John Kenneth Galbraith, the Harvard economist and author of *The Affluent Society*. These men—politicians, philosophers, academics, and journalists—had one thing in common: they were all part of the non-Communist left.

Rowe also told me that he had an urgent problem: the $25,000 budget for the film he had received from foundation grants did not include travel expenses to Athens for himself, his crew, and the filming equipment. He had tried to make a product placement deal with Olympic Airlines (which was then owned by Aristotle Onassis), but he learned the day before our fateful coffee that the Olympic deal had fallen through, leaving him with no money to get to Greece. As I had a car and nothing to do, I offered to drive him, his crew, and his equipment there. I had no reason to stay in Paris and I needed a credential for my empty résumé. I wanted him to put me on the production crew in Rhodes. "You got a deal," he said. "You will be the interview assistant."

I had to pay all my expenses including gas, tolls, and the ferryboat charge. The Congress for Cultural Freedom only paid for my room at the Grand Hotel de Roses, a luxury Venetian-style hotel built in 1927 when Rhodes was under Italian occupation.

My job as "interview assistant" consisted of carrying the cans of film to and from the location every morning and positioning the canvas deck chairs for the guests, the interviewer, and Tom Rowe, who was both the director and producer. My only other duty was to fetch glasses of water for the interviewees.

The first interview was with John Kenneth Galbraith, a six-foot, nine-inch giant of a man with a craggy face and unruly gray hair. Born in 1908 in Ontario to Canadian farmers of Scottish descent, he got his PhD in agricultural economics from the University of California, Berkeley. He had worked for the Office of Price Administration during World War II and then became a professor at Harvard. Spry and ironic, with a great sense of humor, he provided by far the liveliest interview.

The interviewer, whose fee made up a hefty part of the budget, was Woodrow Wyatt, the cohost of the BBC program *Panorama*. Born on America's Independence Day in 1918, he was named after the American president Woodrow Wilson. He attended Oxford, fought in World War II, and, in 1945, was elected to Parliament as a Labour MP. Wyatt went on, as I only learned later, to work for the Information Research Department (IRD), a secret branch of the UK Foreign Office that engaged in state-sponsored disinformation, before becoming a producer for *Panorama*. I spent a good deal of time with him since he arrived early in Rhodes. He was a short, stout man who waddled and flapped his hands, reminding me of an irate penguin. He brought with him to Rhodes his young wife, Moorea Hastings Wyatt. Exceedingly tall, lithe, and beautiful, Moorea was also an aristocrat, the daughter of the sixteenth Earl of Huntingdon. While Wyatt was interviewing intellectuals at various locations, Moorea spent her days at the beach in front of the hotel. After each filming session I also went to the beach, where I befriended stray intellectuals. It was my first networking opportunity, and I wrote to my parents about it. Since my mother saved my typed letters from Rhodes in an album, I can quote from them. In one I reported, "I sat on the beach with Gunnar Myrdal and [Robert] Hutchins and discussed politics." Myrdal was the Swedish economist whose famous book, *An American Dilemma: The Negro Problem and Modern Democracy*, would be cited by Earl Warren in *Brown v. Board of Education*, and was now the head of the UN Economic Commission for Europe (he would win the Nobel Prize for Economics in 1974). Hutchins, a former president of the University of Chicago, was head of the Ford Foundation. If I discussed any political topic with these eminent thinkers, as I reported to my mother, it could only have been tidbits of what I had heard in the filmed interviews.

The main excitement on the beach came when Woodrow Wyatt, dressed in a heavy suit, came on the beach frantically looking for his wife. It turned out Moorea, apparently bored with the beach talk, had flown to Italy with Galbraith without informing Wyatt. (A few years later, when Kennedy became president in 1961, he appointed Galbraith the US ambassador to India.)

As the Congress for Cultural Freedom event wrapped up, I had time to get to know its organizers, including Julius "Junkie" Fleischmann, whose Fairfield Foundation was writing the checks for the conference, and Nicolas Nabokov, who was the Paris-based secretary-general for the Congress for Cultural Freedom.

Nabokov, a composer who born in 1903 in czarist Russia, was a first cousin of Vladimir Nabokov. After I told him about my gig as a movie reviewer for his cousin at Cornell, he invited me for a drink at the Grand Hotel of Roses. As we sipped ice tea on the terrace, he told me that he had just finished an opera, "Rasputin's End," whose libretto was written by Stephen Spender (also at the conference). Before we could get to the subject of his cousin's book *Lolita*, an athletic-looking man in sunglasses joined us. Nabokov, who seemed well acquainted with him, introduced him as Clint Hunt. I had not seen him before and asked if he was part of the conference.

He answered in a slow drawl that he was the "conference expeditor." I shrugged: "Whatever."

He then asked what I was doing in the film.

I answered, "Interview assistant."

"I'm not sure I've heard of that job description before," he said, finally taking off his glasses.

"I am not sure I ever heard of a conference expeditor before."

He turned to Nabokov and spoke in a whisper of an "urgent matter," and they both excused themselves and left.

Although my suspicions were aroused by these men, I had not yet developed journalistic ambitions and so only noted in my diary about this odd encounter, "This Rhodes gathering gets curiouser by the day." I learned seven years later, when *Ramparts* magazine sensationally revealed that the Congress for Cultural Freedom was partly a CIA front and that John Clinton "Clint" Hunt was one of the CIA officers involved in the operation, that I had missed one of the biggest coups of the Cold War.

The documentary was not a great success. As it turned out, its entire soundtrack, which had been recorded directly onto the film, had somehow been destroyed in a lab accident. So ended my short but educational career as an interview assistant.

When I returned to New York that October, I decided to get business cards for myself. Since Clint Hunt had looked with suspicion on my title "Interview Assistant," I identified myself on my cards, more in wishful thinking than reality, as "Producer." I believed it was a step up.

# CHAPTER THREE

# MY *ILIAD*

Finally, on September 11, 1961, after three years of seeking a calling in life, I had justified the movie producer title on my extravagantly printed business card. The movie was *The Iliad*. The production included a cast of 1,200 extras, provided by the Greek government. The crew, which arrived from Munich in early September, included Werner Kurz, a director of photography; Karl Baumgartner, a special effects supervisor experienced with playing with fire; and one Pia Arnold, a script supervisor. We began shooting the film on September 9 at Tolon, a beach about 120 miles from Athens.

My far more talented collaborator was Susan Brockman, with whom I had fallen head over heels in love at Cornell four years earlier. I had met Susan, standing alone in the lobby of Willard Straight Hall, the student union. She was looking so intently at a mural depicting a youth trying to subdue a unicorn that she didn't notice me. I asked her if she identified with the youth or the unicorn. Without turning her head, she answered the unicorn. When I tried to keep the conversation alive by saying unicorns don't exist, she replied, walking away, "Neither do I."

Despite that inauspicious beginning, I persisted with a tenacity of which I did not know I was capable. As I got to know her, I realized that though we had come to Cornell from fairly similar Jewish middle-class backgrounds in Brooklyn, she had ascended to a world that I had only read about in books and magazines. She knew such illustrious figures as the surrealist Salvador Dali, who, while I watched, splattered an egg on the wall of her home in New York to gift her what he called an "original Dali"; the conductor Leopold Stokowski, who invited her to all his performances at the New York Philharmonic; the photographer Robert Frank; and the abstract expressionist Willem de Kooning, who was pursuing her. When I was temporarily suspended from Cornell in 1956, I had no idea what to do with my idle days or how to continue seeing Susan. I asked her if she had an ambition and, to my utter surprise, she said that she had always dreamed of playing the part Helen of Troy in a movie of *The Iliad*. A few weeks later, I read a *New York Times* story saying that Zervos Pictures in Athens and Mosfilms in Moscow had tentatively agreed to make a Russian-Greek coproduction of *The Iliad*. I was taken by an absolutely insane idea: If I produced *The Iliad*, I could cast Susan as Helen of Troy. Seizing the opportunity, I dashed off a telegram to Zervos Pictures in Athens:

IF YOU ARE NOT IRREVOCABLY COMMITTED TO THE RUSSIANS, WOULD YOU CONSIDER DOING INSTEAD AN AMERICAN COPRODUCTION WITH MARLON BRANDO AS ACHILLES, JAMES MASON AS AGAMEMNON, RICHARD BOONE AS ODYSSEUS AND SUSAN BROCKMAN AS HELEN OF TROY.

I could not send it immediately because I was concerned about my return address. I was living at my parents' home in Rockville Centre and feared that asking Zervos to reply to Ed Epstein c/o Betty & Lou Epstein might cast my credibility as a producer into question. Susan's sorority house at Cornell,

Alpha Epsilon Phi, had a similar problem, but Susan found the solution: her father.

David Brockman, a successful financier, had an impressive cable address: Gilesact New York, which I used as my return address. About a week later, David Brockman received a telegram from George Zervos, the president of Zervos Pictures:

I AM WILLING TO PUT UP 7 MILLION DOLLARS FOR BELOW-
THE-LINE PRODUCTION STOP PREFER TO DO THE ILIAD
WITH EPSTEIN'S COMPANY INSTEAD OF THE RUSSIANS.

As David Brockman had not seen my original telegram offering to provide Marlon Brando, he was impressed that someone would offer a friend of his daughter $7 million (the equivalent of $56 million in 2022). He asked Susan to arrange for me to meet him and Arnold Krakower, a successful New York divorce lawyer. The meeting then expanded to include another of Brockman's business associates, Ben Javits.

Ben was the brother, éminence grise, and law partner (Javits & Javits) of New York senator Jacob Javits. He reveled in the idea of influencing world events, or at least Grecian ones, by blocking a Russian coproduction. He offered to have his brother write letters to everyone who mattered in Greece.

Even though I had not previously conceived of my adventure as part of the Cold War, I accepted his offer. Why not block the Russians? At Krakower's suggestion, we formed a partnership—Iliad Productions, Inc.—in which Javits, Brockman, and Krakower would provide the initial money for preproduction.

"You have to go to Athens right away," Javits said with urgency.

On September 15, 1959, Susan and I made our initial trip to Greece. Her father, who owned a travel agency among many other companies, provided us with first-class tickets to Athens on a KLM "sleeper" flight. As promised, Javits had opened every door for us. Over the next week, we met government ministers, shipping magnates, and others in the Athens power elite who had responded to Javits's letters. We had a great time being wined and dined in tavernas.

The first deal I made was with Spyros D. Skouras, the namesake nephew of Spyros Skouras, chairman of 20th Century Fox. Skouras owned a local film studio in Athens (Skouras Films), as well as the lucrative Eastman Kodak film franchise for all of Greece. After he listened to my plan for *The Iliad*, he asked who would play Achilles. When he heard Brando's name, he became so excited that he wanted to sign a contract that day.

"Forget Zervos, forget the Russians. I will be your partner—but you must get Brando."

I told him Brando had not yet agreed.

"He will," Skouras said.

Two days later, Skouras and I signed a memorandum of understanding stipulating that I would supply Brando, the script, and the director, and Skouras would pay for the production in Greece. Next, Minister of Industry Nikolaos Martis, moved by Javits's letter, offered a battalion of soldiers from the Greek army, horses from the King's Guards, and whatever else I needed. He then said he would also like to host a small dinner at his home for Brando.

"When will Marlon arrive?"

I explained that Brando would need to approve the script.

"Just give him Homer's *Iliad* to read," Minister Martis suggested. He wrote a letter stating, "I will do everything in my power to ensure that every reasonable facility is provided by the authorities."

With this impressive-looking letter from Minister Martis and the agreement with Skouras Films, Susan and I triumphantly returned to New York. A telegram was waiting from Skouras:

DEAR ED, IT HAS BECOME AN OBSESSION WITH ME. WE MUST GET BRANDO FOR OUR PICTURE...SPYROS.

By this time Arnold Krakower had taken a hand in the search for a director. He suggested Sidney Lumet, whose divorce from Gloria Vanderbilt he was then handling. To accommodate Krakower, Lumet invited me for breakfast at his penthouse at 10 Gracie Square, which overlooked the mayor's mansion.

Lumet, though only 36, was no amateur. The son of an actor and a dancer, he had made his stage debut in 1928 (at the age of four) at the Yiddish Art Theater. He had been nominated for an Academy Award for directing *Twelve Angry Men.*

After selecting my breakfast from a large platter of smoked salmon, I asked him about Brando, whom he had just directed in *The Fugitive Kind.* He said Brando would be perfect, and he would be "keenly interested" in directing it once Brando signed on.

"Do you have a script?"

"I'm still working on it."

In fact, all I had was a 30-page treatment written on spec by a very talented playwright, Sloane Elliott, an aficionado of Homer who had traveled to almost all the Greek islands. He was not, however, interested in writing a shooting script. A script was not my only problem.

"Once you have a script, you will need to put $500,000 in an escrow account before Brando's agent, Audrey Wood, will allow him to read a page of it."

I had neither a script nor $500,000. Having made these cold facts of the conventional movie business clear to me, Lumet politely ended the breakfast and walked me to the elevator. While awaiting it, I told him that the Greek government was providing its army for the battle scenes and that Spyros Skouras was willing to finance the shooting of those scenes.

"I guess you could shoot the battle scenes with a second unit," he said, as the elevator doors opened.

"With Achilles wearing a mask?" I asked. "So Brando could still be used by the first unit?"

"Let's see how they turn out. Bye."

I decided on a new strategy: first, I'd shoot the battle scenes in Greece with a Greek unit and then get Lumet to direct Brando in a studio in America. Yet I still had to worry about the United States. Having been suspended from Cornell, I could be drafted at any moment. The alternative to the draft was joining a reserve unit, but, given the number of men with the same idea, all the reserve units had long waiting lists.

As it happened, my cousin David Rockower had the means to jump the cue; he knew the civilian administrator at the 442nd Army Reserve unit in New York, Mario Puzo. So I paid Mario $50 to jump the queue. Though only 39, Puzo was overweight and balding with unkempt hair, but he had a sort of street wisdom I did not. He would take me over the next five years to places I otherwise would not have seen, such as an illicit high-stakes poker game in Hell's Kitchen, my first, a bookie parlor in the Bronx, and a Mafia-favored restaurant on Mulberry Street in lower Manhattan. He also introduced me to his pal Joseph Heller, whose *Catch-22* was one of my favorite books, at his "Gourmet Club" dinner in Chinatown. When he told me he was a writer for magazines with names like *Stag*, I told him I desperately needed a screenwriter for *The Iliad*. A deal was instantly struck to kill two birds with a single stone: Mario would slip me out of my reserve unit in such a way that it would not interfere with my activities as a movie producer; I would pay Mario $400 for a 40-page shooting script for the battle scenes. After I brought Puzo to meet Krakower, he said, "I'll give him the $400 and a contract, but no one will ever believe this guy is a writer." Puzo did deliver, however, the promised script.

Krakower showed no enthusiasm for a bifurcated movie. "You need a single director," he said authoritatively. He then found a candidate: Lewis Milestone. Milestone was an old-timer par excellence. In 1927, he had won the first (and only) Academy Award given for

Best Comedy Director. Krakower had recently met Milestone at a Hollywood dinner, and Milestone had complained that because of age discrimination he could not get a picture to direct. Krakower proposed *The Iliad* and Milestone showed "real interest in getting back in the game," as Krakower put it.

After our initial meeting, at which I gave him Puzo's script, Milestone and I carried on a month-long correspondence about Homer. On first reading Homer's *The Iliad* the previous year, I had envisioned the foot soldiers like pawns in a chess game. They were protected from the front by giant ox-hide shields but without armor, entirely vulnerable from the rear. In my concept, only the heroes—Achilles, Ajax, Hector, and Diomedes—had bronze armor. Once a hero cut his way through the line of enemy shields, he could slaughter the entire Trojan army unless opposed by an enemy hero, also in armor. This disparity could visually explain why heroes play such a decisive role in *The Iliad*.

Milestone—who had won an Oscar for *All Quiet on the Western Front* in 1930—found my idea impractical. After I described the shields in more detail in "production notes for *The Iliad*," he wrote back, on March 18, 1960:

> The prospect of doing *The Iliad* is exciting and inspiring and my interest could not be more thoroughly aroused. However…your notes state that the extras will carry giant shields from which only their naked feet and head protrude. I must assume that the author of that sentence does not expect an extra to fall, nor to turn around, nor to pass the camera and be photographed from the rear.

Milestone had 30 years of experience as an action director, but I had an idée fixe. When he decided not to direct after discovering I had no funds to pay him, I proceeded with my giant shield obsession.

Returning to the idea of splitting the movie, I assumed, without any real basis, that I could find a Greek second unit director for the battle scenes and later induce Lumet to take over as director.

On July 15, I returned to Greece with Susan. She would supervise the design of the costumes, chariots, and other artwork. She took the costume design from vases she found in museums. They were loincloths, helmets, and sandals. We used student interns from the art school to fit them to the soldiers.

By this time I had raised $50,000 from Brockman, Krakower, Sloane Elliott, and my stepfather. We also got our plane ticket gratis from Brockman's travel agency, We moved into the King George Hotel, where the owner, George Calcannis, anticipating the arrival of Marlon Brando, had given us the bridal suite. Finding the right location for *The Iliad* proved much more time-consuming than I had anticipated. In late July, the Greek navy provided us with a spare gunboat, the BB36, to scout locations on various islands. We saw almost as many islands as Odysseus—Skiros, Andros, Hydra, Patmos, Lesbos, and Thera—all with beautiful beaches, but none had the requisite electricity, hotels, or airport connection. Fortunately, by the time we returned from our futile search, Minister Martis had found the ideal location: a not-yet-occupied hotel on a deserted beach at Tolon that the Ministry of Tourism would provide free.

"Brando will be the first guest," he added.

Meanwhile, the Greek Defense Ministry had appointed a colonel as our liaison with the Greek army. I drew call sheets based on both Puzo's treatment and my imagination specifying how many extras were needed each day.

The script opened with a huge battle around the Greeks' beached ships. For that spectacular scene, Susan and I had meticulously assembled ships, 500 shields, 2,000 costumes, and the other requisites. The Greek government had been most cooperative. For ships, the port of Piraeus contributed six waterlogged hulls long sunk in a caïque graveyard outside the harbor. Shipping tycoon

Stavros Niarchos contributed a floating crane to raise and load the hulls onto an LST landing craft—the L188—supplied by the Greek navy. The LST ferried them to the location. (Unfortunately, the LST broke its propeller unloading the cargo in shallow water.) Local authorities supplied a work gang of prisoners to reconstruct the ships. For masts, I had the prisoners borrow telephone poles from the surrounding area (temporarily interrupting local telephone service).

At this point, with shooting scheduled to commence in two weeks, I still had to fill the directorial gap. I cabled the London talent agency that was supplying me with three stuntmen in September. Could it also supply a second unit director? Enter, on September 7, Desmond O'Donovan, an ebullient Irishman with a great gift of gab. He told me he had produced a British TV show about a dog called *Whirligig* when he was just a teenager and, more recently, had worked (unaccredited) with his half-brother Kevin McClory on *Around the World in 80 Days*. With just five days to go before shooting, I was in no position to challenge even these scant credentials. So I sent him by taxi, along with the three stuntmen—Joe Powell, Pat Crane, and Frank Haydon—directly from the airport in Athens to the free hotel in Tolon.

O'Donovan decided that it was too cloudy to shoot battle scenes. Instead of following the script, he wrote a "weather contingency" scene in which a dog snatches a piece of meat from a pot at a campfire. He said it would provide a "cinematic metaphor" to depict the hard times the Greeks were suffering in their siege of Troy. In the aptly named Apollo screening room in Athens, I watched the results of this contingency with horror. There were 37 retakes of the mangy dog.

Meanwhile, I was being billed daily for the cases of orangeade and mounds of shish kebab the 1,200 hungry extras consumed while waiting for the sun, draining a significant portion of my $36,000 production budget.

Watching the rushes with me were three visitors from Hollywood: Polish-born Rudy Mate, Russian-born George St. George, and a 19-year-old Italian actress, Maria. (I never learned her last name.) Rudy Mate had been a legendary cinematographer—photographing Dryer's classic *The Passion of Joan of Arc*—before becoming a Hollywood hack director. He was in Athens to scout locations for his next film, *The Lion of Sparta*. George St. George—who had escaped the Russian Revolution via Shanghai and wound up in Hollywood—was Rudy's producer and sidekick. Maria was, as became clear, Rudy's lover. I had met them earlier in the day in the lobby of the Hotel Grande Bretagne and invited them to the screening.

"Interesting," Rudy said after the dog's twentieth lunge at the bone. (I later learned from Maria that "interesting" was Rudy's code word for "awful.")

"I'm not sure I am familiar with this director, O'Donovan."

"It is his first film," I replied. I added that the script was also by a first-time writer. His name was Mario Puzo.

"How did you get the Greek army?" asked George, intrigued by the cooperation I was getting from the Greek government.

"How did you get into this mess?" asked Maria, more to the point.

Over dessert in Cafe Floca, I explained how what had begun as a love story had turned into an organized flight from reality, with me as tour leader.

"That's how we got the dog scene," I concluded.

"Fascinating," Rudy said. He, Maria, and George rose in unison to leave the Floca. "By the way, I wouldn't want to contradict your director, but the best battle scenes I've shot were in cloudy weather."

When I went back to Tolon, I gave O'Donovan new marching orders. Tomorrow, without any further delays, he was to shoot the establishing shot for the battle of the ships, which, according to Puzo's script, was to be shot from a platform mounted in the water.

"I wish that it was possible, but you can see it's going to be overcast tomorrow," he said, pointing to the night's sky. "But don't worry. I have written a great contingency scene. It has a magnificent-looking old man—he must be ninety—tussling with the dog for his bone. It represents…"

"No old man, no dog, no more metaphors," I angrily interrupted. Since Rudy Mate had told me his best shots in *The Passion of Joan of Arc* were shot in cloudy weather, I said, "Clouds or no clouds, rain or shine, shoot the battle scene."

Kurz then raised the issue of his reputation as a cinematographer (even though previously he had only been a camera operator). "I will shoot in bad weather if you insist, but I will not put my name on the clapboard."

"Neither will I," O'Donovan said, his gaze still fixed on the set carpenter's 15-year-old daughter.

"Put my name on the clapboard as both cinematographer and director," I volunteered, thereby expanding my portfolio of credits.

Not having been on a movie set before, I had no idea how long it would take to prepare 1,200 extras for a single shot. At 7:00 a.m., the student interns from Athens began the somewhat precarious job of fitting the Greek soldiers into loincloths.

What made the task dicey was that Susan had meticulously copied the Trojan loincloth from a highly stylized vase in the Knossos museum that depicted a row of wasp-waisted Minoan warriors. But modern Greek soldiers did not have the same hourglass figure. Given the embarrassing mismatch, most of the extras insisted on wearing their polka-dotted boxer shorts under the loincloths, forcing the student dressers to make the necessary alterations on hundreds of the plumper (or less exhibitionistic) soldiers.

Building the camera platform on pylons during low tide was also time-consuming. The carpenters waded out to the half-sunk LST landing ship and, using it as a seaward base, began building the platform. They tested it by jumping on it, then rebuilding it when it collapsed.

Onshore, meanwhile, my German pyrotechnician, Herr Baumgarten, used a squad of prison volunteers to load each of the six ships with a ton of kerosene-soaked tires from a nearby waste dump. He then taught them how to smear incendiary napalm on the ship's masts and railings. The stuntmen supervised the erection of stacks of cardboard boxes that would break their fall when they leaped from the fiery decks.

By noon, the wranglers were still struggling to attach two large (and rearing) white horses, supplied by the King's Guards, to a flimsy chariot built by the local blacksmith. The problem again proceeded from Susan's brilliant effort to get life to imitate art. As with the loincloths, Susan had taken the design from a beautiful Mycenaean vase. Our imitation of this chariot overlooked the fact that horses had changed in 3,000 years.

Finally, at 3:00 p.m., after the crew had had their lunch, they waded out to the platform in a rising tide. Kurz tested the camera and signaled that it worked. O'Donovan signaled the assistant director, Eric Andreo. Baumgarten set the ships afire. The extras, all in position, raised their shields. The camera rolled. The clapboard—with my name on it—clapped "Take 1."

"Mache!" shouted Andreo over and over again. *War!* The soldiers did not move. It was a mutiny. They claimed the sand was too hot for their bare feet.

"Cut!" shouted O'Donovan.

While the dressers scrounged up sandals and rags for the soldiers to wear, Baumgarten's crews put out the fires, which was not difficult since the telephone poles and prow heads had already burnt to a crisp. The prisoners sent out a foraging party to gather more telephone poles from the road to Athens (thus adding to the area's communications failures).

Meanwhile, the tide had risen nearly to the level of the camera platform. It was now 5:00 p.m. The army was again placed in position, but this time, at my suggestion, the untested chariot (driven by Joe Powell) was set just behind the extras.

The fires were relit, the camera rolled, the clapboard clapped "Take 2," and the wranglers released the chariot from the guide ropes. The horses reared, hoofs flashing.

"Mache!" Andreo shouted. This time the soldiers charged forward into the gauntlet of burning ships, pursued by the chariot. The expressions of fear on their faces were not entirely pretense: they, like everyone else on the set, knew that the chariot had no brakes and was completely out of control.

"Cut! Great. Print it," O'Donovan yelled, along with his one Greek word: "Efcharisto" (thank you).

Water now partly submerged the camera platform.

Then, finally, it happened. Six ships on the beach, doused in napalm, were set on fire. Since their hulls were waterlogged from the many years they had spent beneath the Aegean, all that burned were the local telephone poles and the plywood prow heads. And 1,200 scared Greek solders wearing loincloths and helmets ran into the blazing gauntlet between what remained of the ships.

O'Donovan strolled over to me in a bathing suit and suggested cutting out the Myrmidons, proposing to write a "cover scene" in which an old man with a lyre sings of the Myrmidons rescuing the ships. "It would be like the gods intervening."

"Shoot the charge of the Myrmidons," I insisted.

So Achilles's Myrmidon contingent, carrying huge figure-eight shields that made them look like a swarm of ants, charged onto the beach toward the Greek ships. But, as in the last five takes, many of the extras stumbled or fell under the weight of their shields. Others stopped dead in their tracks. O'Donovan again yelled, "Cut."

It was clear, alas, that Milestone had been right. As magnificent as the shields looked when stationary—an army of ant-men silhouetted on a ridge—they caused chaos in motion. Not only did they restrict the movement of the soldiers (not even the fear of the snorting chariot horses could prod them to run), but they also limited the angle of the camera.

Such unplanned battle scenes could not go on. "We are out of telephone poles," the assistant director informed me. Apparently, the production inferno had consumed every pole for 30 kilometers. I suggested burning more rubber tires to mask the background ships in a cloud of smoke.

"Baumgarten says we are out of tires—and napalm," Andreo added.

I suggested using diesel fuel from the LST, reasoning that with a smashed propeller it did not need fuel. Andreo sent the special effects crew out to get the fuel.

As the sun set, the special effects crew doused the ship in navy diesel oil, which Baumgarten somehow managed to ignite. The smoke began rising.

The soldiers again picked up their shields, the clapboard clapped "Take 7," and I quietly slipped away. I had seen enough takes of the battle of the ships. I headed back to Athens to look at the new footage—and to consult again with Rudy Mate.

"The minister would like to know if Brando is in Greece," said Spyros, Interior Minister Marti's persistent assistant. Despite the report of a sighting of Brando reported in the English-language *Athens News*, I assured Spyros—as I had the hotel owner, the tourism minister, the army liaison, and the waiter at Cafe Floca—that it was a false sighting.

Nor would he likely arrive during my stay: I planned to depart Athens the next day for New York.

Back at the location, O'Donovan informed me he had exhausted the supply of diesel fuel from the LST as well as German napalm, junkyard tires, plywood prow heads, rope nets, and cardboard boxes (to break the fall of the stuntmen). The work crew of prisoners had also so denuded the region of telephone poles that the telephone company had declared a state of emergency.

Nor were there any extras. The previous day, the colonel, who would go on to join the junta that overthrew the Greek government, had not only withdrawn the 1,200 troops but informed me as well that Iliad Productions would be billed for the expenses, including the missing diesel oil and the propeller for the stranded LST landing craft.

O'Donovan, who was still planning on shooting his "contingency scene" of an old man and a dog, was disappointed when I told him the shoot had ended and there was a bus was waiting to transport him, the three stuntmen, and the German technicians to the airport.

"What about our wrap party?" he asked.

"Have it on the bus," I offered.

For me, reality was beginning to poke its finger through the haze. All the money invested in *The Iliad* was gone—even the $20,000 supplement Susan's father had generously added the week before. My Diners Club card was fatally encumbered with debt, including charges for the crew's air tickets to Germany. I anticipated with dread the scary bill that would arrive any day from the Defense Ministry for disabling its one and only landing craft.

Susan, who had seen the rushes the previous night, was rightly concerned about the many gaps in the battle of the ships. She wanted to know why I ended the shoot so abruptly.

"Rudy Mate told me it was enough for a great battle scene," I said to reassure her. In truth, Mate's advice, after seeing all the footage, was expressed in a single word: "Enough."

"But will you be able to do the rest of the movie in a studio?"

"First, let's get it edited," I temporized, spotting the huge frame of Spyros Skouras rising from a nearby table and approaching us.

"Is it true Brando arrives tomorrow?" Skouras asked. "Everyone is waiting…"

It was clearly time to leave Greece—Susan agreed.

Soon after Susan and I returned to New York in October 1961, she moved to East Hampton, to try her hand at avant-garde art. Her parents had a home on Huntting Lane near the ocean and invited me to stay there so we could attempt to write a new screenplay of *The Iliad*. The home had a small theater in the basement, which Susan used to act out the Helen of Troy scenes. In early 1962, Susan told me that she had become romantically involved with Willem de Kooning. With little on the horizon in New York, I decided to return to Europe.

I rented a one-room apartment on Viale Dei Parioli in Rome. I chose Rome because George St. George and Rudy Mate were there completing the postproduction work on their movie *Lion of Sparta* at Cinecittà, then the epicenter of sword-and-sandals epics. I thought that if I could find an Italian producer willing to resuscitate *The Iliad* and found a way to finish the film, I might be able to win back Susan. I met numerous producers but, unlike the Greeks, they required more than Lattimore's translation of *The Iliad*, Puzo's treatment, and the hope of getting Brando. Nor were they impressed with the battle scene footage.

I came up with the idea of a movie in which *The Iliad* would be told from the prophetic point of view of Cassandra. It would be called *Cassandra's Iliad*. I even found a possible Cassandra, Marie Devereux, who had been a body double for Elizabeth Taylor in *Cleopatra*. I met her on the set at Cinecittà and offered her the part. When I asked Puzo to write a screenplay for *Cassandra's Iliad*, he turned me down cold, saying he was no longer interested in writing a movie that didn't get produced. He wanted to write novels. He said he had an idea of a Mafia version of Dostoyevsky's *The Brothers Karamazov*, which he considered the most powerful book ever written about power.

I next turned to my friend Sloane Elliott, who was a playwright, independently wealthy, and a scholar of Greek archeology. Sloane had earlier expanded Puzo's initial treatment for *The Iliad* into a screenplay and, to help finance the project, invested $10,000 in it. Even though he never recovered a penny, it was not a total loss. When he came to Greece in 1961 for the shooting of the battle scenes, he fell in love with Drusilla Vassiliou, the daughter of the movie's production designer, married her, and moved to Greece. I now outlined to him my idea for telling *The Iliad* from Cassandra's point of view. "Would you be interested in writing the screenplay?" I asked.

He replied with his own question: "Haven't you spent enough time on *The Iliad*? You need to move on."

He was right. As the Arabs say, when you've dug yourself in a hole, stop digging. Not only had I failed at producing *The Iliad*, but I had also used up every penny of the modest inheritance of $6,000 I had received on turning 21. I could charge dinners on my Diners Club card, but I couldn't pay the bill when it came due. The question was, move on to what?

When we were working on *The Iliad* in Athens in 1960, Susan Brockman and I met Constantinos Doxiadis, an international town planner who was the father of ekistics. He had coined the word to describe the field of planning new cities. Over a number of impressive dinners at his apartment overlooking the Acropolis, he told me how he was drawing up the master plan for the new city of Islamabad, which would replace Karachi as the capital of Pakistan. He also spoke of his projects to design other new capital cities on a human scale. His concept so fascinated me that I kept in touch with him after I left Greece, writing to him about my utopian ideas for new cities. Now in 1963, with my prospects of being a movie producer rapidly fading away, I wrote to him again, asking if I could work for him creating new cities.

He answered that he could employ me only if I could draw architectural renderings for his projects. He suggested I send some samples of my drafting ability. Alas, that was not possible. Not only had I no aptitude for drawing, but I could hardly write a legible signature. So ended my short-lived fantasy of being a master planner.

It was becoming increasingly clear that without a college degree, my employment prospects were exceedingly dim. That left only one viable option—one which I hated: giving up my megalomaniacal ambitions and going back to college. If I could get readmitted to Cornell as an undergraduate and qualify for a student loan, I could get a degree. It was going backward, but I saw no other way of going forward.

# PART TWO

# THE JFK ASSASSINATION

# CHAPTER FOUR

# THE MAGIC OF SELF-ACTUALIZATION

Fast-forward 29 months. On June 14, 1966, Clay Felker, the visionary editor of the *New York* magazine section of the *Herald Tribune,* and his wife, the movie star Pamela Tiffin, hosted a book party for me in their duplex apartment at 322 East Fifty-Seventh Street. The living room was 20 feet high and decorated with original Toulouse-Lautrec posters. Looking over it, there was a stage-like balcony where Clay and I stood. Below us was a veritable who's who of the literary and journalism worlds: Tom Wolfe in his signature white suit, Gloria Steinem in her iconic aviator glasses, Saul Bellow, Norman Mailer, Peter Maas, Arthur Schlesinger Jr., Nancy Sinatra, David Frost, Milton Glaser, and Paul Newman (who Pamela Tiffin had just co-starred with in the detective movie *Harper*). Susan Brockman, my once and hopefully future muse, standing in the back of the crowd, gave me a much-needed encouraging wave.

I had found a new career as an author. The party was for my book *Inquest: The Warren Commission and the Establishment of Truth.* Copies were piled high on every table. Clay, standing next to me on the balcony, made an overly laudatory introduction about the book and then called on me to speak. My back became drenched with nervous sweat. As I struggled to find words for this impressive audience, my mind ran back through the sequence of unexpected events that had brought me from the brink of despair over the collapse of *The Iliad* to speaking on this balcony. It began some 29 months earlier, on the day of the assassination of President John F. Kennedy.

On November 22, 1963, I had driven in a green Oldsmobile belonging to my stepfather from New York City to Ithaca, New York. The purpose of my 12-hour drive was to get myself readmitted to Cornell after the six-year hiatus during which I failed to be a movie producer. The only person I knew there now was my former government professor, Andrew Hacker. When I took his course on American politics in 1956, I had found it a far cry from the other courses on government, which treated the formal requisites of the Constitution as a satisfactory explanation of the political system. Hacker had a very different approach. He focused on the extra-legal mechanisms of power, such as elites, corruption, and interest groups. His contrarianism so appealed to me that when I took my involuntary leave of absence from Cornell in 1956, the year before I was due to graduate, I kept in touch with him. Inspired by C. Wright Mills's 1956 book, *The Power Elite*, I rolled up and sent him a 10-foot-long chart I had put together with a wild array of multi-colored lines, connecting possible relations between business elites and political parties. Hacker's somewhat ambiguous response was that I needed to finish my undergraduate studies.

In 1963, after realizing my talents were not in movie production, I asked Hacker if he could help me get back into Cornell. Though only 27, he had become by then a full professor in the government department.

He advised that I first had to appeal in person to the dean of admissions in Day Hall in Ithaca and, on a friendlier note, invited me to dinner at his home on the night of my arrival. I made my appointment to see the dean on Friday, November 22, 1963.

When I arrived on campus, I found that the admissions office in Day Hall, where I had an appointment, was closed. So was every other office in the building. The entire campus seemed eerily deserted, except for a lone coed sitting on the steps of Willard Straight Hall. When I asked her why everything was shut, she replied, "President Kennedy has been assassinated in Dallas."

It was the first I had heard of the assassination. My good friends Jack and Janet Gatto had accompanied me on the drive, but instead of listening to the car radio, we had played my favorite car game, 20 Questions. Since it was pointless to remain on the ghostlike campus, the three of us took a long walk along the shore of Lake Cayuga as we listened to news bulletins about JFK's murder on Jack's portable radio.

Then, armed with a bouquet of flowers for his wife Lois, I arrived for my 7:00 p.m. dinner at Hacker's home. Over a well-seasoned coq au vin, we had a conversation about the academic requirements I needed to get back into Cornell, but by dessert, talk turned to the tragedy in Dallas that afternoon. Television news had identified the alleged assassin, Lee Harvey Oswald, as a former Marine who had defected to Russia and then had involved himself in left-wing causes after his return to America. When he was arrested, he claimed that he was merely a "patsy."

"How would the truth ever be known?" I asked.

Hacker said that establishing the truth would be "a test of American democracy."

Thanks to Hacker's help, I was quickly readmitted and returned to Cornell in September 1964. Walter Berns, the soft-spoken chairman of the government department, offered me an unusual dispensation to earn a master's degree while completing the coursework for my undergraduate degree. As I needed a professor to supervise the master's thesis, I went to see Hacker, who asked, "What topic do you have in mind?"

For a moment I was stymied. I had not taken a government course in nearly seven years; I was unfamiliar with all the current jargon, like "charisma," that other students used. So I proposed the only subject that I had reason to believe might interest him: the Kennedy assassination. President Lyndon B. Johnson had appointed a commission "to ascertain, evaluate, and report on" the facts of the assassination. It was headed by Earl Warren, the chief justice of the United States, and known as the Warren Commission. On September 24, 1964, the commission submitted its final report to President Johnson, concluding that Lee Harvey Oswald, acting alone, had killed the president.

"My subject would be the process by which the commission reached this verdict," I proposed to Hacker. After pausing to light his pipe, he suggested I first read the 889-page *Warren Report*, as well as the 26 volumes of documents. He would then write a letter to the members of the Warren Commission on my behalf.

After I satisfied him that I had read the material, he wrote a letter to seven of the most powerful men in America, including the chief justice of the United States, the former director of the CIA, the former high commissioner of Germany, and four ranking members of Congress. It read:

Edward Jay Epstein, a student in the government department at Cornell University, is currently writing a thesis under my supervision. His subject is the commission on which you served. Epstein will call your office to ask if he can have an appointment with you. I hope you can give him some time for he has several questions he would like to ask you.

His thesis is a scholarly study in political science. Its theme, in general terms, is as follows. The country was faced with a unique and critical situation, and there were few precedents for dealing with it. How, then, did the government set about handling the whole question of the assassination? Mr. Epstein has prepared some queries about the organizational arrangements of the Commission and the activities of its counsel and staff. He and I would be extremely grateful if you would discuss these questions with him. Let me say that Mr. Epstein is one of our best students and I am confident in his ability to carry out an objective and informed study. He has read the full hearings as well as the *Report* and, in directing his research, I have been impressed with his mastery of the record. I recommend him to you as someone who has entered this area with an open mind and scholarly temperament.

I next wrote a shorter letter to each of the seven commissioners specifying when I would call his office. Even with Hacker's support, it seemed like a long shot, as none of the commissioners, or their staff, had given anyone outside of the government a single interview on the subject.

# CHAPTER FIVE

# THE SEVEN MOST POWERFUL MEN IN AMERICA

On March 21, 1965, I tepidly began my own inquest by calling the offices of seven of the most powerful men in America, the members of the Warren Commission. Born in 1891 in Los Angeles, California, Earl Warren had been governor of California from 1943 to 1953, was the Republican nominee for vice president of the United States in 1948, and was appointed the chief justice of the Supreme Court in 1953 by President Dwight D. Eisenhower. As chief justice, he arranged the unanimous decision in the landmark case of *Brown v. Board of Education*, which desegregated education in America. Allen Dulles, the former head of the CIA, had helped create the postwar American intelligence establishment. John J. McCloy, the former high commissioner of Germany, had helped build Europe. The Warren Commission's four congressional members—Gerald Ford, Hale Boggs, John Sherman Cooper, and Richard Russell—were among the most powerful member of the House and Senate.

To my astonishment, all but one of them agreed in principle to see me. The notable exception was Chief Justice Warren, who wrote me a polite note saying he had promised the president that he would not discuss the work of the commission with anyone.

There was a silver lining, however. The chief justice recommended I speak to J. Lee Rankin, general counsel to the commission.

Seizing this opportunity, I fired off a letter to Rankin, beginning, "I am writing to you at the suggestion of Chief Justice Warren. He strongly recommends that I discuss the work of the Warren Commission with you." Rankin, who had served first as Dwight D. Eisenhower's White House counsel and then as the solicitor general of the United States, immediately agreed to see me, since, as he told me on the phone, he would never turn down a request from the chief justice.

When I went to Rankin's office on the 14th floor of the Bar Building at 36 West Forty-Fourth Street in New York City, I felt as if I had been transported to another world, an adult world of serious men of power, a world for which I had little preparation. I had still not graduated from college. I had no experience in journalism. I had never even worked on a school newspaper or known a reporter. Indeed, this was the first time I had ever interviewed anyone.

Rankin was a short man in his late 50s with silver-gray hair. A slight Midwestern twang in his voice betrayed his origins as a native of Nebraska. "Relax," he said, sensing my nervousness. "We have all the time in the world." He sat back in his leather chair, lit a pipe, and patiently waited for me. He said, as if confiding in me, that he was surprised the chief justice had picked him to run the staff of the commission investigating the murder of a president, a task for which he had no prior experience, but that the chief justice had such a compelling presence, he had no choice to accept. "What questions do you have?"

It took me a moment to find the 3x5 card that contained my initial question. Putting on my glasses, I read directly from it. "I assume finding the truth about an assassination can be very difficult. How did you go about organizing such an investigation?"

He drew boxes on a yellow pad, depicting how he had divided the investigation into seven key areas, each of which was assigned a senior and junior lawyer. The lawyers worked as consultants getting $100 a day.

"Did some work more days than others?" I asked.

"Yes. Some of the investigations were more complex."

The conventional wisdom was that the Warren Commission had based its report on an exhaustive investigation. I realized immediately that the payroll records could provide me with a way of testing that assertion. If I could determine how much each lawyer was paid, it would tell me how many days the staff had spent investigating the seven different areas.

"Do you have payroll records?" I asked.

He replied that they were in the administrative file at the National Archives. He called in his secretary and told her to retrieve the administrative files and make them available to me.

Rankin then settled back in his chair, telling me this was the first time he had talked about his experiences on the commission. "It was a learning experience for me."

"About the assassination?"

"Yes, and about human nature. Establishing the truth was a heavy burden for all the lawyers. And I was their taskmaster."

"But didn't they have help from the FBI and local police?"

"We could call on them and other agencies of the government, and did, but the chief justice wanted us to do an independent investigation."

When I left his office two hours later, he gave me two gifts. The first was a black-and-white photograph of the commission's first meeting, personally signed by every member of the commission. I had it framed and, a half century later, it still hangs in my den. The second gift was even more valuable. It was advice about preparing for an interview. "I am not sure that this is helpful, but I've always found that the iron rule of cross-examination is not to ask a question to which you do not know the answer." His iron rule proved extremely helpful. In the thousands of interviews I conducted since that first one, I never forgot it.

On May 3, I took the train to Washington, DC. Rankin had arranged for me to meet with two key members of his staff: Howard P. Willens, his administrative deputy at the Warren Commission and the deputy head of the criminal division of the Department of Justice, and Dr. Alfred Goldberg, a Defense Department historian who had written a large part of the initial draft of the *Warren Report*. I had also made appointments with two members of the Warren Commission: Gerald Ford, a Republican, who was the House minority leader, and John Sherman Cooper, a Republican and the senior senator from Kentucky, both of whom had promptly answered my letter.

As I had no money for expenses, I relied on the kindness of strangers for two nights' lodgings. The strangers were General Michael West, a military attaché at the British embassy, his wife Christine, and their 16-year-old daughter Carinthia, whom an acquaintance of mine in New York knew. I had arrived at the West home that evening, suitcase in hand, amid a family drama: Carinthia, who had walked in the door minutes before I did, had been detained by Washington police for chaining herself to a gate in Dupont Circle during an anti–Vietnam War protest that evening.

The next morning, I met Willens in a reception room in the attorney general's suite of offices in the Justice Department. I decided to follow Rankin's advice in preparing my interview with Willens. I would ask him only questions to which I already knew the answers. This was not difficult since I had the administrative file and could determine from it a precise chronology of each lawyer's work, travel, and even expenses.

A tall, broad-shouldered lawyer in his early 30s, Willens bounded into the room in a burst of energy. Even while looking at me, he shouted instructions to each of his three secretaries in the outer office. One responded by snapping open her pad. He clearly enjoyed being in command. He motioned me into his inner office, which was not air-conditioned. He wiped the sweat from his brow and with a wave of his other hand, pointed for me to sit on the leather couch across from his desk. "I can only give you 15 minutes. Is that enough?"

"I only have a few questions," I replied accommodatingly.

I began with a softball question. "How did you become Rankin's administrative deputy?"

He said that in December 1963 he had been a US attorney working as an aide to Deputy Attorney General Nicholas Katzenbach, who "detailed" him to serve as a liaison between the Justice Department and the Warren Commission. His job had initially been to obtain the investigative reports that the commission sought from the FBI and other units of the Justice Department. As the reports piled up, he packed up his desk at Justice, moved to the commission's offices, and worked full-time for Rankin as the de facto administrator for the commission.

Rankin described Willens's role somewhat differently. He said Willens had acted as an informal liaison with Attorney General Robert F. Kennedy, the assassinated president's brother. In an attempt to clarify his role and the relationship of Robert Kennedy to the commission, I asked Willens, "Had Attorney General Robert F. Kennedy approved your move?"

"Yes," he answered tersely. "I briefed Kennedy."

"On the progress of the investigation?" I asked.

"No comment." His clenched jaw made it clear that he did not want to discuss the role of Robert Kennedy.

"On the drafting of the report?"

"No comment again."

"Did the attorney general have any input at all?" I asked.

"I can't discuss that. Let's move on," he said curtly.

I made a mental note of his unwillingness to discuss any involvement of Robert Kennedy in the commission's work. It was a subject I intended to pursue with others on the staff.

He looked at his watch impatiently, as if to say my time was running out. "Your letter said you wanted to discuss how the investigation was organized."

So applying my newly discovered iron rule, I tepidly began my first attempt at a cross-examination. "You said you began organizing the investigation in December 1963. How soon afterward did the teams of lawyers begin their investigation?"

"January '64, right after the Christmas holidays."

"They all began simultaneously?"

"More or less." He looked at his watch again.

"I assume that establishing what happened at the crime scene in Dallas was of primary importance. I believe it was team number one's responsibility."

He shrugged affirmatively.

"So they went immediately to Dallas in January?"

"I guess so. I would need to consult my records for the exact date."

I had jotted these dates down on my 3x5 cards. "As I understand it, the senior lawyer on Team One was Frank Adams, and he never went to Dallas. The junior lawyer was Arlen Specter, and he did not go to Dallas until March 17th."

He glared at me for a minute and shook his head. "How the hell do you know that?"

I decided not to tell him I had obtained the payroll records. Instead I said, "I've been speaking to the commission's lawyers."

"Then you know that Warren forbids any of the lawyers to set foot in Texas while the trial of Jack Ruby was going on. I didn't think it made any sense but he was afraid we might get subpoenaed."

I didn't know that. I continued, "So you had to delay the crime scene investigation to late March?"

He exploded, shouting, "It was a total mess! Warren and Rankin hired a bunch of lawyers who didn't understand that this was not some kind of honorary position. They had to do the footwork, travel around the country and take depositions. The FBI was also confused by Warren's idea of an independent investigation. J. Edgar Hoover wasn't keen on amateurs doing the FBI's work."

"Did you tell Kennedy about these problems?"

"What do you think? He was the attorney general."

A knock at the half-opened door ended my interview. His secretary stepped in, pointing to her watch.

As if she had entered on cue, he rose and extended his hand. "I have a meeting. Good luck with your college paper."

Before leaving the building, I passed the main offices of J. Edgar Hoover's FBI headquarters. Leading to it, 68 murals celebrated the achievements of American justice, all painted during the presidency of Franklin Delano Roosevelt. I mused about the optimism reflected in this New Deal art that had been so diminished by the assassination of President Kennedy. Even though my interview with Willens had been brief, I learned an important fact. The commission's investigation of the crime scene itself had not begun in earnest until nearly four months after the assassination. The final report was published in September. Did the commission begin writing it before the investigation was completed? I hoped Dr. Alfred Goldberg, one of the principal authors of the draft, could shed some light on that question.

Goldberg insisted on meeting me not at his office in the Pentagon but at the All-State Cafeteria in downtown Washington. He was a thin man with thick horn-rimmed glasses and a hawk-like nose. We had a quick hamburger at an outside picnic table, and he suggested we take a drive. As we drove in slow circles around

Washington in his Ford station wagon, he spoke in a quiet voice, almost a whisper at times, about his role as a "historian" on the commission. He was the only non-lawyer on the staff. He said he was also the only person with an intelligence background (except for former CIA director Allen Dulles, who had suggested Goldberg to Rankin).

Rankin had told me that Dulles recommended Goldberg to Chief Justice Warren, and the payroll records showed that he began his work there in March 1965. I began, "How did you come to be working on the commission?"

Goldberg replied that he was told that the commission needed a professional historian with the proper security clearances and an understanding of the national security issues on the periphery of the investigation. He had those credentials. During World War II, he rose to the rank of colonel writing field narratives of air battles. After retiring in 1946, he worked as a historian for the US Air Force Historical Division and other government agencies, where he met Allen Dulles, then the CIA director. Part of his job was to provide, as he put it, "perspective on the national security dimension" of the investigation.

"Rankin said you wrote a large part of the report."

"I wrote some of the draft chapters, but the commission was the final author of them."

His tone had a ring of false modesty, but my interest was not in ascertaining credit for the authorship. It was in finding out when the writing had taken place. "When did you begin writing your chapters?"

"May."

"Were you given a deadline?"

"The chief justice said the report needed to be finished well before the 1964 election. He didn't want the campaign tainted with assassination conspiracies."

"Were you given a firm date?"

"The initial deadline for the draft was July but that was impossible."

"Because the investigation was still going on?"

"Because it takes time to write a proper history. The deadline was extended to August."

He mentioned protecting the "national security dimension." I asked whether that entailed removing material that conflicted with it.

He looked at me sharply. "You are treading on very sensitive ground here. Not a word of this can be mentioned in your thesis because there are issues that cannot be made public."

"Was the FBI aware of these issues in its investigation?"

"Not all of them," he replied and fell silent.

A few minutes later, he dropped me back at the All-State Cafeteria. Lingering over a cup of lukewarm coffee, I realized I needed to build a timeline of the Warren Commission. With that, I could precisely determine the dates that the teams of lawyers both began and ended their investigations, when the writers of the report began and ended their work, when witnesses were deposed, and when the FBI, Secret Service, and other investigative agencies turned over their reports to the commission. In short, I needed to reconstruct the time that had elapsed between the commission's birth and its final report. Such a reconstruction of reality was appealing to me. Ever since I was a child, collecting postage stamps and assembling model airplanes, I had a compulsion to arrange things in an unambiguous order. Constructing the commission's timeline fit that bent.

I next saw House Minority Leader Gerald Ford, the first of the commission members I planned to see. Born in Omaha, Nebraska, in 1913, Ford began his political career in 1949 as the US representative from Michigan's fifth congressional district, a position he held for 25 years, and was chosen by his Republican colleagues as the House minority leader. He would later become vice president and then president of the United States.

I already knew something about his participation in the Warren Commission since it had released 26 volumes of testimonies from the witnesses the previous November. From them, I had been able to determine how many hearings each commissioner had attended when he departed and the questions he had asked. Ford and the three commissioners from Congress—Russell, Boggs, and Cooper—had been absent during most hearings and, by my reckoning, heard only a small fraction of the testimony. I knew Ford was an eminent political leader with a reputation for candor, but I wanted to know more about his role in supervising the investigation.

He asked me to come to room 230 in the Sam Rayburn Building. When I arrived promptly at 3:45 p.m., Ford greeted me personally, pumping my hand with the powerful grip of a former football star. He was taller than I expected, with somewhat unruly patches of flaming red hair. He directed me to a chair next to his desk. Conspicuously displayed on it was a copy of an article by Andrew Hacker in the *New York Times Magazine*. He had done his homework on my professor. He turned on his office tape recorder for "his office record."

The interview lasted exactly one hour. I asked the questions; Ford gave the answers.

Q. What role did the commission play in selecting its staff?

A. We agreed on J. Lee Rankin—as it turns out, a good choice—then Rankin submitted staff and biographies, and we approved. We, more or less, took his word. I didn't know any one of them. We approved purely on Rankin's say-so.

Q. Did the commission act as a sort of board of directors?

A. I didn't. I had my own independent investigation. I had [Gerald] Stiles, and ex-Congressman Ray, and a Harvard lawyer, Frank Fallon, on my payroll, and they evaluated testimony.

Q. Their names are not listed in the commission's administrative file.

A. You have the files? I kept these people from the commission because I wanted to be sure they were independently there.

Q. Was there disagreement on the bullet that hit Governor Connally?

A. There was a wide spectrum of opinion among the commission. I was closest to the staff position that the same bullet that hit Kennedy hit Connally. Senator Russell was at the opposite extreme. He believed that a separate bullet hit Connally. The other members ranged in between us.

Q. Were there other areas of disagreement?

A. Yes. I can note two. The first draft of the report categorically stated there was "no conspiracy." But after objections, it was changed to "No evidence was found." And in the chapter on Oswald's motivation, I added "Marxism."

Q. How was it determined when to wind up?

A. The deadline for a completed report was September 1964. We wanted to finish the report before the November election. Otherwise, it might become an issue.

When I asked him about the division of responsibility in the investigation and showed him the chart that J. Lee Rankin had given me, he looked flustered and asked a staff aid to turn off the recorder. "I left all the nitty-gritty to Rankin. He was Warren's man, and I had the Republican side of Congress to run." Ending the interview, he said, "By all means, write your thesis," adding "I'm writing a book on the subject."

I was less impressed by his knowledge of the workings of the commission than with his keen grasp of its ramifications it would have for the stability of the American government. He was masterful at seeing each issue in its political context. Indeed, it was from him that I first heard the term "political truth," a concept in which facts may be tempered to fit political realities. (Less than nine years later, he would be sworn in as the thirty-eighth president of the United States.)

Leaving Ford's office, I took the private subway that links the House and the Senate to the Senate Office Building for my 5:00 p.m. appointment with John Sherman Cooper, who called the subway line the "Congressional Express." Born in 1901 in Somerset, Kentucky, Cooper had graduated Harvard University and Yale Law School and won a Bronze Star for bravery in World War II. He then was elected twice as the Republican senator from Kentucky and, in between those terms, served as the US ambassador to India. Since he was known for candor, I was anxious to ask him about the Warren Commission. But when I got to the Senate Reception Room, I was told Senator Cooper was still on the Senate floor. His staff assistant, Bailey Gard, escorted me to the Senate gallery, from which I watched Senator Wayne Morse delivering a speech on Vietnam to a nearly empty room. Among the handful of senators in attendance was Senator Cooper. "The senator is too much of a gentleman to leave," Gard said to me. "Do you mind waiting?"

The speech went on for nearly an hour, and then Senator Cooper met me in his office. He was a distinguished-looking man with thinning white hair who weighed his words carefully. Unlike Ford, he did not record our conversation.

When I asked him how the commission worked, he said, "Every member made his own unique contribution to the commission. We didn't take any evidence at face value. We thrashed out our ideas at executive meetings." I asked him how the lawyers on the staff handled the investigation. "Frankly, I don't know. Except for the chief justice, commission members did not get involved with the operations of the staff." Indeed, he did not even know the names of the lawyers who had supervised the investigation, took the depositions of the witnesses, and drafted the chapters of the report. I asked him whether he had questioned any of the commission's conclusions.

"I had my doubts about the finding that a single bullet had wounded both the president and the governor."

"Were they eventually satisfied?"

"The staff insisted there was no other logical explanation."

"So you went along with it?"

"Begrudgingly," he said with a wistful smile. "Warren insisted on a unanimous report—and he got it."

Forty-five minutes into the interview, a bell rang, signaling the Senate was back in session. Senator Cooper courteously excused himself, saying, "It is a busy day."

I drove back to New York that evening.

I next went to see John J. McCloy. He was one of the two independent commission members. McCloy had been born in 1895 in Philadelphia to poor parents—his mother worked as a hairdresser to support the family – and rose by dint of his legal skills to become such a power behind the scenes that by 1956 C. Wright Mills, in his classic book *The Power Elite*, put McCloy at the very epicenter of the American establishment. His career in government began in 1917 when, as a 22-year-old lawyer in the Justice Department, he was assigned the task of investigating the Black Tom munitions explosion in Hoboken, New Jersey. Through brilliant investigative work, he identified it as German state-sponsored terrorism. He then moved back and forth between the private sector and government, serving as assistant secretary of war, president of the World Bank, high commissioner for Germany, and finally, under President Kennedy, disarmament advisor. President Lyndon Johnson chose him to represent the private sector on the Warren Commission.

I met McCloy at 2:35 p.m. on June 7 in his office on the 46th floor of the Chase Manhattan Bank, of which he had been chairman. He was now, in his early 70s, a senior partner at the corporate law firm of Milbank, Tweed, Hadley & McCloy. As he rose slightly to greet me, his body seemed much too small for his massive head. He asked his secretary, Miss Wilson, to hold all his calls.

He began the interview by telling me that he viewed his appointment to the Warren Commission as a continuation of his government service. He joked that since he was unemployed at the time (unlike the four congressional members of the commission), he had time to attend all of the hearings in which witnesses had testified. He leisurely told me how his work on the Black Tom explosion had led him to believe that an investigation should have its own investigators. So he convinced Chief Justice Warren to set aside the FBI report and organize an independent investigation staffed by young lawyers.

I asked him why he opposed using FBI agents for the investigation. He replied coolly, "J. Edgar Hoover likes to close doors. I told Warren we had to reopen them."

Had the commission's investigation faced limits in what it could report? I asked.

He answered by describing Thornton Wilder's novel *The Bridge of San Luis Rey*, in which an investigation uncovered a series of unrelated sexual liaisons. He compared the book to the investigation, saying, "We had uncovered a lot of minor scandals, but they were not relevant to our investigation. We decided not to publish them in the report."

When I pressed him on what these scandals involved, he replied, "It was as if someone picked up a rock and the light caused all sorts of bugs to run for cover." He said the Secret Service needed to obscure the indiscretions of its agents the night before the assassination, the FBI had to expunge embarrassing incidents from its reports, and the CIA had to hide its unauthorized domestic activities. He added that even Attorney General Robert Kennedy, the president's brother, had put his own man, Howard Willens, on the staff to deal with "inappropriate revelations."

I had already interviewed Willens at his office at the Justice Department. He told me that the attorney general had dispatched him to the commission to make sure it had assistance from the Justice Department, but he said nothing about suppressing any material. I asked McCloy what Willens had done.

"He locked away material in his desk," he replied. According to McCloy, Willens did not believe the staff had any need to see it. He said it concerned a "national security issue" he was not free to discuss.

I knew that McCloy had seen a dark side of international intrigue of which few others were aware. From his investigation as a young lawyer of state-sponsored sabotage to his dealings with Russian machinations in postwar Germany when he was high commissioner of Germany in the 1950s, he had seen the capacity of intelligence services to manipulate their adversaries' view of reality. Had he applied this perspective in the JFK assassination? I asked him as tactfully as I could whether the commission had fully explored Oswald's foreign connections.

He said that while no one on the commission had any doubts that Oswald was the shooter in the sniper's nest, the real mystery for him was "why Oswald was there with a rifle." He believed there was persuasive evidence that Oswald had been trained in espionage in Russia and that Oswald might have been "a sleeper agent who went haywire." Warren did not buy his theory, and he lost the argument because "Warren was, you need to understand, stubborn as a mule."

Toward the end of the interview, McCloy briefly excused himself to use the restroom. Left alone, I couldn't help noticing his open appointment book on his desk. What caught my eye was that I was his only listed appointment that day. Based on my reading of Mills's *The Power Elite*, I had imagined that a man who had been president of the World Bank, US high commissioner of Germany, chairman of Chase Manhattan Bank, chairman of the Council on

Foreign Relations, and an advisor to every president since Franklin D. Roosevelt would be busier. Apparently, even the power elite's schedules fade away in time.

We spoke for another half hour about the Warren Commission when he returned. In my opinion, he was the sharpest and most focused member of the commission. I left him at 4:30.

After writing up my notes on the McCloy interview, I had dinner with Susan Brockman, my former collaborator on *The Iliad*, at the Puffing Billy, a restaurant on Madison and Eighty-Sixth Street in New York. Susan had just broken up with de Kooning, whom she told me she had been living with since November 22, 1963, the day Kennedy was assassinated. It seemed an odd coincidence that we had both changed directions, for different reasons, that day. As I had not seen her since I reentered Cornell, she knew nothing of my interest in the assassination. So when I told her about my interview that afternoon with McCloy and his insights into the Kennedy assassination, her eyes widened.

"Why were you seeing him?" she asked.

"I am investigating the Kennedy assassination."

"Are you an investigator now?" she asked with a broad smile. The last time we dined, my profession was a failed movie producer.

"Not yet, but I am learning how."

"And how do you do that?"

It was a question I had been wrestling with since I had begun my interviews. For my first interview, I prepared 10 questions on blue 3x5 cards and then nervously reeled them off as I flipped the cards. Unfortunately, this method yielded short, pro forma answers that were not informative. So I threw away the 3x5 cards. Instead, I committed to memory my questions and engaged in a free-ranging conversation with the person I was interviewing. This method produced longer but less-focused answers. I realized that what was critically necessary was precise and spontaneous follow-up questions. That required listening for what was omitted as well as what was said.

"I asked a lot of unexpected questions."

"You were always good at asking 'why,'" Susan said.

One week later I returned to Washington to interview the two remaining members of Congress on the Warren Commission, Senator Richard Russell and Congressman Hale Boggs. Born in 1897 in Georgia, Russell, as head of the Conservative Caucus and chairman of the Senate Armed Services Committee, had enormous power in the Senate. I arrived at Russell's office for our noon appointment, but he was not there. His administrative assistant, Bill Jordan, told me the interview would have to be rescheduled because Russell had been called away for an "emergency meeting" in Georgia, the state he represented.

Again, I took the handy Congressional Express to the Sam Rayburn Building, where I had a 2:30 p.m. appointment with Hale Boggs. Boggs, born in 1915 in Mississippi, had been elected as a Democrat to Congress at the age of 26 in 1946, making him the youngest congressman in history. A charismatic old-style politician with a southern drawl, he was now the majority whip in the House, a job that entailed rounding up enough votes to pass a bill. He was also the youngest member of the Warren Commission. Even though Boggs had attended only a few meetings of the commission, I wanted to get his perspective as a politician on how the commission conceived of its job.

Boggs arrived 45 minutes late, shouting orders to his young staff. Looking at his watch, he told me that he could give me only a half hour.

I began the interview by asking whether he could account for the differences between the initial reports of the Secret Service and FBI and the commission's final report.

"There were none."

"What about the sequence of the bullets?" I asked.

He held up a hand as if to stop traffic. "I did not involve myself in the minutiae of the investigation. I left all the conflicts to our very able lawyers," he said.

I saw there was little purpose in pursuing this point, so I asked why the commission decided to wrap up its investigation in May 1964.

"We had to get the report out well before the November election," he answered. "It wouldn't look good to delay until after the election. People would think something was wrong."

As a skilled politician who had climbed the rungs of power in the House, he knew how to evade a potentially embarrassing issue. He concluded the interview. "We tried to do the best job possible for the country. If you say something about the commission, you should say something good." Seven years later, he vanished on a private plane that presumably crashed in the wilds of Alaska. Neither the plane nor its passengers were ever found.

The final commissioner I met with was Allen Dulles, the other independent member. Born in 1893, he had spent most of his career in the spy business. He served briefly as counselor to the US delegation in Peking and then joined the New York law firm of Sullivan and Cromwell, of which his brother, John Foster Dulles, was a senior partner. He next joined the Office of Strategic Services, the forerunner of the CIA, where as a master spy he helped arrange the surrender of German forces in Italy in World War II. After the CIA was established in 1951, Dulles served as its deputy director, and in 1953, President Dwight D. Eisenhower appointed him CIA director. He had retired in November 1961, some two years before his appointment to the commission. What especially interested me about him was his vantage point in the CIA, an organization he had a large hand in creating as a weapon in the Cold War. He likely knew more about the covert side of Russian intelligence than anyone else on the commission.

Dulles had invited me to his home on Georgetown's Q Street. While his wife, Clover, served us a leisurely tea on the shaded veranda, he told me about his career in intelligence before being appointed a member of the Warren Commission. He took pride in having been the longest-serving director of the CIA.

He recalled that at the very outset, in January 1964, Rankin called an emergency meeting to report there was uncorroborated information that Oswald was a paid FBI informer. "I knew it was bunk from the start," he said. "J. Edgar Hoover would never employ anyone like Oswald. He was too unstable."

Dulles said he was proven correct when Lonny Hudkins, the reporter who had originated the rumor, admitted it was baseless. Dulles added that it was part of the commission's job to discredit such rumors because they injured American credibility in the world.

I asked whether the CIA would have conducted the investigation differently.

He smiled. "In the CIA, we usually have a greater problem with verification. In the Warren Commission, most witnesses were ordinary people." He added cryptically that there was one defector who might have helped if the CIA had been handling the case. He did not name him, though that defector would later become a very important part of my investigation.

The interview lasted almost two hours.

By now, these interviews were making it increasingly clear to me that the members of the Warren Commission had been only peripherally involved in the investigation itself. Certainly, President Johnson had a reason for picking the top Democrat and Republicans in Congress, a former CIA director, and a principal member of the foreign policy establishment. They lent bipartisan credibility to the conclusions that the assassination was the work of a lone assassin. They had accepted the task out of a sense of duty, but I was realizing that they had consigned most of the day-to-day investigative work to a dozen or so staff lawyers. I now intended, with a recommendation from J. Lee Rankin, to see them all. There was no other way to learn about the investigation.

# CHAPTER SIX

# THE LIEBELER FILE

As I would learn on June 30, 1965, an investigation often turns not on diligence but on luck. On that day I had again borrowed my stepfather's Oldsmobile to drive to Newfane, Vermont. The reason for the five-hour road trip was a 2:00 p.m. appointment with Wesley J. Liebeler. This 34-year-old lawyer had spent more time than anyone else on the Warren Commission investigating Lee Harvey Oswald's alleged role in the Kennedy assassination.

I pulled up to Liebeler's rustic house just before 2:00 p.m. There was no car in the driveway. I rang the bell several times, but no one came to the door. I waited in my car. Shortly after 3:00, Liebeler's wife, Celia, arrived in a battered pickup truck with their two young sons. When I introduced myself, she said she had not heard from her husband but expected he would be arriving shortly. I helped her unload a chainsaw from the back of the truck, and, after she demonstrated how it worked, I spent the next three hours sawing off limbs from a fallen maple tree. I then joined her and the children for dinner in the kitchen. Still no Liebeler. I kept checking my watch, knowing that I had promised to get the car back to my stepfather that night.

It was not until 8:00 p.m. that Liebeler arrived. He was a slightly overweight man with uncombed blond hair and eyes set far apart in his head who was surprised to find me waiting in his home. He explained that he had forgotten to enter our appointment in his office calendar. He said he was too exhausted after his long car trip from Washington to answer my questions about the Warren Commission. (I later learned that he had actually been with his mistress.) Instead, he suggested that I stay over in the guest room, where I could read through his "chronological file," and then he would answer my questions in the morning.

After I called my parents to get permission to keep the car another night, Liebeler brought the file to the guest room. It began in January 1964 and it was the first time I realized that lawyers keep a day-by-day record of their work. I stayed up until 5:00 a.m. reading through it.

At breakfast, Liebeler gave me his own account of the investigation. He ridiculed the seven commissioners, saying the staff called them the Seven Dwarfs because they refused to question the claims of Oswald's Russian wife, Marina (who was Snow White). He said Dopey was Chief Justice Warren, who dismissed any testimony that impugned Marina's credibility.

I asked him, "Who was Sleepy?"

He said Allen Dulles, the former director of Central Intelligence. Dulles received this appellation because he often fell asleep during the testimony of witnesses and, when awakened, asked inappropriate questions. For example, an FBI fiber expert was describing the bullet holes in the front of Kennedy's shirt when Dulles woke up, looked at the blowup of the bloody shirt, and said, "He wears ready-made shirts, huh?" At another point, he spilled a wad of tobacco on a photograph of three bullet fragments and said, as if he had discovered new evidence, that he saw four fragments.

McCloy was Grumpy. According to Liebeler, he became angry when staff lawyers did not pay sufficient attention to his theories about possible foreign involvement.

Liebeler was also scathing about the initial FBI investigation, which he called "a joke." As for the CIA, he said one of its theories was that Oswald might have been "brainwashed" into serving as a "Manchurian Candidate" assassin. He noted the agency had no basis for this "ridiculous theory" other than a decade-old study it had conducted on brainwashing techniques.

He answered questions for about two hours and gave me a tour of his farm in his truck. Along the way, he stopped by a fallen birch tree and, with his new chainsaw, cut it into firewood. As he worked, Liebeler told me that the commission had come under enormous pressure to complete the report before the 1964 election campaign began in September. One result was that investigations were not always completed, as happened with the allegations made by Sylvia Odio. Odio, a young Cuban exile living in Dallas, testified that Oswald had visited her in the company of two "Cuban underground fighters" on September 25, 1963. She said he was introduced to her as "Leon Oswald," and after Kennedy's assassination, she recognized him as Lee Harvey Oswald. Her sister, Annie Odio, corroborated this identification. Since September 25 was the day before Oswald arrived in Mexico, Odio's allegation, if accurate, could mean that Oswald had been with two unknown associates during at least part of his trip.

"You need to see Odio," Liebeler said.

Despite the serious implications, the commission had not investigated the allegation further because of a staff lawyer's analysis of bus schedules between New Orleans, where Oswald boarded a bus on September 24, and Mexico City, where Oswald arrived on September 26. The analysis concluded that Oswald must have gone via Houston and caught the 2:35 a.m. bus from Houston to Mexico City on September 25. That would not have left Oswald enough time to visit Odio in Dallas on the evening of September 25.

When Liebeler read this timeline in the draft chapter in July 1964, he decided, as he put it, "to play Sherlock Holmes" by checking for alternative buses between New Orleans and Mexico City.

He found Oswald could have traveled by bus from New Orleans to Dallas on September 25, visited Odio at her home, and then had ample time to board the Houston-to-Mexico bus at Alice, Texas. Odio said Oswald left her home in an automobile with the two Cubans. If so, they could have driven him the short distance to the bus station at Alice.

Liebeler wrote a torrid memorandum showing that the earlier analysis used to dismiss Odio's testimony was wrong. He suggested to Rankin that he go to Dallas to question Odio and her sister. Rankin wrote back, "At this stage, we are supposed to be closing doors, not opening them."

This suggested to me that the investigation, far from being exhaustive, had been badly flawed by the time pressure imposed by the White House.

I asked Liebeler if the commission had prematurely foreclosed other investigative avenues that could have identified associates of Oswald.

"You'll need to see my files in July to answer that question," he answered, loading the firewood into his truck.

"Where can I see your files?" I said, as if I was asking routine directions at a gas station.

He stepped, cocking one eye at me suspiciously. "What exactly are you doing?"

"I am writing a paper on how the commission went about establishing the truth," I said, paraphrasing what I had said in my letter to him.

Continuing to squint, he asked in a very dubious tone, "Do students usually travel to Vermont to do their term paper?"

Given that the last thing I wanted to discuss with him was my decidedly shaky academic credentials, I diverted to my interview with John J. McCloy. "McCloy told me that there were missing pieces in Oswald's background. And Oswald's background was your area."

"So Grumpy piqued your curiosity," he cut in, using his pet name for McCloy. "Did you ever hear that curiosity killed the cat?"

I smiled as if he was making a joke rather than a threat. "I am curious about finding missing pieces."

"OK, be my guest."

He went back into the house and returned with two cardboard boxes. "I feel bad about making you wait in your car yesterday. Everything you need to know about the Warren Commission," he said, handing me the boxes.

That afternoon I returned to New York. I couldn't believe he had given me his files. I realized that they were an unexpected treasure trove for me. They contained hundreds of memos to and from the lawyers, entire draft chapters, a commission symposium on Oswald's possible motives, and, most importantly, FBI reports. Back then, in 1965, there was no Freedom of Information Act, and FBI reports were rarely, if ever, released to journalists or academics. Indeed, few people had seen one before. And I had two blue-bound volumes of them concerning one of the great mysteries of the 20th century. They consisted of over a hundred pages of preliminary FBI reports and photographs that had been given to President Johnson and the commission, but as far as I knew, no one outside of the FBI and the Warren Commission had seen them. Although they fell into my hands through a stroke of sheer luck, they would allow me to determine the extent to which the commission changed the findings of the original investigation. There were also Liebeler's memos on his effort to find the missing pieces in Oswald's life.

I now tried to fill these and other gaps. The Liebeler files were an enormously useful tool for preparing my next interviews because I could read what the various staff members had written to him, citing the precise date. As I learned, having access to documents is the secret of effective cross-examination.

By July, I had seen seven lawyers on the commission's staff, but

I still needed to see Francis Adams in particular, for two reasons. First, Rankin had appointed him to supervise the single most important part of the investigation, the place of origin of the shots that killed President Kennedy and wounded Governor Connally. Second, the payroll records showed that he had worked only two days and then, Liebeler told me, abruptly quit after a meeting in Rankin's office. But why?

Unlike the other members of the commission staff, Adams had years of experience in criminal investigations. He had been a well-regarded police commissioner of New York City in the mid-1950s when he initiated Operation Efficiency to eliminate police corruption. That was why Warren had chosen him. Even to Liebeler, his sudden departure was a mystery.

I arrived at Adams's Park Avenue law firm at 2:30 p.m. The photographs on the wall showed him with every important Irish politician in New York. With his silver hair and finely chiseled features, he looked the part of a police commissioner. He was also very blunt with me.

"Let's be straight," he began. "I know very little about the investigation because in all but name I quit after the first organization meeting. I did not want to officially announce my resignation because it might raise questions."

"Can I ask why you quit so early in the investigation?"

"I disagreed with Warren's plan for the investigation. I told Rankin that the entire staff, 14 lawyers, should work on the evidence concerning who shot the president. Warren wanted to divide the investigation so that only two lawyers would work in each area."

"You and Arlen Specter," I said.

"Yes, and Warren did not want to begin with the investigation in Dallas until the trial of Jack Ruby was concluded in March. That meant we had only two months or so to take the testimony of scores of eyewitnesses, doctors, and forensic experts."

"What did you tell Rankin?"

"That a compartmentalized investigation would not work. He replied that Warren had already decided on it. That was that."

As a result, Arlen Specter alone had to carry out the entire investigation into who shot the president.

Though only 35, Arlen Specter had already had a brilliant career. After graduating Phi Beta Kappa from the University of Pennsylvania, he became an editor of the law journal at Yale Law School. He was now an assistant district attorney in Philadelphia. It took until August 21, well over a month, before he could find time to see me. I met him in his office on the 28th floor of the Philadelphia Saving Fund Society building at 2:10 p.m. in downtown Philadelphia.

Specter began by explaining what happened on the Warren Commission. He had been hired to assist Francis Adams on Panel 1, which was charged with establishing the central facts of the shooting. When Adams failed to show up for the investigation, Specter assumed the job of establishing the sequence. Specter said that on March 15, 1964, Chief Justice Warren called him into his office and told him it was of the utmost importance "to clear up the confusion over the bullets." The confusion arose because the FBI summary report said all the bullets that hit Kennedy had been fired from the sixth floor of the Texas Book Depository, which was behind the motorcade. A Dallas newspaper reported, however, that doctors in Dallas had identified Kennedy's throat wound as an entry wound, which suggested that Kennedy had been shot from the front. Specter asked when he should leave for Dallas. Warren replied, "I'd hoped you could catch the evening plane tonight."

Over the next nine days in Dallas, Specter deposed the doctors who had seen the wounds and the pathologists who had conducted the autopsy. All agreed that there was no basis for concluding the throat wound was an entrance wound.

"I cleared up that problem," Specter said, "but I found another problem." It was the sequence of the shots. He discovered a blatant contradiction between the FBI summary report, which concluded that a single rifle accounted for three separate hits—the first shot wounding Kennedy in the back, the second shot wounding Governor John Connally in the wrist, and the third shot hitting Kennedy in the head—and the photographic evidence from the Secret Service reconstruction, which showed that there was not enough time for the rifle in question to have fired the first two of these shots. Either the FBI was wrong about the number of shots or there had been a second gunman. Despite this critical inconsistency, the commission set a June deadline for ending the investigation, so Specter said he "rushed back to Dallas" to re-interrogate the doctors and other witnesses. It was then that he came up with the so-called single-bullet theory.

At this critical point in the interview, his secretary barged in to remind him he was due at court at 4:00 pm. Specter politely excused himself, suggesting that, if I was free for dinner, we could continue at his house at 6:00 p.m. He wrote down his address.

When I arrived, his wife, Joan, took me to the backyard, where Specter, wearing a chef's apron, was in the backyard grilling lamb chops on a small Weber grill. She then left us alone.

I reminded him, as he brought the chops to the table, that he was explaining the single-bullet theory. I asked, "When the Secret Service did a reconstruction on December 7 [1963], why didn't they arrive at your single-bullet theory?"

"They had no idea at the time that unless one bullet had hit both Kennedy and Connally, there had to be a second assassin." He added that the FBI had also missed this problem. So he had to find a way to explain how one shooter could have hit both men in the available time. The best explanation he found was that two, not three, bullets had hit the occupants of the car.

"How did you convince the commission about the single-bullet theory?"

"I showed them the Zapruder film frame by frame and explained that they could either accept the single-bullet theory or begin looking for a second assassin."

He had given them no real option if they were to conclude Oswald acted alone. Yet his single-bullet theory had to be squared with the main medical evidence, the autopsy results. A bullet passing through Kennedy into Connally would leave a path through Kennedy's body that could be seen in the autopsy photographs. So I asked whether the color photographs taken at the autopsy revealed such a path.

"I assumed they did." He chewed on his lamb chop bone.

Up until this point, Specter had given definite answers to my questions. He seemed to pride himself on his precision. But his tentativeness about the autopsy photos raised a red flag. He had been by far the sharpest lawyer I had interviewed yet. Why would he now use the weasel word "assume." He certainly could determine whether or not the commission had seen the autopsy evidence since he had conducted much of the questioning of the pathologists for the commission. Something seemed amiss. I waited for him to finish eating before asking, "Did you examine the color autopsy photos?"

"No," he answered. "I never saw the autopsy photos."

"Did anyone else on the commission or staff see them?"

"Not to my knowledge."

Obviously they were missing. Looking him straight in the eyes, I asked, "Why not?"

Specter shook his head. "You need to ask Rankin."

I immediately called Rankin to get an answer to the question Specter raised. He accommodatingly scheduled an appointment. We met again in his office in New York. I reminded him of the advice he had given me about not asking questions to which I didn't know the answer.

"Was it useful?" he asked cordially.

I replied it was part of my continuing education, adding that I had learned more in this investigation that I had learned in my entire time in college.

"I understand you saw Specter last week."

I assumed Specter had called him after the backyard barbecue.

"Yes, he told me the autopsy photos had not been examined. Aren't the autopsy photos crucial pieces of evidence?"

Rankin appeared distressed at my question. "It is," he answered. He said he had "directed" Specter to examine the autopsy X-rays and photographs but that Specter had been blocked.

"By who?" It was a question to which I already knew the answer.

"Robert Kennedy." Rankin explained that when Willens told Kennedy about the request, Kennedy went to see Warren. Kennedy expressed his concern to the chief justice that the gory autopsy photographs might leak to the tabloid press, and in deference to the Kennedy family, Warren ordered them directly locked away in the National Archives as sealed evidence. Consequently, the Warren Commission never saw the most direct evidence of the path of the bullets.

This crucial omission showed that the Warren Commission, no matter how decent and virtuous its seven members, did not conduct an exhaustive investigation. Indeed, it did not even examine the basic autopsy evidence of how the president was killed. What I turned up in my investigation did not necessarily prove that the conclusions of the commission were wrong, but it did show that its investigation was incomplete.

# CHAPTER SEVEN

# THE NIGHT THIEF

The JFK investigation had gone beyond the requisites of a school project. Unlike anyone else, I had managed to interview the members of the Warren Commission and its staff and to obtain FBI summary reports and the chronological files of the investigators. But other than writing my investigation up as a thesis, I had no plans to publish it. That changed when I received a phone call from a stranger on December 18, 1965. The man on the line identified himself, falsely I later learned, as "Ed Victor," an editor at the British publishing house of Jonathan Cape. He said he had gotten my number from Emile de Antonio, who had told him I was working on a book on the Kennedy assassination based on FBI reports. If so, he was interested in publishing it.

I had no reason to doubt him. De Antonio, or just De, as he liked to be called, was a friend of Susan Brockman, who met him through her liaison with de Kooning and then introduced him to me in 1963 as "the real brains behind pop art." Born in 1919 in the coal-mining town of Scranton, Pennsylvania, De was in the same Harvard class as John F. Kennedy, served as a bomber pilot in World War II, and befriended many artists in the New York art scene, including Jasper Johns, Robert Rauschenberg, John Cage, and Andy Warhol, who reportedly said about him, "Everything I learned about painting, I learned from De." It was no doubt hyperbole, but De certainly was close with Warhol. He took me to Warhol's "the factory," a rundown studio on East Forty-Seventh Street, which had silk-screen printings of Jackie Kennedy on the walls, and told Warhol I would "crack the JFK case." Warhol responded by snapping my picture with a Kodak camera and, at De's suggestion, showed me a few silk screens of Jackie Kennedy. Although they all looked identical to me, I nodded appreciatively at each one, wondering if he expected me to buy one. I did not appreciate that I was on the cusp of what would become the pop art revolution.

After I indiscreetly told De about my thesis on the Warren Commission, he said he was a friend of the lawyer Mark Lane. Born in Brooklyn, New York, in 1927, Lane made a name for himself organizing rent strikes, leading bomb shelter protests, defending accused anarchists, and, in 1962, unsuccessfully running for Congress. In January 1964, he had gotten Marguerite Oswald, the mother of Kennedy's alleged assassin, to retain him as the lawyer for her deceased son, thereby giving him the opportunity to proclaim himself as the legal investigation of the putative plot to frame Oswald for the JFK assassination. De had suggested I speak to Lane, but I refused. Now it appeared De had told this editor about my book.

When I told the caller that my thesis was based on unseen documents, including FBI reports, I had obtained from Warren Commission lawyers, he said he would like to obtain the British book rights, offering to immediately pay me $500 for a first-refusal option. I was flattered by his bold offer and, more to the point, I could use the $500 to help pay the next term's tuition.

He was coming to Ithaca that evening and staying at the Ithaca Hotel. Could he come to see me?

I suggested the following day but he said that was not possible since he had to drive then to Toronto, 250 miles from Ithaca, to see one of his authors. So it had to be that afternoon.

After I agreed, he said he would come to my apartment at 3:00 p.m. to read the thesis, and if it was appropriate for publication, he would give me a check for $500.

I excitedly awaited his arrival. As I had never before dealt with a publisher, I was not sure how I should present my only-partially written thesis. I placed 80 typed pages on the coffee table and also put on a jacket and tie. But he did not show up at 3:00 p.m. I waited for another hour and called the Ithaca Hotel. The desk clerk told me that no one by the name of Ed Victor was now registered there or had been that morning. I sadly wrote off the phone call as a practical joke by one of my fellow students.

Professor Hacker had invited me to join him that evening at Berry's, a fancy seafood restaurant in Oswego, New York, about an hour from Ithaca, to celebrate the completion of my thesis. Because of a heavy snowstorm, I did not get back to my apartment until after midnight.

Around 2:00 a.m., there was a loud, unrelenting knocking at my front door. When I opened it, a short man in his early 30s stood there covered in snow.

Shaking the snow off like a shaggy dog, he introduced himself as Ed Victor. He profusely apologized for missing our early appointment, saying that his car had skidded into a snowbank. I offered him tea, which he refused, explaining that he was in a hurry to leave for Toronto. Even though his excuse seemed lame, his disheveled clothes were not what I expected a British publisher to wear, and his guttural accent was unmistakably acquired in Brooklyn, I accepted him as the person he claimed to be.

We sat at the coffee table as he leafed through the pages of my thesis. "This is publishable," he said, tossing the pages back on the table, "but I also need to see the FBI reports you mentioned."

I went to the breakfast nook, which served as my office, and brought back a blue-bound 87-page FBI summary report entitled *Investigation of Assassination of President John F. Kennedy, November 22, 1963.* It was one of the reports Wesley Liebeler had given me. When I handed him the report, his eyes widened. The expression of glee on his face was so clear that it reminded me of someone who had just drawn the winning numbers in a lottery. Plainly, he had found what he was after. I suddenly realized that it was not my book that had brought him to Ithaca but the FBI reports. Whoever he was, he was not a legitimate book publisher. He had lied about being registered at the Ithaca Hotel. I now assumed the reason it took him 11 hours to get to my apartment was that he was not in Ithaca when he had called me, and he had decided to drive to Ithaca only after I had confirmed that I had FBI documents in my possession. Such are the powers of wishful denial. I had swallowed his unlikely story hook, line, and sinker because I wanted to believe my thesis was of such great interest that a publisher would buy it. Simply put, I had deceived myself.

To try to remedy my mistake, I snatched the FBI report he was reading out of his hands. When he looked up, I told him I would send him a copy in London so he could read it at his leisure. "Could I have your business card?" I asked.

Claiming he had left it back at his hotel, he began writing out his address in block letters on a piece of paper.

As he was doing this, I took the FBI report back to the breakfast nook and sought a place to conceal it. Because the man was short, I put it on top of a tall breakfront.

I returned and looked at the piece of paper he handed me. The address on it—3 Shavers Place, Haymarket, London—further persuaded me he was an imposter. It was the same address that appeared on a letter I had received from Mark Lane. In that note, Lane said he was working on a book on the assassination and asked me if I could share any information I had obtained. Suddenly, all the pieces fell into place. De Antonio knew Lane. He likely told

Lane what I had told him about my investigation. Since I had not answered Lane's letter, he had dispatched this man disguised as a book publisher to find out what I knew.

Voicing my suspicion, I told the man, "Your address is identical to Mark Lane's address. I doubt you are who you say you are."

He bolted from his chair, pushed by me, and rushed into the breakfast nook. I could see him wildly rooting through my papers, presumably intending to grab the FBI report. I threatened to call the police, although it was not a realistic option since I would have to explain to them how I came to possess secret and highly sensitive FBI reports.

He glowered at me, saying as he stormed out the door, "I have never been so insulted in my life. The hell with your book."

The following morning I made several calls. It turned out that, yes, there was an editor at Jonathan Cape named Ed Victor, but he was a tall man whose description in no way matched the appearance of the night visitor. I then called De Antonio, who told me that he had given my phone number just that Friday to some friend of Lane's who worked at Bertrand Russell's Peace Foundation, which was located at 3 Shavers Place, Haymarket. Since Mark Lane was staying at thar address, I thought it likely that Lane had sent the fake "Ed Victor" to get the FBI reports so he could use them for his own book.

I called Arnold Krakower, the New York lawyer who had helped me organize my disastrous production of *The Iliad* and paid Mario Puzo for the script treatment. I knew that he loved a mystery, having been married to the novelist Kathleen Winsor. When I told him about the incident, he said he was going to "read the riot act to Lane's publisher."

Krakower called me back two days later to report that Lane's manuscript, entitled *Rush to Judgment*, was at Viking Press. He had spoken to its publisher, Thomas Guinzburg, who, after hearing the story, no longer wanted to publish Lane's book but would be interested in my thesis. The editor there whom I was to contact was Clay Felker.

I could no longer be angry with my nighttime visitor. Whatever his intent, he had opened a door for me to the New York publishing world. I intended to take full advantage of the opportunity.

I checked *Who's Who*. Felker had been born in 1925 in Webster Groves, Missouri, the son of the editor of the *Sporting News*. He went to Duke and then worked as an editor at *Life*, *Time*, and *Esquire*. He was now both the editor of the *New York* section in the *Herald Tribune* and a consulting editor at Viking. After a brief chat with me on the phone, he asked me to drop by his home.

At 10:30 a.m. on New Year's Eve, I arrived at Clay Felker's apartment at 322 East Fifty-Seventh Street. When he answered the door, he looked as if he had just woken up. He was wearing pajamas, a silk art-nouveau bathrobe, and slippers. He was in his late 30s, with a rugged face and a square jaw. I followed him through an impressive library of leather-bound books in glass-enclosed cases. His duplex had its entrance, library, and bedrooms upstairs. An elegant staircase led down to the living room, which had a 20-foot-high ceiling and casement windows. He suggested I wait there while he got dressed.

In the center of the room was a tall, tinsel-covered Christmas tree with an angel on top. Next to it was a ladder. The Filipino maid, Angela, seated me at a round table and brought me a coffee on a silver tray. About 10 minutes later, a strikingly beautiful woman in a sheer white nightgown descended the stairs, carrying a box and scissors. Unaware of my presence in the room, she climbed the ladder, her blond hair flowing over her shoulders, and began removing decorations from the tree. I did not speak up for fear of startling her.

A few minutes later, Felker bounded into the room and introduced the woman on the ladder as his wife, Pamela. At that point, I recognized her as the movie star Pamela Tiffin. I had seen her act in Billy Wilder's movie *One, Two, Three*. She was even more beautiful in person. Felker apologized for the delay, explaining he had been on the phone with the White House. He said in a grave tone that President Lyndon Baines Johnson might be ill, adding that the news might upset the stock market. He joined me at the table while Pamela, who had put on a robe, brought a basket of croissants. I handed Felker my thesis.

A week later, Felker called with good news. He told me Viking wanted to publish my book based on the 90-page draft that I had given him. Viking would also give me a $5,000 advance, a princely sum. Krakower negotiated the contract and acted as my agent. Aaron Asher, one of Viking's most respected editors, would edit the book. In less than three weeks I had gone from having an imposter editor to having a real one.

# CHAPTER EIGHT

# HANNAH ARENDT'S
# INTERVENTION

On January 13, however, there was a setback. Felker called me in Ithaca to say that Asher had had second thoughts. Since the book was very short, Asher was, as he put it, "toying with the idea" of combining my draft with two other essays, one by Leo Sauvage, a French correspondent for *Le Figaro*, and the other by Fred Cook, an investigative reporter for the *Nation*. The anthology was to be called *New Doubts about the Kennedy Assassination*.

I was aghast. I asked if could change editors at Viking. Felker replied that the real problem was not Asher but the publisher, Tom Guinzburg, who was concerned that, as an undergraduate at Cornell, I lacked sufficient credentials to take on such a sensitive matter as the *Warren Report*.

I was so dispirited by this call that I stopped working on chapter 10, the last chapter, and, despite the freezing weather, headed downtown to see Arthur Penn's film *Mickey One*. It was about a comic who, after a merciless reversal of fortune, becomes the victim of killers. It failed to cheer me up.

But my own fortunes changed on the car ride back home. At the bottom of the steep hill leading to campus, I saw an elderly woman bundled up in a heavy shawl, vainly attempting to hail a taxi. Realizing she had little chance of finding one, I stopped my car and asked her whether she would like a ride up the hill. When she got into the car, I instantly recognized her as the philosopher Hannah Arendt. How could I not? Not only had I audited her lectures on the accused Soviet spy Alger Hiss, but she had been featured in a profile the week before in the *Daily Sun*. Her life story was incredible. Born in 1906 in Hanover, Germany, to a Jewish family, she grew up in Königsberg, the same East Prussian city that the philosopher Immanuel Kant never left, and then moved with her family to Berlin. At the University of Marburg, despite her deep concern about anti-Semitism, she had a long affair with Martin Heidegger, who supported the Nazis even after Hitler came to power and was also considered one of the most influential philosophers of the 20th century. When Hitler began rounding up German Jews, Arendt was arrested by the Gestapo and spent eight days in a Nazi prison. After being released, she escaped Germany via a perilous route over the Erzgebirge into Czechoslovakia and by train to Switzerland, France, and Portugal. In 1941, she arrived in New York as a penniless refugee. The 1951 publication of her masterpiece *Origins of Totalitarianism* established her as one of the leading philosophers of the Cold War. But her reporting in the *New Yorker* on the war crimes trial of Adolf Eichmann in Jerusalem in 1961 made her the center of a bitter controversy over the role of Jewish leaders in the Holocaust. In the midst of the dissension, she came to Cornell as a visiting professor.

In the car I tried to discuss her critique of the FBI's identification of Hiss's typewriter, a part of her lecture that greatly impressed me. Still half-frozen, she remained silent. Halfway up the mile-long hill, the car skidded dangerously on the ice, and perhaps terrified by my driving skills, she asked whether I was an undergraduate at Cornell. Although she retained her German accent, her English was precise. I answered affirmatively, adding that I was also a hopeful author and that Viking was interested in publishing my thesis on the Kennedy assassination. She said Viking was her publisher, too, and asked when my book would be published.

I told her that although Viking had agreed to publish it as a book, the publisher was now considering merely doing it as part of a three-author anthology. She said, "That is reprehensible. They can't do that."

"There is not much I can do about it," I said, as we pulled up to the Telluride House, where she was staying. Getting out of the car, she said she could ask her editor at Viking, Denver Lindley, about it.

The next morning, I went to Arendt's office in Boardman Hall. She looked confused. "Who are you?"

I reminded her of my problem with Viking and of her kind offer to call her editor there. She shrugged, dialed a number in New York, and asked for Denver Lindley. When her editor came on the line, she said, "I have a student here." Holding her hand over the receiver, she asked me my name, which she relayed to Lindley. She told him I had received conflicting versions of how Viking planned to publish my book. After hanging up, she told me that Lindley knew nothing about my book. That was the last time I saw Hannah Arendt.

The issue then disappeared. Asher called a week later to tell me he was rushing the book into production.

"The anthology?" I asked in a dejected tone.

"What are you talking about?" he shot back.

"Clay told me you wanted to do an anthology."

"That was some crazy idea Clay had," Asher explained. He said that Clay only worked at Viking one day a week and he apparently mixed up an agent's proposal for another anthology with my book. As for my book, Asher said Viking was on a "crash production schedule." That ended the issue in my mind.

In June 1966, Viking Press published my book as *Inquest: The Warren Commission and the Establishment of Truth*. Because the text was less than 40,000 words long, below the minimum for a

Viking book, Asher included the two-volume classified FBI report as an appendix. At the time, no publisher had ever published, and the public had never seen, the underlying FBI investigation of a crime. So it provided an unprecedented view of the workings of J. Edgar Hoover's FBI.

The book also changed the way the media looked at the Kennedy assassination. Until that point, writing about the Kennedy assassination fell into one of two categories: blind faith or conspiratorial demonology. The blind-faith writers reasoned that because the members of the Warren Commission were unquestionably men of high integrity, the commission would not conceal evidence of a conspiracy. The demonologists, on the other hand, led by Mark Lane, believed there was a conspiracy and since the commission found no evidence of one, it must have been part of the cover-up. The assumption common to both groups was that the Warren Commission had conducted an investigation that would have uncovered a conspiracy if it indeed existed. My book showed this assumption to be wrong, thanks to the documents provided by Liebeler and other staff lawyers. Just the commission's hourly payroll records, showing how little time the investigators spent on key parts of the investigation, debunked that assumption. Taken together with the memos, they proved that the commission's investigation, far from being exhaustive, had been limited by time deadlines, staff disagreements, missing autopsy evidence, and political pressure.

However honorable were these men, they had not dug deep enough to rule out the possibility of a conspiracy. Once that was accepted, the assumption that it was an exhaustive investigation that had left no stone unturned, which had been the established wisdom before my book was published, was then abandoned. Even though I had found no evidence to contradict the commission's conclusion that Oswald was the lone assassin, I opened the public's mind to the possibility that the shallowness of its investigation meant new evidence could be found. Interviewers and others relentlessly questioned me on missing evidence. Rather than taking "I don't know" for an answer, they often supplied their own. For example, after seeing me speak at an Associated Press–sponsored event in Coronado, California, on November 17, 1966, the comedian Mort Sahl insisted on driving me back to L.A. in his sports car, a 120-mile trip. Traveling at hair-raising speeds, I found myself a captive audience for his loaded questions about the single-bullet theory and his periodic rants about government secrecy. "If the *Warren Report* was a school report, it would receive an I for Incomplete," he shouted as we arrived at my hotel. "It left out the whole plot to murder Kennedy." The revelation that the JFK assassination was still unsolved seemed to torture, if not unhinge, many people aside from Sahl. I soon found that I could not escape the furor I had let loose.

There was still a piece missing from this part of the story that I discovered nine years later. On December 5, 1975, I received a call from Aaron Asher, who by now had become a close personal friend. He said in a hushed voice, as if announcing the death of a relative, that Hannah Arendt had died. He asked whether I was going to her funeral in Chicago.

"Why would I go to her funeral?" I replied, somewhat confused.

"I thought you were her protégé."

I told him that not only was I not her protégé, but that I had met her only twice in my life, and then only very briefly.

Taken aback, Aaron told me what had driven the decision to publish *Inquest* at Viking. He said Tom Guinzburg was against publishing my book because I was an unknown commodity. He owned the company and his word was final. So Asher suggested the anthology, not Clay, and Clay had been correct in telling me that Viking planned to throw my book in an anthology.

"What happened to change Guinzberg's mind?" I asked.

Asher now told the whole story. They were in the middle of an editorial meeting discussing another book when Denver Lindley was called to the phone by his secretary. He came back a few minutes later, his face beet red, and shouted at Guinzburg, "You can't do that to Epstein. He is Hannah Arendt's student. Her protégé. That was her on the phone."

Guinzburg, taken aback by Lindley's vehemence, relented. "If she vouches for him," he said, "there is no reason not to go ahead with publishing Epstein's book." It was a fortunate misunderstanding—at least for me. It was another odd turn on a bumpy road but, thanks to that misunderstanding and Hannah Arendt's accidental intervention, I had finally found my calling in life. I was to be a questioner of received wisdom and a solver of unsolved riddles.

# CHAPTER NINE

# THE JOLLY GREEN GIANT

T he curse of the JFK mystery was its propensity to change its shape. On March 1, 1967, I learned that it was far from over. Jim Garrison, the district attorney of New Orleans, had just reawakened it by charging a prominent New Orleans businessman named Clay Shaw with "participating in a conspiracy to murder President Kennedy."

A few days later, I met with William Shawn, the editor of the *New Yorker*, at his request. When I was ushered into his office, he was partly hidden behind a mound of manuscripts on his desk. As he emerged, I could see a small man with slumping shoulders, a balding head, and timid eyes. He seemed so frail I feared that a loud noise might cause him to duck behind the manuscript pile. I would later discover that, when it came to supporting writers, he was as strong and unbending as steel.

"Please sit down, Mr. Epstein," he said in a low but clear voice.

The office was modestly furnished and far smaller than I had expected for an editor at the center of the literary world. Shawn said Richard Rovere, the *New Yorker*'s Washington correspondent, had recommended me to write on Garrison. I had met Rovere briefly at the Congress for Cultural Freedom conference on the island of Rhodes in 1958, and at my publisher's request, he had written the flattering preface for *Inquest*. Shawn came right to the point, asking in a hushed voice whether I had a view as to why Garrison had arrested Clay Shaw.

I said that I was as mystified as he was by the news of the arrest in New Orleans.

He all but whispered, "But Mr. Epstein, could a local district attorney have solved a mystery that had defied the Warren Commission?"

I told him my investigation had convinced me that the Warren Commission could have left loose ends dangling in New Orleans in its rush to meet a 1964 deadline and that it was possible that a determined DA, using rougher police methods, had found new evidence.

"Would you be willing to go to New Orleans and look into the matter?" he said as if he were asking me a great favor.

As I admired the *New Yorker*, I accepted.

When I called Garrison and said I planned to write a profile on him for the *New Yorker*, he said I should come to New Orleans right away because there had been a startling new development in the case. He could not discuss it further over the phone because an unnamed "agency" was tapping his line.

I had done the research on the Warren Commission on a shoe-string 10 years earlier, but now, thanks to an expense account provided by the *New Yorker*, I could fly first class, stay at five-star hotels, and hire an able researcher from Harvard Law School. It greatly enhanced the experience, if not the substance, of investigative reporting.

I booked a seat on a flight to New Orleans on April 13 and then arranged a car and driver to take me on a tour of the places Oswald had worked and lived in 1963. Garrison had scheduled dinner for us the next night at 8:00 p.m. at Broussard's, a well-known restaurant in the French Quarter.

I arrived a half hour early, as I often do for fear of being late.

While I was waiting for Garrison, the manager, who knew I was writing for the *New Yorker*, explained that the ubiquitous Napoleonic statuary in the restaurant was the result of founder Joe Broussard's near worship of the French general. The manager added that "the jolly green giant," the common nickname for Garrison, was also "a fan of Napoleon."

Garrison made his entrance shortly before 9:00 p.m. There was no mistaking this giant of a man. He was six feet, six inches tall, with glassy eyes and a jutting jaw. He walked to my table with a slightly askew gait, stopping at nearly every table to extend his hand to well-wishers. When he finally reached my table, he welcomed me to New Orleans, saying that my book on the Warren Commission had helped shape his decision to launch his investigation. I was duly flattered. When I asked about the exciting news he had to tell me, he fixed me with a walleyed stare and, after a long pause, replied, "First let me tell you a little about myself. You are writing my profile, right?"

"Right."

He told me that he owed everything to two individuals. The first was Ayn Rand, whose book *The Fountainhead* had impressed on him the need for individuals of higher consciousness to act like supermen. His second "hero" was Huey Long, the late governor of Louisiana, or, as Garrison called him, "the Kingfish." Before Long was assassinated in 1935, he had won enormous political support by attacking putative government conspiracies.

Neither of his intellectual heroes reassured me. I had already done some research on him in Harvard's Widener Library. Garrison's career had not gone smoothly. Born in 1921 in Iowa, Garrison served briefly in the Louisiana National Guard, but he was relieved of duty after a military doctor diagnosed him as suffering from a disabling neurosis. Garrison appealed to the surgeon general, who allowed him to complete his service. He then decided to enter politics. After legally changing his name from Earling

Carothers Garrison to Jim Garrison, he defeated the incumbent district attorney, Richard Dowling, and once in office indicted Dowling for criminal malfeasance. (The charge was dismissed for lack of evidence.) He also accused a New Orleans judge he had taken issue with of racketeering and conspiracy, which, when he furnished no evidence, led to Garrison being convicted in 1963 of criminal defamation. (The conviction was thrown out by the US Supreme Court two years later.)

I asked him about the army doctor who had diagnosed him.

Garrison said he was a "personal enemy, out to get him." He then told me his side. He relayed his extraordinary story of persecution while he compulsively consumed three dozen oysters.

I wanted to know the specific evidence he had discovered implicating Clay Shaw, but he evaded that issue by telling me about a tangle of characters emanating from the putative plot he claimed to have uncovered. I jotted down their names as he rambled on, then asked, "How did these people connect to the JFK assassination?"

Over the next two hours, Garrison spelled out the elements of the conspiracy he had established. It came—like the Creole specialties that the chef personally delivered, dish by dish, to our table—in sporadic doses. He identified the central character as David W. Ferrie, a former airline pilot and self-styled soldier of fortune, whom Garrison described as "one of the most bizarre men I have ever met." At one point, Ferrie had professed to be a bishop in a quasi-political cult called the Orthodox Old Catholic Church of North America. He had also worked as a freelance pilot, a pornographer, a hypnotist, and a gas station operator. He came to Garrison's attention on November 24, 1963, two days after the JFK assassination, when Garrison's office got a tip alleging that Ferrie had trained Oswald in marksmanship. Garrison detained Ferrie for questioning. When the tipster, a former partner of Ferrie's, recanted his story, Garrison had no choice but to release Ferrie. Four years later, he reopened the investigation when he had found other witnesses who claimed that Ferrie had become involved with Oswald. By March 1967, he had decided, as he put it, "to break Ferrie." But before he could re-arrest him, Ferrie was found dead. It was either suicide or murder, he said, but, in either case, he had lost his suspect.

Why had he arrested Clay Shaw? I asked.

"It's exactly like a chess problem," he answered. "The Warren Commission moved the same pieces back and forth and got nowhere. I made a new move and solved the problem."

What he had done in his chess analogy was to add new pieces to the board. I gently reminded him that he had told me on the phone he had new evidence.

He looked at his watch. "It's past midnight. Come to my office tomorrow and you can see the evidence for yourself." He finished his wine and was off, shaking the hands of the few people still in the restaurant on his way out.

I arrived at 10:00 a.m. at the district attorney's suite of offices in the Criminal District Court Building. Jones Harris, wearing a straw hat and blue blazer, was waiting for me in the outer office. Harris was part of a rapidly disappearing tradition, the gentleman amateur sleuth. Born in Paris in 1929 to movie star Ruth Gordon and Broadway producer Jed Harris, he did not need to work for a living, so he devoted his time to solving mysteries. He was not only well connected socially, dating a Vanderbilt, but he had a bloodhound's ability to tenaciously, if not obsessively, track down people. He had helped me find people I needed to see in my original investigation of the Warren Commission, and, as he was good company, I asked him to join me in New Orleans.

Garrison was not there yet. His receptionist said that he had been called away on another case. He had left word that I "should start going through the evidence."

Andrew "Moo Moo" Sciambra, an assistant DA, took Harris and me to a small office in the rear of the suite. When we got there,

Sciambra pointed to a table full of whips, masks, and other bond-age paraphernalia and said, "Jim wanted you to see what we seized from the home of Clay Shaw." Shaw, who had been director of the International Trade Mart in New Orleans, claimed to Garrison that these items were part of his Mardi Gras costume.

Sciambra asked mockingly, "Does this look like an innocent Mardi Gras costume to you?"

It didn't, but even if it was S&M gear, I didn't see the connection between this part of Shaw's private life and the Kennedy assas-sination. I asked Sciambra how this gear was relevant to the case.

"Jim will explain that when he arrives," Sciambra replied. Pointing to a stack of six cardboard cartons on the desk, he said as he left, "Jim suggests you familiarize yourself with the rest of the evidence."

For the next two hours, Harris and I sifted through the boxes. They contained Shaw's personal letters, photographs, manuscripts, checkbooks, address books, calendars, and even his blueprints for the renovation of a house in the French Quarter.

Harris then found a five-digit number in Shaw's address book that partly matched an entry in Lee Harvey Oswald's phone book: the number 19106 preceded by the Cyrillic letters for the English letters *DD*. Shaw's book contained the same five digits attached to the name Lee Odom, followed by *PO Box 19106, Dallas, Tex.*

By the time Garrison finally arrived, I had gone to lunch. Meanwhile, Harris, who remained in the office, told Garrison about the entry he had discovered and Garrison, without waiting for confirmation, announced to the press that he had linked Shaw to Oswald.

Garrison stated that Shaw's phone book and Oswald's contained the identical entry "PO 19106" (which was untrue) and that this number was "nonexistent" (which he had not yet determined). He then went a step further in saying that the number was a code he had deciphered. His method involved arbitrarily rearranging the digits, subtracting another number, and adding the letters *WH*. So it yielded *WH 1–5601*, the telephone number of Oswald's killer, Jack Ruby, and, Garrison claimed, "no other number on earth" (which was false). When asked by a reporter from the *New Orleans Times-Picayune* for a fuller explanation of how *PO 19106* became Ruby's number, Garrison, without missing a beat, explained that one simply transposed its third, fourth, and last digit (so it became *PO 16901*) and subtracted the difference.

I had breakfast with Garrison at Brennan's the next morning. He said the phone number was a major break in the case. I asked how he had derived the *WH* portion of Ruby's number. He answered that the code was "subjective." In other words, he used hocus-pocus to connect Shaw to Oswald and Ruby. Meanwhile, he still avoided answering my questions about the "new evidence" he had told me about on the phone. I left New Orleans.

I didn't tell Garrison that I had received a phone call from Thomas Bethell, a 27-year-old British academic who was working in Garrison's office. After graduating from Trinity College at Oxford in 1964, he had gone to New Orleans to write about jazz and was hired by Garrison as a researcher. The disturbing news he conveyed to me was that the decoded number Garrison had shown me was "pure nonsense." According to Bethell, Garrison's staff had determined that the entry in Shaw's address book, *PO Box 19106*, not only existed but had been assigned to Lee Odom, the exact name listed in Shaw's book. Further, the same number in Oswald's address book could not possibly have referred to the same thing because Dallas Post Office records showed that the post office box number did not exist in Dallas before it was assigned to Odom in 1965. He further said Garrison had ordered that no one on his staff discuss this embarrassing mistake.

I did not return to New Orleans until June 22. Garrison had called the night before to tell me he was about to "haul a key witness before the Grand Jury." The witness, according to Garrison, linked Shaw directly to Oswald. I flew Eastern Airlines from Boston to New Orleans, arriving at 2:40 p.m., and went straight to Garrison's office.

Moo Moo Sciambra met me there. Despite the city's sweltering heat, Garrison had gone for a sauna at the New Orleans Athletic Club. "The dry heat helps him think," Sciambra added.

Sciambra said Garrison's "key witness" was Dean Andrews. I recognized the name. Andrews was the lawyer who had told the Warren Commission three years earlier that Lee Harvey Oswald had sought his legal help in appealing his dishonorable discharge from the Marines and that someone called Clay Bertrand had sent Oswald to him. Andrews had no address for Bertrand and said he knew him mainly as "a voice on the phone." The Warren Commission had been unable to find Bertrand.

"There is no Clay Bertrand," Sciambra said. "It was the alias used by Clay Shaw."

I asked how Garrison uncovered that match.

Sciambra told me that Garrison assigned him the task of questioning every bar owner in the French Quarter to find anyone with the first name Clay. He came up with a list of a dozen or so Clays, and Garrison further narrowed it down to one—Clay Shaw.

Recalling the legerdemain that Garrison had used to decode the phone number, I asked Sciambra how Garrison decoded *Bertrand* as *Shaw*.

"Jim figured it out."

I met Garrison that evening for dinner. He told me he had made progress since the arrest, and release on bail, of Shaw. "I can now prove that Oswald, David Ferrie, and Clay Shaw met at Ferrie's apartment in 1963," Garrison said. "During that meeting, they planned out the assassination."

I asked how Garrison could establish such a meeting took place since two of the alleged participants, Oswald and Ferrie, were dead and the third, Shaw, categorically denied ever meeting Oswald.

Garrison said there was another witness named Perry Russo, who happened to be in Ferrie's apartment at the time and had overheard the conversation. Unfortunately, Garrison said, Russo had repressed his memory of the assassination meeting when he was initially questioned by Sciambra, so no mention of it was made in Sciambra's memorandum of the interrogation. Garrison then told me that he had "reconstituted Russo's memory" by using both sodium pentothal injections and hypnosis. As a result, Russo was able to recall Oswald, Ferrie, and Shaw at the assassination meeting. The problem for Garrison was that the Sciambra memo could be used to discredit Russo's reconstituted memories in court. Therefore, Garrison said, he needed a witness to connect Oswald to Shaw. This made Dean Andrews, in Garrison's view, a key witness, since he might be able to identify Shaw as the Clay Bertrand who had sent Oswald to him.

"Will he?" I asked.

"He will when we press him." Garrison squeezed a lemon over his oysters as if demonstrating his ability to squeeze a witness.

I met Dean Andrews the next day at the Marlboro Club at 4:00 p.m. He was in his late 40s. A plump man with a boyish face, he wore a badly crumpled suit, a loud tie, and round dark glasses. After waving me over with exaggerated hand gestures, he told me he had served as an assistant DA in Jefferson Parish and knew "how the game is played." Andrews had a colorful way of describing people. He called Garrison "a thousand-pound canary."

"Is Clay Shaw the person you called Clay Bertrand?" I asked.

"Absolutely not," he answered. "Shaw is just an unfortunate who was grabbed out of the sky by the jolly green giant, and his wizards and practitioners of voodoo labeled him Clay Bertrand, and bang, he's been tagged 'it' ever since."

"Is there a Clay Bertrand?"

"I can't answer that question without running into a legal meat grinder," he said, laughing out loud. All Andrews could say was that someone he knew had called him at the Hotel Dieu in 1963 and told him he had sent him a client. That client turned out to be Oswald, who wanted his military discharge reclassified from dishonorable to honorable.

"So you know who called you?" I interjected.

"Of course," he answered. "If those lazy bums on the Warren Commission had even bothered to check my phone records, they would have found out no one named Clay anything ever called me."

"Would they have found another name?"

"They might have found that I got a call from Gene Davis."

"And you invented the name Clay Bertrand to protect him."

"I am not saying I did, and I am not saying I didn't. All I am saying is that it was not Clay Shaw."

The *New Yorker* published my 10,000-word "Reporter at Large" article on Garrison on July 6, 1968. Shawn, who chose clarity over wit, changed the title from "The Thousand-Pound Canary" to "Garrison." The article, as I knew, did not please Garrison. It described how he had used raw power and demagogy to build an entirely bogus case against an innocent man. It concluded: "In the year I have been studying Garrison's investigation, and have had access to his office, the only evidence I have seen or heard about that could connect Shaw with the assassination had been fraudulent—some devised by Garrison himself and some cynically culled from criminals or the emotionally unstable."

# CHAPTER TEN

# THE GREAT JFK DEBATE

Nearly a quarter century after Garrison's case fell apart, Oliver Stone demonstrated that a fraud can have a second life in fiction if not in the universe of fact. He accomplished this by casting Kevin Costner in the role of a truth-telling Garrison in his 1991 movie *JFK*. In the film, unlike in reality, Garrison uncovers a CIA-backed conspiracy to kill Kennedy.

The movie created such an immense controversy over the Kennedy assassination that Victor Navasky, the editor of the *Nation*, America's oldest continuous magazine, came up with the idea of a *Nation*-sponsored debate about whether the movie *JFK* was fact or fiction at Town Hall in New York. Stone, who was claiming that his movie was fact, not fiction, was eager to participate. Navasky asked me to join the debate to provide a counter-view because I had written about the actual Garrison inquest in the *New Yorker*.

I readily agreed. Navasky, the author of *Kennedy Justice*, had been a friend of mine since we both learned to play tennis together 20 years earlier in the Hamptons. In light of his intelligence and wit, I had full confidence that, as moderator, he would keep the debate on track. When he asked me about other participants, I suggested Norman Mailer.

Born in 1923 in Long Branch, New Jersey, Mailer was a prize-winning author, journalist, film director, and political activist. Three years earlier, in August 1989, Mailer had asked me to join him in forming a monthly dinner discussion, which he self-mockingly called the "Dynamite Club." The other founding member was Don DeLillo, the author of *Libra*, a novel about Oswald. Mailer hoped that we would come up with a dynamite revelation about who was behind Kennedy's assassination. Initially, the three of us had pleasant, if not enlightening, dinners at Mailer's house in Brooklyn Heights. We then moved the dinners to my house and gradually expanded the club to include such leading conspiracy investigators as Jim Hougan, the author of *Spooks*, and Bernard "Bud" Fensterwald, the founder of the Assassination Archives and Research Center. At one dinner held at Fensterwald's house in Washington, G. Gordon Liddy, the organizer of the infamous Watergate break-in, attended and suggested that the FBI had orchestrated, if not the assassination, a massive cover-up of it. Mailer himself concluded that JFK was killed as part of an apocalyptical struggle to change history. As he had just written *Harlot's Ghost*, a roman à clef suggesting the involvement of a rogue faction of the CIA in the Kennedy assassination, I thought he would be a lively participant in the debate. He readily accepted.

Navasky chose the film writer-director Nora Ephron as the final participant because she had to deal with the compromises Hollywood makes on reality-based subjects in *Silkwood*. Nora also had a brilliant eye for irony and absurdity, which would be useful in the debate.

The event took place on March 3, 1992. Some 1,200 people jammed into Town Hall. It was scheduled to begin at 7:45 p.m. Oliver Stone arrived five minutes late accompanied by two young aides: Jane Rusconi, his chief researcher on *JFK*, who sat next to him on stage, and Kristina Hare, his production assistant, who sat in front of him in the first row. The almost 10-minute standing ovation he received made it clear to that Stone all but owned the audience.

When the applause for Stone subsided, Navasky opened the discussion with a well-received joke. He asked, "Will all of you out there that think you don't belong on this panel, please stand up?" No one did.

Mailer spoke first. He began by saying that the JFK assassination should be "seen not as history but as a myth in which the gods warred and a god fell." About Stone he said, "Of course, like many a movie man beforehand, he mislabeled the product. He did not make cinematic history, and in fact, to hell with that. He's dared something more dangerous. He entered the echoing halls of the largest paranoid myth of our time: the undeclared national belief that John Fitzgerald Kennedy was killed by the concentrated forces of maligned power in the land." After hearing him espouse Manichaean conspiracy theories at Dynamite Club meetings, I was not surprised at his deification of Kennedy as a "god." For him, great evil needed a god to battle.

Next came Nora Ephron, who was as insightful in person as in her books and movies. "I'm not here to talk about *JFK* per se," she began, "but about what it is like to have written a movie based on something that happened." She provided immensely entertaining anecdotes about the filming of *Silkwood* and how a factual story had to be varnished with a layer of fictive embellishment, such as adding "spoons at a table," to create the illusion of reality. Her account neatly evaded the issue of Stone's movie.

So it fell to me to point out that Stone's *JFK* had diverged so far from the facts of the case that it was nothing short of a total misrepresentation of reality. But surveying the audience, I said: "I'm going to be in the minority. But I believe there is a difference between nonfiction and fiction. I don't believe the difference is trivial. Stone has every right to present whatever view he considers valid—or even entertaining—in a work of fiction. Everyone else does it. And as such, it may contain much truth in it, and it may look like a news documentary, but it cannot be considered nonfiction because it blends in fictional characters and fictional episodes. But, as we all know, a real event also happened in New Orleans in 1967."

I pointed out that in that event, there was a flagrant abuse of prosecutorial power by Jim Garrison. Clay Shaw, whom Garrison had charged with conspiring to assassinate President John F. Kennedy, had been acquitted and exonerated. Over a dozen people were arrested or charged with a crime by Garrison (though they were never prosecuted). Three were members of the press—Walter Sheridan of NBC News, David Chandler of *Life* magazine, and Richard Townley of WSDU-TV. Arrest warrants were issued for them on charges of libel because they had claimed that Garrison was fabricating evidence. Three were members of Garrison's staff. They were charged with larceny for leaking Garrison's purported evidence to the press. Six were potential witnesses. They claimed Garrison asked them to perjure themselves or plant evidence in return for legal favors or cash. Garrison also arrested someone called Edgar Eugene Bradley, charging him with "conspiracy to kill JFK." The arrest was just a desperate effort to divert public opinion. After Bradley—whoever he is—was released, Garrison forgot about him. The assistant DA said, "It was a mistake." You won't find Bradley's name in the movie *JFK*.

At this point, having appealed to the civil liberties side of the *Nation* audience, I was not booed. So I proceeded to make the points I had prepared.

Stone was the final speaker. Born in 1946 in New Yok City, Stone had directed such critically acclaimed films as *Platoon*, *The Doors*, and *Wall Street*. He strode over to the podium and responded, "I obviously would like to address some of your questions, Mr. Epstein, but we'll wait till afterward." He said that his film represented the mythic "common man, Jim Garrison, risking a comfortable life to do battle with the forces of overwhelming evil. He cannot in the end, of course, be triumphant because this would mean a successful political revolution against this invisible government. He must fail and become a martyr in his quest for truth." The audience gave him another standing ovation.

The debate ended at 11:00 p.m. Afterward, we gathered backstage, where my guest, Sonserai Lee, joined me. A 27-year-old Korean-born practitioner of Asian traditional medicine, she had accompanied me on a three-week trip to China, Inner Mongolia, and Japan in 1990. She instantly caught Stone's eye. Although he had not previously spoken to me off-stage, he suddenly shouted from across the room, "Hey guys, where are you going to dinner?" Sonserai said, "The Royalton," and next thing I knew, he joined us for dinner. He brought with him his production assistant Kristina Hare.

At dinner, Stone proved to be far more insightful than I had expected from his JFK movie. He also was completely charming. I realized that charm was a skill that a successful movie director like Stone needs to get peak performances from his actors. (Stone would later give me a small part in his movie *Wall Street 2: Money Never Sleeps*.) Toward the end of dinner, he brought up the CIA's former counterintelligence chief, James Jesus Angleton. When I mentioned I knew Angleton, he exclaimed, "Wow. Did he say if the CIA killed JFK?"

"Angleton is a story for some other time," I replied. What I didn't tell him was that Angleton had had an enormous influence over the way that I viewed the work of intelligence services.

# CHAPTER ELEVEN

# JAMES JESUS ANGLETON

No one I ever met in government had the raw intellectual capabilities of Angleton. How he employed them was another matter. His story, like the man himself, was tangled in convoluted concepts of deception. He changed my understanding of the business of espionage and began my education in its inseparable twin, deception. Up until December 1975, when I read in the *New York Times* that a man called James Jesus Angleton had been fired as the chief of the CIA Counterintelligence Staff, I didn't even know that the CIA had a Counterintelligence Staff, let alone that Angleton had headed it since its inception in 1954.

The *Times* story caught my eye because of a book I was just beginning that December. A week before the *Times* story, I had been invited to the University Club on Fifth Avenue—a club so staid that it banned reading any book or paper in its dining room—by two top *Reader's Digest* editors, Fulton Oursler Jr. and Edward Thompson. They proposed that I write a biography of Lee Harvey Oswald that the *Digest* would finance. I was not interested. After all, 13 years had passed since the assassination of President Kennedy and little, if any, new evidence had emerged about the alleged assassin Oswald worthy of a biography. Thompson, measuring his words carefully, told me that there was indeed a new source of evidence whose knowledge had been kept from the Warren Commission by the CIA. He now had my attention.

"Is the name Yuri Nosenko familiar to you?" he asked.

I knew, from a file given to me in 1966 by Wesley Liebeler, that Nosenko (misspelled in it as "Nossenko") was the KGB officer who had been involved in Oswald's case in Moscow. I also knew that this "Nossenko" had defected to the United States and been held under tight wraps by the CIA.

"He was Oswald's KGB case officer," Thompson said.

"We could make him available to you for this book," Oursler added.

If so, Nosenko was in a position to fill in the blanks regarding Oswald's relationship with Soviet intelligence during the two and a half years he had spent in the Soviet Union. I agreed to consider the book if they could produce Nosenko.

True to their word, Thompson and Oursler arranged for me to meet with Nosenko at the *Digest*'s Washington offices on Rhode Island Avenue on January 4, 1976. Oursler was waiting for me, along with Jamie Jamieson, a retired CIA officer, who was on crutches. Jamieson, who had a contract from the CIA to handle Nosenko, assured me that "Colonel Nosenko is as good as gold."

"Meaning?" I asked.

"Meaning everything he has told us has proven to be true." Jamieson spent 10 minutes briefing me on the case. Nosenko had defected in 1964 and over the past 12 years, according to Jamieson, had provided "a hundred or so" invaluable leads that had unmasked many KGB agents abroad. As far as the JFK assassination went, Jamieson said the CIA had established that Nosenko had full access to the KGB's Oswald file and was therefore in a position to reveal to me Oswald's relationship with the KGB.

At 11:30 a.m., the KGB defector whom the CIA had kept secret for over a decade, Yuri Ivanovich Nosenko, arrived. He stood six feet tall, with a massive jaw and dark brown eyes set deep in their sockets. He walked with a slight limp. His English, though adequate, was marked with a heavy Russian accent.

Jamieson, after making introductions, left the room. Oursler remained to take notes (as a tape recorder was not allowed). I began the interview by asking Nosenko about his prior life in Russia.

Nosenko said he had been born October 30, 1927, in the town of Nikolayev. His father, Ivan Nosenko, was part of the Communist elite, an alternate member of the Central Committee of the Communist Party, who served as the Soviet minister of shipping. He died in 1956 when Nosenko was 29. At his funeral, many leaders of the Soviet Union, including Nikita Khrushchev, Georgi Malenkov, Nikolai Bulganin, and Kliment Voroshilov, formed the honor guard. Yuri Nosenko said he saw himself at this time as a rising star in the KGB.

He described his career with great precision. In 1953, he had transferred from Naval Intelligence to the KGB's Second Chief Directorate, which was responsible for counterintelligence against potential enemy agents inside Russia. He became deputy chief of the American-British section of its Tourism Department in 1962, which monitored the activities of American visitors in Russia.

This piqued my interest. Oswald was residing in Russia in 1962. "So Oswald came within your purview?" I asked.

Nosenko nodded. "Yes."

He explained that he had assumed supervisory responsibility for any efforts the KGB undertook to watch, recruit, or otherwise exploit Oswald. Therefore, after Kennedy's assassination, he was charged with conducting a complete after-the-fact investigation of all contacts between Oswald and Soviet intelligence officials. He said a plane was put at his disposal so he could rush all of Oswald's files to Moscow. He also sent his investigators to the city of Minsk, where Oswald had resided. As Nosenko described it, he was the post-assassination "inspector general" for the KGB on Oswald. After completing his investigation, he became concerned that the

KGB had learned he was also working for the CIA. So he decided to defect to America.

When it came to Oswald, Nosenko's answers were far less detailed, often no more than "Yes" or "No." I asked him directly whether the KGB had recruited Oswald.

"No." He said that neither the KGB nor any other Soviet service had attempted to recruit or exploit Oswald. According to Nosenko, Oswald was too unstable to be of any use to the KGB. Although the local police in Minsk watched him, Oswald, again according to Nosenko, was never drawn into any relationship with any of the Russian security services. On the contrary, Russian intelligence was relieved when he decided to return to the United States with his Russian wife, Marina. Nosenko further said he had determined from his personal access to the KGB file on Oswald that no effort was made to recruit him after he returned to the United States. He spoke with great authority, insisting that he was in a unique position to know if there had been a liaison between Oswald and the Russians.

"As much as I despise the KGB," he said, "and would like to implicate them, the fact is that they were blameless in this matter."

I continued questioning him for nearly six hours. I found some of his answers, which he seemed to be giving by rote, at odds with the documentary evidence. As the interview wore on into the late afternoon, he said he was hungry and suggested we stop for dinner.

Oursler had made a 6:00 p.m. reservation at Jean-Pierre, a posh French restaurant on K Street. At dinner, Nosenko consumed a great deal of wine—so much that I thought he might be an alcoholic. The alcohol also seemed to feed his fury at the man who was his nemesis at the CIA.

"He put me through hell," Nosenko said.

"Who?" I asked.

"Angleton."

I recalled the name from the *Times* story. I asked what he would say to Angleton if he met him.

He replied that he did not want to speak any further about him. He raised his hand, as if to wave me silent. Getting up abruptly, Nosenko lurched out of the restaurant. I followed him outside. A car was waiting for him. Jamieson waved to him from the back seat, Nosenko got in, and the car sped off.

To check out Nosenko's story, I wanted to go to the Soviet Union to interview Oswald's acquaintances in Moscow and Minsk. These interviews might allow me to determine if what Nosenko had described from the KGB files matched the recollections of those whom Oswald had met, befriended, and worked with. For this enterprise, I needed a Soviet visa, however, so I arranged to meet with Igor Agou, a political assistant to the Soviet ambassador. At a cordial lunch at the Madison Hotel, I told him I needed to go to Russia to interview Oswald's acquaintances. I asked if he could expedite my visa application. Agou replied, "There is no need for you to go to Russia. The best source on Oswald's visit to Russia is in America—Yuri Nosenko."

It seemed odd to me that a representative of the Soviet government would recommend that I seek information from the very same source that a CIA representative had recommended. Nosenko, if a true defector, should have been viewed as a traitor to the Soviet Union. So why did Minister Agou tell me to see and believe Nosenko?

I told Oursler that I was not comfortable using Nosenko as a source unless I knew more about how he was received at the CIA.

"Jamie said he was good as gold," Oursler said.

"But Nosenko said Angleton put him through hell," I replied. "I need to know why."

The next morning, I received a call from Ken Gilmore, who headed the *Digest*'s Washington bureau (and would later be the editor-in-chief of the *Digest*). He told me it would be a grave mistake calling Angleton since it would risk offending Jamieson and losing access to Nosenko.

That conversation further provoked my curiosity. Even before I put down the phone, I had decided to call Angleton.

Oddly, Angleton evidenced no surprise that I called him or that I had met with Nosenko. I told him Nosenko had mentioned his name, but he did not comment. I next told him that a Soviet diplomat I had seen earlier that day had vouched for Nosenko's credibility. He remained silent.

I broke the silence. "I would like your perspective."

"I am away most of this week," he said. "Can I invite you for dinner next week?"

We met in the lobby of the Madison on January 18, 1976. Angleton, in a black homburg and gray raincoat, looked like someone that central casting in Hollywood might have chosen for the part of a master spy. Even though he was six feet tall, he shuffled down the hall with a stoop that made him seem a foot shorter. He was in his late 50s but looked older. As he drew nearer, I saw that he was ghostly thin with finely sculptured facial features set off by arched eyebrows.

In the dining room, he told me about his history. During a punitive raid on Mexico in 1916, his father, William Angleton, a cavalry officer in the Idaho National Guard, courted and married his mother, a 17-year-old Mexican beauty. The family then moved from Idaho to Italy, where his father worked for the National Cash Register Company. Living in a magnificent villa overlooking Rome, James became quickly accustomed to the wines and cuisine of Europe. He attended school at Malvern, an elite public school in England. In 1937, with war tensions building in Europe, he returned to America and enrolled at Yale. While there, he founded and edited *Furioso*, a quarterly devoted to original poetry. To write for it, he recruited several world-renowned poets including Ezra Pound,

Archibald MacLeish, and E.E. Cummings. After he graduated in 1941, he went on to Harvard Law School. A year later, both James and his father volunteered for service in the OSS. After the war, he served in an elite counterintelligence unit in Rome called only X-2, which became part of the newly created CIA in 1947. He returned to Washington in 1949 to take over as the liaison with other allied intelligence services, a position that brought him into direct contact with the British liaison to Washington, Kim Philby.

When it emerged in the spring of 1951 that Philby was a likely KGB spy, Angleton persuaded Allen Dulles, the director of Central Intelligence, to create a new CIA unit, a Counterintelligence Staff, which Angleton would head. For the next three decades, Angleton was responsible for keeping the CIA's central registry of its foreign agents and, even more important, determining which of these agents were deemed "bona fide" sources. It was Angleton's job to make that determination for the entire CIA. An agent not labeled bona fide by Angleton was assumed to be a possible double agent under the control of the KGB, and whatever information he supplied was not to be trusted. Angleton thus assumed immense power over the CIA's flow of information from its human sources.

Angleton chain-smoked Virginia Slims cigarettes as we spoke.

I asked him directly, "Was there any problem with Nosenko's veracity?"

Angleton put out his cigarette. "Truth is always complicated when it comes to defectors." He added that since the case was "still sensitive," he could not discuss it. With that, he abruptly cut off the conversation about Nosenko and moved on to a subject of which I had no understanding at all: orchids.

Over the next hour, he provided me with elaborate details about the pollinating conditions for dendrobium, phalaenopsis, cattleyas, cymbidium, and other "tribes" of orchids, stressing their use of deception. He explained that the perpetuation of most species of orchids depends on their ability to misrepresent themselves to useful insects. Having no food to offer, they have to deceive insects into landing on them and carrying their pollen to another orchid. For this vital task, orchids depend on deception. In this curious universe, it was not the fittest but the most deceptive orchid that survived.

It gradually became clear to me that he was talking about more than the manipulation of insects. I asked him whether intelligence services could be similarly duped, provoked, and lured down false trails. "Could Nosenko have been sent to deceive the CIA?"

He shrugged, finished his wine, and got up to leave. "I told you I could not discuss cases," he said. "But you might want to buy orchids for your greenhouse."

"I don't have a greenhouse."

"Why don't you come with me to Kensington Orchids next week."

So, on January 26, 1976, I met Angleton in Kensington, Maryland.

The high humidity in the hothouse so fogged my glasses that I could hardly see Angleton. He was examining a long, spiny orchid with a flashlight. "See this oncidium orchid," he said as I approached through the corridor of plants. "It has an almost exact replica of a bee's head on its petals." He meticulously traced the upside-down bee's head for me with his flashlight. "Here's the illusionary foe— the killer bee. Unable to distinguish the simulacrum from the real bee, the wasp is triggered to attack. When it plunges its stinger through the petal, the orchid's pollen pod adheres to it. The wasp flies away and, if it sees another similar orchid, attacks again. But this time its stinger deposits the pollen from the first orchid onto the second," Angleton continued.

I was impressed by his lyrical description of the elaborate deceptive disguises in nature. It brought to mind my former teacher and employer Vladimir Nabokov's fascination with the imitative disguises of butterflies, writing in his memoir *Speak, Memory* that they were "a game of intricate enchantment and deception." Angleton was no less fascinated with this game.

Surveying the orchid, I asked why this deception worked.

Angleton answered, "Because the deceived wasp does not have the means to differentiate the real from the fake."

To switch to the subject I needed to learn about, I asked him if the CIA possesses those means.

"It once did," he said, speaking in the past tense. "The means was the Counterintelligence Staff." This was the unit Angleton had headed.

"Did the Counterintelligence Staff determine if Nosenko was real or fake?"

He brushed the question aside with a wave of his hand, as one might a pesky fly. He guided me to a nearby odontoglossum orchid. He said that it deceived the carrier it needed by blinding it. He explained, as he traced out the mechanisms in the orchid, that the carrier, in this case a mosquito, is first lured into the coils of its fleshy tubes. Its eye then collides with a spike of pollen pod, which blinds it. The blind mosquito backs out of the tube, carrying the pollen in its eye. Blinded, it follows a scent trail from a different orchid, which, repeating the procedure, it pollinates with the pollen in its eye. I assumed that his point was that deception might rely on blindness.

Angleton afterward drove me back to the Madison Hotel in his Mercedes. A violin soloist was playing on the tape deck. He said that an Israeli violinist had privately recorded the tape for him.

At the bar of the Madison, Angleton asked me what I planned to ask Nosenko in my next meeting with him.

"Any suggestions?" I replied.

He dictated, with extraordinary precision, 13 questions. Each contained names and aliases I had never heard before. After I wrote them down, I asked Angleton if he could further elaborate on these esoteric questions.

"I can't do that. I would be revealing secrets. All you need to know—and all I can tell you—is that Nosenko never got his bona fides while I was at the CIA."

I asked him in more general terms how the KGB used bogus defectors in their deception operations. "Can they be controlled once they defect?"

Angleton said I could not even begin to understand Russian intelligence services without acquainting myself with one of its classic operations. It occurred in the 1920s and was called "The Trust." He recommended that I learn about it from "The Rock," his former head of research, who had, according to Angleton, pieced together the story with "monk-like devotion."

So began my trip into Angleton's private wilderness of mirrors. "The Rock" was Angleton's pet name for Raymond Rocca. Angleton told me that his research had been vital in the Nosenko case. He lived, as did many other former CIA executives, in Fall River, Virginia. I arrived at his modest house on February 6, 1976. Rocca was a tall, bearded man in his early 60s. There were two giant cattleya orchid plants on either side of his front door. Had Angleton's staff adopted Angleton's fascination with these flowers of deception? I wondered.

"They are prize winners," Rocca said as he ushered me in. He walked with the same slight stoop as Angleton. He said he was recovering from a serious heart operation, and he had agreed to see me only because Angleton said that I needed "perspective" on Soviet deception.

Rocca had served under Angleton almost his entire career in intelligence. He was first employed by him in 1945 in the OSS in Italy to keep track of the fragmentary intelligence reports taken from German, Italian, and Vatican archives. These provided clues to individuals who might be vulnerable to blackmail, bribery, or other forms of coercion. He followed Angleton to the CIA. When Angleton organized his Counterintelligence Staff, Rocca became his head of research. He took charge of what Angleton called "the serials." These were the pieces of information left over from previous cases, which might someday fit into still other jigsaw puzzles. Angleton believed that the past, present, and future were somehow all connected in the universe of counterintelligence. Others in the CIA disagreed. When Angleton was fired from the CIA, Rocca also left.

"The Trust," Rocca explained, was a clandestine organization that operated in the Soviet Union from 1921 to 1928. Its official title was the Monarchist Union of Central Russia. Supposedly, its purpose was to overthrow the Communist regime in Russia and to restore the czarist monarchy. Since its headquarters, and cover, was a municipal credit association in downtown Moscow, it became known among anti-Communist conspirators outside of Russia as "The Trust."

Anti-Communist exiles in Europe first heard of the existence of this resistance organization in September 1921, from a Soviet official named Aleksandrovich Yakushev. On his way to an international lumber conference in Oslo, Norway, he slipped away from his delegation and contacted a leader of the anti-Communist movement in Estonia. He said that though he was outwardly working for the Communist government, he believed Communism was unfeasible in Russia. He and others who shared his conviction were now working to overthrow the Communist regime in the Soviet Union. The instrument for this subversion was the Trust. According to Yakushev, it had been so successful in recruiting government officials disillusioned with Communism that it was now the underground equivalent of a government-in-exile, and its members had infiltrated key Soviet ministries, including the secret police.

Yakushev asked the exiles to get in touch with other leaders of the anti-Soviet movement abroad, saying that the Trust would act as the "service organization" for them inside Russia. He offered to arrange to smuggle out whatever secret documents these exile groups needed. The Trust would also furnish fake passports and visas for exiles so that they could go in and out of Russia. Furthermore, he offered to undertake sabotage and assassination missions in Moscow. One by one, all the exiled leaders came to accept his version of the Trust. So did the Western intelligence services to which they reported, including those of France, Germany, England, Austria, Sweden, and Finland.

"The Trust was not an anti-Soviet organization, it only imitated one," Rocca continued, lighting his pipe. "It was a creature of the Soviet secret police, designed to supply misinformation to Western intelligence services."

But what did this half-century-old deception have to do with Nosenko—or the JFK assassination? First Angleton lectures me about orchids, and then Rocca lectures me on a defunct credit organization.

Rocca asked me to be patient. In a professorial voice, he said that in the intelligence business, defectors came in two flavors, "real and dispatched." The job of a dispatched agent is to deliver a message prepared for him by his superiors. The defectors from the Trust were all dispatched agents.

Nosenko had delivered a message to the CIA about Oswald. I asked Rocca, "Was there any evidence that Nosenko was a dispatched agent?"

Rocca answered, "Now you're talking about operational data. I was never involved in that."

As if it was some version of an Easter egg hunt, Rocca sent me to other of his former colleagues who held pieces of the Nosenko story. Tiring of the hunt, I went back to see Angleton at his home in Tucson, Arizona, arriving perhaps propitiously on the ides of March.

I was surprised to find that Angleton lived in what amounted to a private park in downtown Tucson. From the porch of his ranch house, one couldn't see the lights of another house or any sign of the city. He showed me, piece by piece, the furniture, which he had himself designed and built. He evidently enjoyed designing his world.

We sat on his terrace, looking into the darkness. He said had I arrived earlier, while it was still light, I could have seen the Superstition Mountains. He proceeded to sketch out with his finger, peak by peak, the view I might have seen. He then asked if Nosenko had answered his questions.

I told him I had not been allowed to see Nosenko again. I had submitted Angleton's 13 questions to him through the medium of Jamie Jamieson but had not received a reply.

"You never will," Angleton predicted confidently. "It is not part of his brief."

I asked what Nosenko's brief was.

"It presumably is exactly what the CIA wants you to write in your book," Angleton answered. "It is Jamieson's job to see you get the message."

Numerous fireflies were blinking in the distance. Calling my attention to them, Angleton said the female firefly uses a sort of Morse code of flashes to signal her availability to males. He added, lest I assume it was a chance observation, "Of course, one can't be sure it's a firefly." He explained that the assassination beetle, which was the firefly's natural predator, had learned over time to replicate this code of flashes. "The firefly responds to this mating call, and instead of finding a mate … is devoured by a beetle." In this case, the assassination beetle provoked the firefly into flying into the fatal trap.

I asked him if a deception run by an intelligence service required more than mere flashes of misinformation.

He replied with a smile that delivering disinformation was "the easy part." The hard part was adjusting it over time to sustain the deception.

"Does that require a mole?" I asked.

"It requires knowing the mind of your adversary."

"Wouldn't that require that the KGB had some way of knowing the mind of the CIA?"

He said he was the wrong person to ask about a mole currently in the CIA. "I was fired from counterintelligence." The FBI, at the insistence of its director, J. Edgar Hoover, had assumed the responsibility for unmasking KGB penetrations in the CIA. "You might try the Bureau."

It was not difficult making contact with the FBI. I quickly discovered that *Reader's Digest* had a direct pipeline to its top executives. Its founder, DeWitt Wallace, had been a longtime friend of both Hoover and his top deputy, Cartha "Deke" DeLoach. So had Fulton Oursler, who arranged for me to meet with DeLoach.

DeLoach was a heavyset man with dark bags under his eyes. He said he would arrange for me to meet with the FBI man in charge of the Nosenko case, William C. Sullivan.

Soon afterward, I got a phone call from Sullivan. He had been the former assistant director in charge of counterespionage investigations. He told me he was calling at DeLoach's suggestion and that he could speak to me because he was no longer with the FBI. He could provide "some background on the Nosenko case."

I met Sullivan, as he requested, at a coffee shop in a large shopping mall in Boxboro, Massachusetts, on June 14, 1976. He arrived almost an hour late. As he walked toward the table, I could see that he was a wreck of a man. Since leaving the FBI, he had had two serious car accidents from which he had not fully recovered. He mentioned that he had been given a "rough time" by the Church Committee in its grueling hearings on the FBI's domestic counterintelligence program, which he had headed. Here was another ruined career. I asked him about Hoover, who had died on May 2, 1972.

He bitterly described how Hoover had not only fired him in 1971 but also had humiliated him by locking him out of his office. He did this, according to Sullivan, to turn him into the FBI's "fall guy."

Sullivan traced his "problem with Hoover" back to an investigation he had conducted of possible Soviet manipulation of the FBI's Counterespionage Staff in the late 1960s. He explained that it had all begun in the winter of 1962 when two Soviet diplomats stationed at the United Nations in New York separately approached American diplomats. Both men were Soviet intelligence officers, working under diplomatic cover. Both said that they had been unable to fulfill their espionage missions and were therefore in grave potential trouble with their superiors in Soviet intelligence. Each then offered to betray their country and work as moles for the FBI.

After speaking to Angleton, Sullivan suspected that they might be Soviet "dangles" who had made their contacts with the FBI at the behest of the KGB. "It all seemed too pat, too contrived," he explained. Nevertheless, Hoover decided to accept their offer and use them as moles. The first of these volunteers was code-named "Fedora," the second "Top Hat." Both Fedora and Top Hat asked the FBI to help them answer the questionnaires supplied to them by Moscow—which meant that the FBI had to do their espionage job for them to help them maintain their credibility in the eyes of their superiors. To "play out this game," as Sullivan put it, Hoover had to give each of them American sources that could provide them with classified military documents. Such "notional agents," as they are called in the intelligence business, are fictitious sources that are in a plausible position to copy and pass on classified documents needed to answer the spies' questionnaires. The data were cleared by a special interagency review board, which decided what secrets the United States could afford to give away to the KGB. When Fedora and Top Hat began pressing the FBI for increasingly sensitive data, Sullivan feared that "the game was getting out of control." He recommended that the contacts be terminated. Again, he was overruled, he said gruffly, "because Hoover wouldn't admit he had been duped."

"How does Nosenko fit in?" I finally asked.

Sullivan shook his head as if I had missed the central point. "They were part and parcel of the same thing. That's what got Hoover in an uproar." He explained that when Nosenko defected, Fedora gave the FBI specific details about the reaction of the KGB that tended to corroborate, point-by-point, Nosenko's story. Sullivan reasoned that if Fedora was providing the FBI with information on behalf of the KGB, as he assumed was the case, then the KGB was deliberately attempting to make Nosenko seem credible.

I asked Sullivan if the KGB could run such a complex deception scheme involving multiple defectors and dangles for years without getting feedback from an inside source.

Sullivan said this was the issue on which Angleton had been pressing Hoover. Was there KGB penetration in the CIA, the FBI, or both security services? Hoover "blew his top," according to Sullivan. He was ordered by Hoover not to pursue the Fedora/Top Hat issue any further. Then Hoover fired him.

"But was there any FBI investigation?" I asked.

Sullivan shook his head. "As far as I know, the cover-up is still going on."

I next contacted the CIA's deputy director, Admiral Rufus Taylor, but he turned down my request for an interview, saying in a letter, "Nosenko is the only source I know of that can supply accurate information on his background."

This left me with only one person who could guide me out of Angleton's wilderness of mirrors: Richard M. Helms. Helms had been chief of the CIA's clandestine division at the time of JFK's assassination, and he would have supervised the defection and debriefing of Nosenko. He had served as CIA director until 1973, when he was fired after resisting Nixon's staff on turning over CIA secrets. As a consolation prize, he was made ambassador to Iran. And I knew him.

I first met Helms in December 1973 on an archeological vacation in Iran. Cyrus Ghani, a well-connected Iranian lawyer, had asked

Helms for permission to invite me and my friend Amanda Burden to dinner at the American embassy. Helms agreed, so long as I did not ask anyone about the Kennedy assassination. I didn't mention the forbidden subject, even though, by coincidence, another guest that evening was Samuel Stern, a Warren Commission lawyer whom I had interviewed in 1965.

As Amanda and I left, we lingered too long at the door to speak to another guest. "Come back in or go, but don't ooze," Helms said with a smile. We left.

Now I was going to Tehran to ask Helms about the very subject he had not wanted to discuss then. I arrived in Iran on November 22. Helms invited me to stay at the embassy residence since Tehran was unsettled by anti-shah riots. He and his wife, Cynthia, had just returned from a trip to the oasis of Bam. At dinner that night, Helms reminisced about his journalistic career in Germany in the late 1930s. Although just a stringer for the United Press, he got an interview with Hitler in Nuremberg. Only when we got to dessert, which was dates he had brought back from Bam, did he ask why I had come to Iran to see him.

"I have been interviewing Yuri Nosenko and I need to clarify his status."

"Nosenko is giving interviews?" Helms shook his head, visibly distressed. He said the CIA "had no business giving you Nosenko in this way." He assumed that whatever the CIA wanted to pass on to me they had given to Nosenko. He said that by using Nosenko, the CIA was sure to reopen "old wounds."

When I mentioned my meetings with Angleton, he cut in, wearily, as if to save time. "Angleton thinks Nosenko was sent by Moscow to mislead us, and it goes much deeper." He explained that in June 1964 Nosenko's reliability was "the key to determining what the KGB had to do with Oswald." Attorney General Robert F. Kennedy knew his importance, as did Chief Justice Earl Warren. Warren sent word to the CIA that he needed to call Nosenko as a witness for the commission. At that point, Helms went to see Warren alone in his chambers. Helms said he insisted that there be no witnesses or notes to the meeting. He told Warren that there were two schools of thought on Nosenko within the CIA. The first was that Nosenko was a legitimate defector and could be believed about Oswald. The second was that he was a KGB plant, dispatched by the KGB to misinform the commission about Oswald. Until the matter was resolved, he strongly advised Warren not to call Nosenko as a witness. Warren accepted his recommendation.

Helms said that the Nosenko case hung over the CIA "like an incubus, and it still does." A few months earlier he had a visit from John Hart, a CIA officer, who told Helms he was reinvestigating the case.

"What did you tell him?" I asked.

Helms smiled. "What I'm going to tell you," he said. "I have no memory of the details of the case." He jotted down three names on a piece of paper. According to Helms, these three men had dealt with the case. "If you can make sense of what they say, it's more than we did." At the top of the list was Tennent Peter Bagley.

Pete Bagley, as he was called, came from a prominent family in North Carolina. Both his older brothers had become fleet admirals in the US Navy, and his cousin served as President Franklin D. Roosevelt's press secretary. Bagley himself had earned a PhD in political science and had been deputy director of the CIA's Soviet Russia Division in the 1960s. Then, in the early 1970s, he had retired. I met Angleton at the Army and Navy Club in Washington, to see why Bagley's career ended so abruptly.

"What happened to his career?" I asked.

"Nosenko," Angleton answered. Up until Nosenko had defected he was, as Angleton put it, "the CIA's golden boy." As Nosenko's case officer at the time of his defection, Bagley got "badly burned."

"Where is he now?"

"He is living on a pension in Brussels." Angleton wrote down Bagley's home address and phone number in Belgium.

It took almost five months to see Bagley. He had not responded to four letters, but I decided to risk turning up in Brussels. Before leaving New York on May 25, 1977, I cabled Bagley at the address Angleton had supplied: "HELMS STRONGLY RECOMMENDS WE SPEAK." I also sent him by express mail an unsigned document I had obtained from the CIA through the Freedom of Information Act, passed in 1966. It contained 44 questions that Bagley had prepared for Nosenko. They were as subtle as a buzzsaw in ripping into the story that Nosenko provided the CIA. For example, since Nosenko had claimed to have been Oswald's KGB case officer, one question asked, "Do you have any information on Oswald's trip to Mexico in September 1963? Whom he saw and what he did at the Soviet embassy?" It was a trap question since the CIA had its own surveillance of the Soviet embassy.

I wrote Bagley's name at the top of the questions, since Angleton had told me he was their author, and asked in a short note, "Were these forty-four questions ever answered?"

On arrival, I called the number Angleton had given me. I told the woman who answered that I would be at the Hotel Metropole for three days. She hung up before I could ask her name.

The situation began to remind me of Beckett's play *Waiting for Godot*, in which the title character never shows up. For three days, I waited. Finally, I received a message from "Pete B." He asked me to call him at a different number than the one I had at 11:00 a.m.

Bagley answered the phone. He said he was returning my call because he had a single question for me: Who had given me the 44 questions I had sent him?

"The questions came from the CIA."

"Why is my name on the top?"

I said that I understood he was the author of the questions.

"Didn't you write them?" He did not answer, so I added, "I used the questions in my interview with Nosenko."

"The CIA arranged for you to interview Nosenko?" he said, with rising fury in his voice.

I said that the *Reader's Digest* had arranged the meeting, but someone from the CIA, Jamie Jamieson, had brought Nosenko to the meeting.

There was another long pause. Then Bagley asked, "Have you seen the battlefield at Waterloo?"

"Not yet."

"Meet me there at 2:00 p.m." He told me precisely where to meet him at the Waterloo battlefield memorial.

I had no trouble finding him. His military bearing and fixed gaze made him stand out like a sore thumb from the other tourists. He was waiting in front of the circular mural of the battle that decided history for Napoleon.

Bagley was in his early 50s, though his blond hair made him look younger. His blue eyes had a sad cast to them. When I approached, he thrust out a hand.

He was more cordial in person than on the phone, and he took me on a whirlwind tour of the Waterloo battlefield. We walked briskly from position to position. At each, he pointed out the strategic weakness of Napoleon's position.

When I asked him if Nosenko was a legitimate defector, he turned to me and asked tensely, "Did the CIA tell you he was?" With a look of painful exasperation, he said, "They had no right to release to you a document as sensitive as the 44 questions."

I had prepared a one-page summary of what I had learned from Angleton and his former staff about Nosenko's defection. As he read it, his jaw tensed. "This is wrong," he said. "You've got it wrong."

I asked in what way my summary was wrong.

"If I told you that, I'd have to tell you everything," he answered. "I am not prepared to do that."

"But there is a reinvestigation of the case." I told him about John Hart's visit to see Helms. "Did Hart see you?"

"Hart is not investigating the case," Bagley replied. "He is whitewashing it." He said Hart had come to see him in Brussels a few months earlier. "I told him even less than I am telling you."

When we left the battlefield, he asked if I wanted to have dinner. He made a reservation at the Villa Lorraine, a three-star restaurant outside of Brussels.

At dinner, he apologized for not answering my letters. He said he had the highest respect for Helms. "You have to understand, Nosenko was not just another case. It was a case at the heart of everything that happened at the CIA for over a decade. Nosenko did enormous damage."

He was more talkative when I asked him about less-sensitive KGB operations. He described in great detail the case of Heinz Felfe, a KGB mole in West German intelligence. He said that when West German intelligence discovered a mole had penetrated it, the KGB attempted to divert suspicion away from the real mole, Felfe, by sending false defectors to West Germany to suggest other possible sources for the leak. As he described it, the KGB diversion was a brilliantly orchestrated deception that was very much like, if not the model for, the one in John le Carré's novel *The Spy Who Came In from the Cold*.

I asked if the false defections in the Felfe case had parallels with the Nosenko case.

Bagley answered, "You might find similarities in the two cases if you had a correct chronology."

Bagley called at 8:00 the next morning. He wanted to hear more about Nosenko's version of his defection. I met him this time in the cloisters of a medieval nunnery in Bruges. It was one of the quietest places I had ever visited.

I quickly summarized Nosenko's story. He had been the officer in the KGB's Second Chief Directorate, which handled the Oswald case. After the Kennedy assassination in early 1964, he defected to the CIA.

Bagley held up his hand, indicating that he had heard enough. "The CIA had no business opening up this can of worms, but since they did, it is important that what comes out of it is the truth. What you heard is a pack of lies."

"What is untrue?"

"To begin with, you have the wrong year that Nosenko made contact," he said. "He started working for us in 1962, not 1964. The chronology is crucial."

I rechecked my notes: Nosenko said he had offered to defect on January 24, 1964, nine weeks after the assassination. If the date was indeed 1962, Jamieson had provided me with an incorrect timetable of Nosenko's engagement with the CIA. So did Nosenko.

"Nosenko defected in place to the CIA before, not after, the Kennedy assassination." Bagley explained that a "defection-in-place" was a term of art the CIA uses to describe an agent who agrees to secretly work for the CIA in his home country, as distinct from an agent who physically defects from his home country. Such an agent is far more valuable because he can supply current intelligence. He is, in spy lingo, a mole. According to Bagley, Nosenko first contacted the CIA in 1962. The CIA then offered him a large sum of money to be its mole in the KGB. Nosenko accepted the offer.

"Nosenko was the CIA's man in Moscow in 1963 when Kennedy was shot?" I interjected.

"Yes. I should know," Bagley said. "I recruited him. I was his case officer."

I asked what had happened between 1962 and 1964 to his defector-in-place in Moscow. Bagley looked at his watch. "We need to find somewhere we would not be disturbed."

Since I was well funded by the *Digest*, I rented a house in Gassin, France, a hill town perched on a rock about two miles from Saint-Tropez. The stone house I rented there adjoined a church graveyard. Bagley arrived on June 8, 1977. He was an avid bird-watcher, and the surrounding forest of cork trees was the nesting ground for a great variety of birds. He took me on long walks in which he, peering through his binoculars, identified the species. Bird-watching seemed to me to be a perfect avocation for a spy.

He had decided to tell me about how he recruited Nosenko 15 years earlier. In 1962, Bagley was, officially, the second secretary at the American embassy in Berne and, unofficially, the CIA case officer in Switzerland assigned with the task of recruiting Russian diplomats, or, as they were called at the CIA, "Redtops."

On June 8, 1962, Yuri Nosenko, a KGB security officer at the Disarmament Conference in Geneva, passed a note in a men's room to an American diplomat. It said that Nosenko wanted to be put in touch with a "representative" of the US government. That meant the CIA. The diplomat called the CIA station in Berne, and Bagley caught the next plane to Geneva.

On June 9, Bagley met Nosenko in a two-bedroom apartment in a large apartment block that served as a CIA safe house. Bagley brought with him a CIA case officer who spoke fluent Russian. He asked Nosenko whether he knew of any imminent attack on America, which was always the required first question. When Nosenko shook his head no, Bagley asked why he had wanted this meeting.

Nosenko replied that he was a KGB officer. He had misappropriated 900 Swiss Francs from a KGB account and needed to replace the funds before he was caught. He wanted 900 Swiss francs, about $500, from the CIA. In return, he offered to furnish the CIA with a KGB manual on surveillance that would explain how the KGB had caught one of the CIA's top agents in Moscow the previous year.

Bagley asked Nosenko if he wanted to leave Russia, and Nosenko answered no. He said he had family in Moscow.

Bagley gave Nosenko the 900 Swiss francs and, as is standard in "redtop" recruitments, made him an offer to be a defector-in-place, a mole. He told him that the CIA would set up a numbered bank account for him in Switzerland into which it would pay $25,000 for every Soviet source in the West that Nosenko helped expose.

Nosenko agreed to the deal, telling Bagley that he would work for the CIA from his vantage point in the KGB's Second Chief Directorate in Moscow. At that time, the CIA had no other mole in the Second Chief Directorate. Since this division had the responsibility in the KGB for recruiting foreigners in Russia and mounting counterintelligence initiatives against the United States, Nosenko's recruitment appeared to be an incredible achievement for Bagley.

When Bagley flew to Washington the next day, he believed he might have had "hooked the biggest fish yet." His triumph was short-lived, however. The next day, Angleton called Bagley into his office and gave him a file on the debriefing of another KGB defector named Anatoliy Golitsyn. It contained startling revelations about a possible KGB penetration of the CIA itself. Golitsyn had also said that in 1962 the KGB would dispatch a false defector from the Second Chief Directorate to mislead the CIA. This was just months before Nosenko contacted them in Geneva. This file persuaded Bagley that Nosenko was the dispatched agent. Angleton's plan was to play out the game with Nosenko for as long it took. He liked to think of himself in this pursuit as a fly fisherman patiently playing with a salmon he had hooked before reeling him in.

I asked Bagley whether the CIA had attempted to contact Nosenko in November 1963, after the Kennedy assassination, to ask about Lee Harvey Oswald's activities in the Soviet Union. After all, since his KGB unit tracked foreign defectors, Nosenko was in a position to cast light on Oswald.

"We were unable to contact him," Bagley replied.

Two months later, Nosenko himself contacted the CIA through a prearranged postcard signal. The signal asked for an immediate meeting in Geneva. Another safe house was used.

When Nosenko walked into the room, he made a stunning announcement. Instead of returning to Russia, he now wanted to physically defect to the United States. He said his life was in peril because the KGB suspected he was working for the CIA. Nosenko then told Bagley that he had information of vital importance. It concerned Oswald's KGB file, which he said he had read before leaving Moscow.

An offer from a KGB man claiming knowledge about the president's alleged assassin could not be turned down. Bagley cabled Helms, who also had little choice, especially since the newly appointed Warren Commission needed a witness to Oswald's activities in Russia. Helms authorized a "crash" defection for Nosenko. That was how Nosenko got to Washington, DC.

"What of the 44 questions that you prepared for him?" I asked.

"He was not able to answer a single one of them truthfully," Bagley answered. "The lie detector test confirmed that."

"So he was a liar?"

"Nosenko was not who he said he was." Bagley said that over the next four years he prepared a 900-page report on Nosenko. It concluded that Nosenko's career in the KGB was a "legend" fabricated by the KGB and that he was a dispatched defector who remained under KGB control.

"What happened to the report?" I asked.

"The CIA buried it," he answered with unmistakable bitterness in his voice.

Then, on September 19, 1977, I learned by pure accident that neither Angleton nor Bagley had told me the full truth about Nosenko. It was also at a very unlikely venue, the 50th birthday party of Steven J. Ross, the chairman of Warner Communications, in the Waldorf Astoria ballroom. The walls were decorated with giant blow-ups of the pages of the *New York Times* from the day Ross was born. While looking at them, I ran into Gloria Steinem, the talented editor of *Ms.* magazine. She introduced me to her date, Stanley Pottinger, a former assistant attorney general at the Justice Department. To make conversation, he asked what I was working on. I told him I had just completed a biography of Lee Harvey Oswald and added, "It is also about a Russian spy no one has ever heard of."

"Not Yuri Nosenko?" Pottinger asked.

I was stunned. Nosenko's identity was supposed to be a closely held secret.

"I spent a year investigating his incarceration by the CIA," Pottinger said.

"He was in prison?" I asked incredulously.

Pottinger explained that in 1975, William Colby, the new director of the CIA, had brought the CIA's so-called "crown jewels" to the Justice Department. These were the CIA's secret operations that Colby believed might have violated US laws. Among them was the CIA's imprisonment of Nosenko from 1964 to 1967. Since Pottinger headed the Civil Rights Division, he was given the task of determining whether the nearly three-year incarceration of Nosenko broke the law. He even visited the windowless padded cell in which Nosenko was held. It seemed cruel to him, but since the CIA "on parole had brought Nosenko to the US," the Justice Department concluded that the CIA had the right to detain him.

I had interviewed a dozen CIA officers involved in the case, including the inspector general, but I had not been told about this extraordinary jailing. Nor did Nosenko tell me he had been imprisoned.

My book was now locked in page proofs, which meant changes would be very expensive, so I urgently needed clarification about what Pottinger had let slip. I flew to Washington the next morning to see Helms, who had finished his tour as ambassador to Iran.

When I met Helms at his office on K Street at noon, he said the imprisonment of Nosenko had been an unprecedented event in the history of the CIA. He recalled that David Murphy, the head of the Soviet Russia Division, and Bagley, then the deputy head, had come to him in April 1964 and said they were concerned that Nosenko was likely to re-defect to the Soviet embassy in Washington and say that the CIA had kidnapped him. If that happened, Helms continued, "he could say we suppressed information on Oswald and all hell would break loose."

Helms found that the CIA had no good options. If the CIA returned Nosenko to Russia and he was a genuine defector, they would be responsible for his execution. If the CIA allowed him his liberty and he was still a KGB officer, he could re-defect to the Soviet embassy.

Helms called Nicholas Katzenbach, the deputy attorney general, who told Helms, "As far as we are concerned Nosenko is not officially in the United States."

Helms said, "I bit the bullet and signed the order to detain him."

I next met Angleton at the Army and Navy Club. I asked him about the imprisonment of Nosenko.

"I opposed it," he said. "I believed we should have let him continue to believe that we bought his story." But Bagley was adamant that Nosenko should be imprisoned and interrogated as a hostile agent. Angleton lost the argument, and Nosenko was locked away.

"Why didn't you tell me he had been imprisoned for three years?"

"You never asked," he replied.

Angleton died of lung cancer on May 12, 1987. Some of the most powerful men in Washington, including senators, ambassadors, cabinet officers, generals, and two former directors of Central Intelligence jammed into a small Congregational church in Arlington, Virginia, to pay their last respects to James Jesus. The wreath of giant purple orchids had been sent by Angleton's former comrades in the OSS, the organization where he had begun his career as a spy 44 years earlier. A poem written by his friend T.S. Eliot described the "wilderness of mirrors," a term which had come to represent for him the war of deception he had waged. The memorial service for the poet-spy was over in 40 minutes.

After his death, Angleton's legend eclipsed his actual achievements. In the media, he was turned into a CIA version of Captain Ahab, wreaking havoc in pursuit of a white whale. Angleton's phantasmagorical monster was an array of KGB moles that had penetrated deep inside American intelligence. Fictive characters based on him became the protagonists of movies such as *The Good Shepherd* (where he is played by Matt Damon), TV miniseries, such as *The Company* (where he is played by Michael Keaton), and novels, such as Norman Mailer's *Harlot's Ghost*. He even made it into the 2020 French TV series *The Bureau of Legends* as the Russia-obsessed "JJA" character.

But had Angleton been right about the CIA? An answer began to emerge with the large-scale defections from the ranks of the KGB after the collapse of the Soviet Union in 1990. The first big jolt came on February 24, 1994, when Aldrich Ames, who had been the head of the CIA's Soviet Russia Division's counterintelligence unit, admitted to having worked for the KGB for more than 10 years. Then, on December 18, 1996, Earl Edwin Pitts, who had been working in FBI counterintelligence against Russian targets, was arrested and admitted that he had been a KGB mole from 1987 to 1992. And on February 18, 2001, Robert Hanssen, a high-level FBI officer, was arrested and admitted that he had been working as a KGB mole for more than 22 years. Clearly, the KGB had been burrowing multiple moles in US intelligence for years. And, as Angleton told me was his worst nightmare, they were in a position to furnish feedback to allow the KGB to run long-term deception operations. To wit, as Timothy Weiner reported in his book *Legacy of Ashes*, the CIA inspector general found that in the 1980s and early 1990s the KGB had dispatched at least six Russian double agents who succeeded in providing disinformation that the CIA passed on to the top echelon of the government, distorted information that no fewer than three American presidents received. So in the realm of reality, if not fiction, Angleton was proven to be right about the vulnerability of the CIA to moles: With them, the KGB could penetrate, deceive, and manipulate American intelligence. For me, it was further confirmation that while Angleton was lost in this wilderness of mirrors, so was the CIA.

# CHAPTER TWELVE

# DE MOHRENSCHILDT'S
# LAST INTERVIEW

I learned more about the CIA from George de Mohrenschildt in March 1977. I had come to Palm Beach to interview him because I believed he might be able to supply a key part of the assassination puzzle. He was one of the few people whom Oswald confided in after his return from Russia in 1962. Indeed, Oswald trusted de Mohrenschildt enough to show him the sniper rifle he had obtained under a false identity and which was used in an attempt to shoot General Edwin Walker, a right-wing activist who lived in Dallas in April 1963. Three weeks after that Walker assassination attempt, de Mohrenschildt went to Washington, DC, and met with high-level CIA officials; right afterward, he moved to Haiti, where he worked on a CIA-related project. De Mohrenschildt was the only person I knew of who had a relationship with both Oswald and the CIA.

Haiti was the penultimate stop on a long migration for de Mohrenschildt. He was born in 1911 in Mozyr in western Russia, the son of a wealthy Russian aristocrat. He spent a large part of his childhood in the nearby city of Minsk. After his father was arrested in the Russian Revolution, he escaped to Poland. He then went to France. In May 1938, he moved to the United States, where he found employment as an insurance salesman, film producer, journalist, and textile salesman. He applied to join the OSS in 1941 but was "security disapproved" because of allegations that he had associated with German espionage agents in Europe.

After the end of World War II, he found another vocation. He became a successful petroleum engineer in Texas, where he also kept in contact with the CIA's liaison office.

In 1962, when Oswald moved from Minsk to Dallas, de Mohren-schildt made a successful effort to befriend him. He began the relationship by driving to Oswald's house and asking about his childhood city of Minsk.

When he returned from Haiti in 1977, I approached him through an intermediary for an interview. De Mohrenschildt told me he wanted an "honorarium." I agreed to pay him $4,000 for a four-day interview. According to our arrangement, I would give him a check for $1,000 each day. He wanted to meet me at the Breakers in Palm Beach, Florida. He also said he needed a car, so I rented a blue Ford LTD sedan from Hertz for him.

We began our meetings in my suite at the Breakers on March 28, 1977. In the initial interview, I asked him mainly about his history: How had he come to be in Dallas in 1962? He told me in great detail how he had been an oil wildcatter, made deals for oil abroad, and dated an impressive number of socially prominent women, including Jacqueline Bouvier Kennedy. I asked him why a person with his social connections would befriend Oswald, an impoverished ex-Marine who had defected to the Soviet Union. He said that was a long story and it was getting late. He offered to tell me the full story when we met the next morning.

He showed up the next morning promptly at 9:00. Nancy Lanoue, my trusty research assistant, was also there. I began by asking de Mohrenschildt (again) his reason for contacting Oswald. He answered that he originally contacted Oswald in Dallas at the behest of a "government official" for whom he had done favors in the past.

I pressed him further and found out that the official was J. Walter Moore, who worked for the CIA's Domestic Contact Division in Dallas. Moore's division had responsibility for debriefing returning visitors from the Soviet Union.

De Mohrenschildt said he had met Moore five years earlier when he was debriefed on a trip he made to the Yugoslavian coast in 1957. This part of his story checked out. A CIA document turned over to the FBI showed that the CIA had disseminated a 1958 report on de Mohrenschildt's debriefing on Yugoslavia to 10 government agencies.

"Did Moore tell you to visit Oswald?" I asked.

"Not in so many words." Moore told him that Oswald had been uncooperative with the FBI and refused to discuss his two years in Russia, including his time in Minsk. From this conversation, de Mohrenschildt assumed Moore wanted him to gain Oswald's confidence and then find out what he could about Oswald's activities in Russia. In CIA parlance, this was to be an "unwitting debriefing."

De Mohrenschildt drove to Oswald's home without an appointment. He introduced himself, charmed Marina Oswald, and told her and Oswald about his own years in Minsk. Oswald reciprocated by showing de Mohrenschildt his photographs of Minsk and other mementos. Oswald told de Mohrenschildt that he had some diary pages that described, among other things, his work in an electronics factory. De Mohrenschildt encouraged Oswald to write a more detailed memoir about Minsk for publication in an American magazine, which he offered to help get published. When Oswald wrote a draft, de Mohrenschildt borrowed it and, according to him, made a copy of it for Moore.

I was impressed with de Mohrenschildt's story because it closely dovetailed with the report of a CIA officer in the Soviet branch of the CIA's Directorate of Intelligence. That officer recalled receiving "contact reports" beginning in 1962 based on the experiences of a US Marine defector to Russia who had worked in a Minsk radio plant. Since Oswald was the only defector who fit this description, and the CIA had not directly debriefed him, the report suggests that the debriefing had been done indirectly.

I asked de Mohrenschildt why he had done Moore this favor.

De Mohrenschildt responded that he did it in the hope of getting the CIA's help in Haiti in arranging an oil exploration deal. He said there was not an explicit quid pro quo, but he had expected that Moore would repay "the favor." He considered it a business transaction. "I would never have contacted Oswald if Moore had not sanctioned it," he said. "Too much was at stake."

I next asked him about an encounter in April 1963. According to Marina Oswald's testimony to the Warren Commission in 1964, de Mohrenschildt had come to Oswald's home immediately after a sniper had attempted to assassinate General Walker in April 1963 and asked Oswald, "Lee, how did you miss General Walker?" De Mohrenschildt, who briefly returned from Haiti to testify to the commission, said this remark was simply intended as a "joke."

When I asked him about the "joke," he told me he had good reason to suspect Oswald might have been the sniper. He had gone with Oswald to many small social gatherings in Dallas, and in one of them in March 1963, Oswald, speaking to three young geologists, described Walker as a "fascist" and compared Walker to Hitler. Oswald then argued that someone should have shot Hitler before he ever achieved power. Soon afterward, de Mohrenschildt said Oswald showed him his rifle.

In early April 1963, just before the Walker shooting, Oswald gave de Mohrenschildt a photograph of himself wearing black and armed with rifle and pistol. It was dated in the European style of day, month, and year: 5-4-63. On the back, it said in Russian "Hunter of Fascists." De Mohrenschildt said he thought Marina Oswald had written the message on the back.

"You had guessed from it that Oswald might have been the shooter?" I asked.

"Call it intuition. I just put two and two together."

I wanted to know if de Mohrenschildt had passed this information, or "intuition," to his CIA contact. "Were you in contact with Moore at the time of the Walker shooting in April 1963?" I asked.

He said he told Moore about the photograph of Oswald with his rifle and pistol shortly after Oswald's wife gave it to him.

I asked if he meant the dated photograph. He nodded.

The 5-4-63 date on the photograph had obvious implications. Oswald had first gone to Walker's home on April 6 with his rifle. Since he had been unable to find the proper opportunity to fire a shot because of a nearby church gathering, he returned on April 10. He then allegedly fired a shot through the window that missed the general by inches. If Moore had viewed the back of the photograph, he would have seen the "Hunter of Fascists" message and the date. It would not be much of a leap to suspect that Oswald was the shooter. That would point to a potential assassin in Dallas. Had Moore passed this information to his superiors at the CIA before the Kennedy assassination?

De Mohrenschildt said he did not know what Moore did about Oswald since he left Dallas shortly after their meeting. Such a meeting had taken place. According to CIA records, de Mohrenschildt met with Tony Czaikowski, a CIA staff officer, in Washington, DC, on May 7, 1963. Clemard Joseph Charles, a Haitian politician and CIA asset, also attended that meeting. Afterward, de Mohrenschildt moved to Haiti almost immediately and worked with Charles on an oil exploration project that never found a drop of oil. I later located Clemard Joseph Charles, who was living in Queens, New York. He confirmed that he and de Mohrenschildt had met with a CIA officer in Washington, DC, in the spring of 1963. He laughed off, with a deep, throaty chortle, the idea that the "oil exploration" ventures were ever about oil. He explained that it was merely a cover for a CIA-sponsored operation aimed at regime change in Cuba. He added that it was terminated a few months after the JFK assassination.

I asked what happened to him after that. Charles answered that as far as he knew, de Mohrenschildt remained on the CIA payroll.

If de Mohrenschildt had indeed told the CIA man in Dallas of Oswald's prior assassination attempt, it could explain why de Mohrenschildt left Dallas. I asked him what had happened to his telltale copy of the photograph he had shown to Moore. He said he had given it to his lawyer, Pat Russell, for safekeeping. He said Russell would make it available to me. He opened his black address book and wrote out Russell's phone number.

It was now 1:30 p.m. I asked my assistant Nancy to try to arrange to get the photograph from Russell. Meanwhile, we adjourned for lunch, agreeing to meet again in the hotel suite at 3:00 p.m.

A few minutes after de Mohrenschildt left the room, I noticed that he had left his address book on the couch and mentioned it to Nancy. Then there was a knock on the door. It was de Mohren-schildt, who had returned for his address book. I gave it to him, and he left again. It was the last time I saw him.

He did not return after lunch. I called the home of Nancy Til-ton in the nearby town of Manalapan, Florida, where he and his 33-year-old daughter Alexandra were staying as her guests. The voice of the woman on the other end of the phone was drowned out by the sound of sirens. I asked again to speak with de Mohrenschildt. She replied, "Mr. de Mohrenschildt can't come to the phone. He is dead."

At that moment, my assistant came into the room and said that there were four police cars downstairs. They had come because I was the last known person to see de Mohrenschildt alive.

A police car took Nancy and me to the state attorney's office, where State Attorney David Bludworth, an athletic-looking man in his late 40s, met us. "Let me fill you in about what happened this afternoon," he began. He did not mince words, saying that de Mohrenschildt had put a shotgun in his mouth and killed himself at 2:21 p.m. in the home of Mrs. Tilton—less than an hour after he left my hotel. I asked how he could be sure of the time of death, since Bludworth said no one heard the shot.

He explained that Tilton had gone to the hairdresser but had left a tape recorder on in her room to record the audio portion of a soap opera. The shot heard on the recording established the precise time of his death.

The body was found about 15 minutes later in the second-floor hallway just outside Tilton's bedroom. The shotgun, which belonged to Tilton, had been found on the Persian carpet next to de Mohrenschildt. No suicide note or other clue was found.

I asked Bludworth how he could be sure de Mohrenschildt was alone in the house.

Bludworth said only a single set of footfalls could be heard on the audiotape of the TV program before the blast. It seemed an open-and-shut case of suicide.

As I was preparing to leave, Bludworth had a question for me. Did I have in my possession de Mohrenschildt's black address book?

"No," I replied, knowing I had returned it to him when he came back to my room.

He politely rephrased the question and asked it twice more. When he received the same negative answer, he turned to Nancy and asked whether she had the black book.

I assumed from the repetitive questioning that the address book that I had put in de Mohrenschildt's hand was now missing. If so, there were three possibilities: First, he had lost it on his way back to the Tilton home. Second, he had given it to someone. Third, someone had taken from his body after he had been shot.

Soon after we returned to the hotel, Pat Russell, de Mohrenschildt's lawyer, delivered the photograph of Oswald to Nancy. Just as de Mohrenschildt had described it, it had a date on the front that closely coincided with the date of Oswald's first attempt to shoot Walker and Cyrillic handwriting on the back. I had a copy of it hand-delivered to Thea Hall, one of the leading graphologists in America, to ascertain if the handwriting on the front matched Oswald's writing and if the Cyrillic handwriting matched that of Marina Oswald. They did, confirming at least part of de Mohrenschildt's last interview.

Later, two FBI agents visited me at my hotel. Both were neatly dressed in ties, suits, and hats. They were also very courteous. They wanted to know about de Mohrenschildt's missing address book. The older agent said that two weeks before de Mohrenschildt had come to Palm Beach, he had been in Brussels, Belgium, staying at the Hotel Metropole. He had left behind his luggage, raincoat, and pipe but had taken with him his black address book. He asked if I had it.

I said that I had given it back to de Mohrenschildt.

The younger agent asked if de Mohrenschildt had given me any of his personal papers.

I said no. They did not ask about the photograph that his lawyer had given me after his death.

After I returned to New York, the coincidence of de Mohrenschildt's violent death just a few hours after he offered me photographic evidence that could embarrass the CIA weighed heavily on my mind. Had it been a real suicide or a murder disguised as a suicide? As I knew from my interviews with James Jesus Angleton, intelligence services had the skills to kill someone and make it appear to be a suicide. In intelligence-speak, it was called a surreptitiously assisted death. I deciding to investigate further in Palm Beach a year later.

Bludworth, who seemed otherwise bored with his job as state attorney, was more than happy to cooperate. He furnished me with the police report, which contained the statements of five other people on the staff who worked in or around the house at the time the shot was fired. None of them saw anyone else enter or leave the house.

Besides, the downstairs doors were connected to a Rawlins Alarm System that beeped when there was movement. The beeps were recorded on the same tape that was recording the TV show, and the timing of each beep could be matched to the times reported by staff members and guests as to their opening the doors. From this reckoning, there were no unaccounted for entries into the house before or after the shooting.

I spoke to de Mohrenschildt's daughter, Alexandra, who said she had left the Tilton home to get her father a gift in nearby Boynton Beach before he had returned from his interview with me. He was dead when she returned. She also told me her father had been treated for severe depression.

In light of his history of depression, the verdict of suicide was likely correct. It was a very sad ending to a promising interview.

My book *Legend: The Secret World of Lee Harvey Oswald* was published later that year. The unfortunate graphic design of the cover, which placed the name "Lee Harvey Oswald" toward the bottom in block letters much larger than my name, created an odd misunderstanding on one of the talk shows for which I was interviewed remotely by telephone. On the highly rated *Michael Jackson* show on KABC (the ABC affiliate in Los Angeles), Jackson, a British expatriate who spoke with a pronounced accent, mistook Oswald's big-type name for that of the author and introduced me by saying, "Please welcome our next guest, Lee Harvey Oswald, who has written a stunning book about the Kennedy assassination." Although I was able to correct his understandable error before he asked me many questions about why I shot the president, I decided there and then that this would be my last book on the Kennedy assassination.

# CHAPTER THIRTEEN

# SPECTER IN JAKARTA

E ven though I had written books on a wide range of subjects, including diamonds, television news, oil, spies, and corporate crime, the JFK inquest, as if it had a mind of its own, persisted in haunting me. New leads kept emerging in the oddest places. For example, on November 16, 1988, almost a quarter century after the assassination in Dallas, I ran into Arlen Specter, one of the main investigators for the Warren Commission, in Jakarta, Indonesia. At the time, I was a guest of the US ambassador, Paul Wolfowitz.

I had met Paul and his wife Clare at Cornell in the early 1960s through Professor Allan Bloom, who lived at Telluride House, a sort of intellectual version of a fraternity house. It could afford to house promising students because it was endowed by the Telluride silver mine in Colorado. Clare lived there while Paul was in Chicago, getting his PhD in political science at the University of Chicago. Paul, though not a student of Bloom's, had been heavily influenced by his critique of American politics. While at the University of Chicago, he became a protégé of Albert Wohlstetter, the hawkish defense intellectual, who he studied under at Chicago and who persuaded him to enter government. In the 1970s, Paul served as assistant undersecretary of defense under President Carter and headed the State Department's Office for Policy Planning under President Ronald Reagan. In 1986, after Paul served as his under-secretary of state for East Asia, President Reagan appointed him to his post in Indonesia. (He would go on to be the architect of the disastrous war in Iraq.)

Paul loved Jakarta and invited me to stay at the embassy residence. Soon after my arrival on November 9, 1988, Paul, changing from a dark pinstripe suit to a colorful batik shirt-jacket, took me on a walking tour of the slums in Jakarta. Paul, born in Brooklyn of Polish and Jewish descent, spoke to passersby in the Indonesian language, which he had learned from his driver, ate local delicacies from street carts, and had immersed himself in the Javanese culture.

As we walked, a single Marine guard, Paul's bodyguard, followed at a discreet distance. I asked Paul about an issue that had long interested me: the CIA's Team B, which Paul helped organize in 1976. Whereas Team A was made up of the CIA's top analysts, who did the national intelligence estimates (or NIEs) concerning the Soviet Union, Team B was composed of 16 outsiders, all of whom had prior experience in government and top-secret clearance. Both teams were given exactly the same intelligence data to analyze. The competition was an unprecedented event, and never to be repeated, meant to determine if the built-in biases of government intelligence agencies affected their evaluations.

"Who won?" I asked.

"Team B indisputably won on the two technical issues, Soviet missile accuracy and Soviet air defense capabilities," he answered. He acknowledged that Team B had been less successful in resolving the crucial issue of whether Soviet doctrine accepted the idea that a nuclear war was unwinnable because it would result in the mutually assured destruction of both the Soviet Union and the United States or whether, as the Team B panel argued, it believed it could win a nuclear war.

This extraordinary competition between inside and outside intelligence experts was never to be repeated and, in Paul's view, did little to erase the purported biases and "mirror thinking" in the CIA's appreciation of a potential adversary.

Two days later, I accompanied Paul in an embassy minibus to the airport to meet three top Republican senators—Bob Dole, the Senate minority leader, John McCain from Arizona, and Arlen Specter from Pennsylvania. At first, I did not remind Specter that I had interviewed him when he was a lawyer for the Warren Commission, and he gave no sign of recognizing me.

The senators came with their wives in an air force plane specially equipped with beds for congressional junkets. Dole explained they were on a fact-finding mission to assess charges of Indonesian genocide in East Timor. When Paul told him on the bus that it was an eight-hour flight to Timor from Jakarta, Dole suggested they spend a few days fact-finding in Jakarta. Cindy McCain, Senator McCain's wife, who was an heiress to a beer fortune in Arizona, suggested they do some shopping in Bali. (As it turned out, the Senate fact-finders never made it to Timor.)

As our minivan crawled through the jam of bicycles and motor scooters in downtown Jakarta, I pointed out to Senator McCain a hand-painted 15-foot-tall sheet depicting Bruce Willis scaling a skyscraper in the movie *Die Hard*. As was often done in these hand-drawn movie posters, the facial features of the American star had been altered to make him look more Javanese.

"Do you like Bruce Willis's ethnic makeover, Senator?"

McCain, who was not given to irony, looked askance at me for a painful few seconds of silence until Elizabeth Dole, who had a keener sense of humor, joked, "Local artistic license." At their hotel, the embassy had arranged a press conference for the delegation. Before it began, Paul asked Dole to be "diplomatic" in referring to the regime as an "authoritarian government," not as a military dictatorship (which it was). Dole nodded his understanding, but in his speech, while looking straight at Paul, he described Indonesia as a dictatorship.

At the reception that followed, I approached Arlen Specter with some reluctance. The last time we met, in 1965, I was an undergraduate writing my thesis on the Warren Commission and he was a young lawyer temporarily working for it. Based on that interview, I divulged in my book *Inquest* that he had come up with the so-called single-bullet theory, which made him the center of the raging controversy.

"Senator Specter, you may not remember but ages ago you barbecued lamb chops for me in your backyard," I said hesitantly.

"I remember well," Specter replied. "It was the only interview I ever gave on the Warren Commission and I got hell for it."

"I needed to see you because you were the one and only person on the staff investigating the crucial issue of the bullets."

"As you said, that was ages ago," he answered. "Would you like to join Joan and I tomorrow for an early dinner?"

"Aren't you going to Timor tomorrow?"

"The trip has been delayed."

We had dinner the next day at the Mandarin Hotel, where they were staying. Joan Specter was a lovely and soft-spoken woman in her early 50s. She also had a genius for making pies. While Specter was still an assistant district attorney, she began selling them to local restaurants. They proved such a success that she distributed them throughout America as America's first gourmet frozen pies. Specter told the story of her success with great pride. He was less satisfied with the performance of the Warren Commission.

"It was a total screw-up when I got there in 1964. Warren had wanted an independent investigation of the bullets, so he hired Frank Adams, naively assuming that as New York's former police commissioner he would put together an investigative task force. But Adams didn't understand that. He thought he was just window dressing for an FBI investigation. He never showed up. Instead, he hired me."

"Just you?"

"Warren's investigative task force was mainly me. Even worse, they gave me only four weeks to investigate the shooting."

"You told me you didn't even have autopsy photos," I said.

"What I didn't tell you is that Robert Kennedy had taken them. He wanted no complications. The only thing I could do without them was to get the Secret Service to do a reconstruction of the shooting."

That reconstruction led to the conclusion that Oswald did not have time to fire the three bullets. Specter realized that the only way to stick to the single-shooter hypothesis was to posit that one of the bullets did double duty and wounded both President Kennedy and Governor Connally. As implausible as the single-bullet theory sounded, the commissioners had little choice but to accept it since Oswald did not have time for three well-aimed shots in the reconstruction. The alternative to it, Specter argued, was a second shooter.

"If you hadn't done the reconstruction, the commission could have evaded the issue."

"Probably, but I was a gung-ho district attorney in those days," he said with a nostalgic smile. "I didn't give a damn about the politics of the commission."

I asked if Robert Kennedy had agreed with the single-bullet theory. Spector answered, "All I know is that Howard Willens, who was his man on the commission, rewrote my draft chapter to make it stronger."

# CHAPTER FOURTEEN

# DICK CLARK GETS
# A CONFESSION

Public interest in even the highest-profile murders usually has a half-life of only a few months. The opposite was true in the case of the JFK assassination, into which tabloids and talk show hosts breathed new life, even though little, if any, credible new evidence had emerged. The Garrison farce, reanimated by Oliver Stone's movie *JFK*, drove public interest to such a high that, in 1994, NBC decided, as I learned firsthand, to use a highly dubious "confession" to boost its ratings during sweeps week, when networks establish the price of their ads for the coming quarter. For NBC, the expected increase in its rating during sweeps week could increase its profits by as much as $50 million. A high Nielsen rating on sweeps week was therefore crucial to a network's profitability.

This economic motive was made clear to me in April 1994, when John Agoglia, the president of NBC Enterprises, called to offer me a job as a consultant on a program. All I knew about him then was that he had made headlines a few years earlier by replacing Johnny Carson with Jay Leno on NBC.

"Consult on what?" I asked.

He spoke in a deep Brooklyn accent, explaining that NBC urgently needed my help to validate the bona fides of an hour-long special on the Kennedy assassination the network planned to run during the sweeps in May.

I assumed he was calling me at this late date because he had a factual problem with the program. I asked how I could help.

"I need someone to do due diligence."

I agreed to help verify the facts in the program. "Does this documentary say anything new?"

"We have the assassin confessing to killing Kennedy on camera," Agoglia answered. "And it is an NBC exclusive."

"That would be news," I said.

"But we need you to check out his story before we air it." Agoglia offered me a generous consulting fee of $20,000. He would also cover all my expenses, which included a weeklong stay at Shutters on the Beach in Santa Monica.

The confessed "assassin" was James Files, a 52-year-old convict at Stateville Correctional Center in Crest Hill, Illinois. He was serving a 50-year sentence for the attempted murder of two policemen in 1991, so he didn't have much to lose by telling a Texas television producer that he had shot Kennedy from the grassy knoll in Dallas on November 22, 1963. He further claimed he had done it on orders from the Mafia.

With this confession in hand, the producer made a deal with Dick Clark, whose Dick Clark Productions also produced *Dick Clark's New Year's Rockin' Eve*, a show that had aired every December 31 since 1972. Clark built the hour-long special around the confession, which it sold to NBC for sweeps week. To find out more about the putative assassin, I made an appointment to meet with Clark.

Born on November 30, 1929, in Bronxville, New York, Clark was determined to be a disc jockey since the age of 10 and, with his perpetually youthful looks, succeeded in becoming an icon of the youth culture. His *American Bandstand*, a weekly TV program launched on ABC in 1957, is credited with introducing rock and roll music to America with lip-synched performances of hit records, interviews with teenage idols, and his weekly "Rate-a-Record." Although I had not met Clark before, I recalled his description of himself as "America's oldest teen." Even though he was now 65, he still hit me with the toothy smile and facial energy of a teenager. While I recognized his incredible role in enabling, if not creating, teenage culture, I found it somewhat incongruous his producing an NBC special that claimed to solve the mystery of the JFK assassination. I immediately asked him about the provenance of the evidence surrounding the confessor, James Files.

"The Files files?" he jokingly asked.

I nodded, assuming this pun was his standard opener.

He told me with great enthusiasm how he had bought the television rights to the Files confession, because "it finally solved the JFK assassination." He added with a beaming smile, "A televised TV confession is going to break the bank. It will revolutionize television."

"Are you sure Files was the assassin?" I asked.

"Let the American public decide," he replied.

When I told him that my job was to check out the factual basis of confession for NBC, he said only, "Good luck. The program airs in a week."

Since I had just one week to validate a jailhouse confession, I turned for help to my friend Jules Kroll, now the leading private investigator in America. He had helped me with several other investigative problems, and since NBC was reimbursing my expenses, I could pay him.

Kroll assigned a team of former police investigators to find out where Files was on November 22, 1963. It determined that Files could not be in Dallas because phone and hospital records showed that he was at a hospital in Chicago the entire week.

I brought their report (and bill) to Agoglia. "Unless there is some explanation Kroll missed," I told him, "Files could not have been on the grassy knoll in Dallas on November 22."

But he did not seem overly concerned that Files had confessed to a crime he could not possibly have committed. He showed more concern with how Dick would explain this on the air. "You need to ask Dick Clark about this immediately," he responded. "I am sure he has a good answer."

The office of Dick Clark Productions was just across the street from NBC in Burbank. When I walked in, Clark was waiting. He said, "I hear there is some kind of a problem."

I guessed that Agoglia had already told Clark what my investigation had turned up. "The problem is that a man can't be in two places at the same time." I added for emphasis, "James Files was in Chicago, not Dallas, when Kennedy was shot."

"He says he was in Dallas, I believe him." Clark bounced back with a smile as if his personal belief settled the issue.

I patiently explained that the Kroll investigator had faxed me hospital records establishing Files's presence in Chicago on November 22.

"I guess that could be an issue," Clark answered. "We will need to directly ask Files about this conflict." He called the producer of the program and asked him to arrange the call with Files. I waited almost an hour while the producer phoned the warden and arranged the emergency call. Finally, Files was put on speakerphone.

"I was in Dallas," said Files in a raspy voice.

"Why do hospital records show you were in Chicago instead of Dallas?" I asked.

"That was my brother using my name," he answered. He explained that he had an identical twin brother, and they looked so much alike that not even his wife could distinguish them. This twin was in the Chicago hospital creating an alibi for Files.

Clark breathed an audible sigh of relief. "Problem solved."

But I was far from satisfied with this contrived explanation. Still on speakerphone, I asked Files if his twin could corroborate his story.

"He's dead," Files answered.

I asked when he had died.

Files said he died soon after the assassination, and Files personally buried him in an unmarked grave. There was no death certificate.

Clark nodded as if it all made sense. "What about your twin's birth certificate?" I asked.

He replied that his mother had never taken one out or had any papers identifying his twin. She kept his very existence a secret, and, since his mother was dead, no one but Files knew he had ever had a twin.

When the call was completed, I told Clark I found the twin story to be unbelievable.

"We can't prove it's not true," Clark answered.

"I doubt NBC will want to air a confession when it has evidence that the man confessing couldn't possibly be the assassin," I said.

"OK, we can add something at the end about the hospital records to cover ourselves and NBC." Clark made another phone call, again on speakerphone, and to my amazement, Agoglia seemed comfortable with his end-of-the-program addition.

I walked back across the street to NBC and told Agoglia that Files's story was ridiculous.

"Dick has offered to put a tag at the end about the twin. I think that covers NBC," Agoglia said.

I replied that a large part of the audience would not watch the program to the very end and many NBC viewers would not find out about the substantial evidence showing that Files could not have been in Dallas at the time of the assassination and that therefore his NBC exclusive confession was a hoax.

"Ed, remember that you are working for NBC Entertainment, not NBC News," he cut in. His point was that NBC's Entertainment division had different standards of verification. "The tag line solves the problem."

But it didn't. NBC planned to list my name on this very dubious program as its consultant and associate me with an obvious fraud. I turned for help to Gus Russo, a very knowledgeable producer at PBS who had researched the four-hour PBS documentary on the JFK assassination (in which I appeared). "Did you ever hear of James Files?" I asked him over the phone.

Russo told me that he read a newspaper story about Files's putative "confession" that had been published about a year earlier in the *Houston Chronicle*. Files's claim "was such nonsense that even Oliver Stone wouldn't touch it."

In these days, the fax was the fastest means of communications, so I asked Russo to fax the published story in the *Houston Chronicle* to both Agoglia and Marjorie Neufeld, the NBC lawyer working for Agoglia. I also left a message on both their voice mails stating that NBC couldn't accurately say that the Files story was an exclusive scoop because it had been published a year earlier in the *Houston Chronicle*. I knew it would cause a reaction since NBC's and Clark's selling point for the special was that it was a news-making exclusive.

After making sure the faxes had arrived, I went for a leisurely lunch with my friend Laurie Frank at the Polo Lounge in the Beverly Hills Hotel. When I returned after lunch to NBC's headquarters in Burbank, the guard at the parking lot told me that my pass was no longer valid and I could not enter. I had him call the president's office. Neufeld came on the line and told me Agoglia had canceled the Files documentary and NBC no longer needed my services. She suggested that I return to New York on the red-eye that evening.

It was not without irony that whereas the evidence of a hoax did not seem to faze NBC, the evidence that it was not an NBC exclusive sunk it. I breathed a sigh of relief and hoped that this debacle would be the end of my JFK assassination saga.

# PART THREE

# DISCOVERING POLITICS

# CHAPTER FIFTEEN

# THE MOYNIHAN CONNECTION

On February 10, 1976, a particularly chilly evening in Manhattan, I met with seven men in my penthouse on East Eighty-Sixth Street to further, if not a conspiracy, a political enterprise. All of the invitees were steeped in New York politics. With a minimum of small talk, I took their coats, offered them a drink, and sat them in order of their arrival around the circular black granite table in my living room.

The purpose of the meeting was to induce Daniel Patrick Moynihan, who was then the US ambassador to the UN, to run as a Democrat for the Senate in 1976. I presumed that the men in attendance were sympathetic to the idea. They also each had a connection to Moynihan. Leonard Garment, Nixon's former White House counsel, was now Moynihan's legal advisor at the UN. Richard Ravitch, the chairman of the New York State Urban Development Corporation, was an increasingly powerful player in New York politics. He would later serve as chairman of the Metropolitan Transportation Authority and as the lieutenant governor of New York. Laurence Tisch, the billionaire chairman of Loews Corporation, was one of the principal financiers of the Democratic Party. Dan Rose, a leading real estate developer, headed a number of civic organizations in New York City. Norman Podhoretz, the editor of *Commentary*, was

Moynihan's informal political advisor. Irving Kristol, the editor of *The Public Interest*, was influential in the conservative wing of the Democratic Party. And Bruce Kovner, a PhD candidate at Harvard, had helped organize the Senate campaign of Nelson Gross. Each invitee was also a personal friend of Moynihan.

After everyone was seated at the table, I related a conversation that I had with Moynihan at the Harvard Club. He said that he was tired of the State Department bureaucratic squabbles that went with his job as UN ambassador and, as someone who prided himself on artful wordcraft, he bristled at the State Department's requirement that he clear every line of every speech with Washington. Would he consider running for Senate against the Republican incumbent James Buckley? I had asked. He answered with a smile, "Running for the Senate is a very expensive proposition. It is not anything I can afford on my civil servant's salary." I pressed on, asking if he would run if he had assured financing. He said, "But I don't."

The response of the men around the table was anything but surprising. I had invited them because I knew they were keen admirers not only of Moynihan but also the positions he espoused at the UN. So everyone immediately agreed that Moynihan should run for the Senate and agreed that if a lack of financing was holding him back, it should be concretely assured to him. I turned to Tisch since, as one of the wealthiest men in America, he was in a position to provide that money. "What do you think, Larry?"

Tisch said in his usual down-to-earth voice, "The money is not a problem. I can set up a finance committee for him tomorrow. The issue is: Does Pat want to commit himself to run?"

At that point, Garment left the table and called Moynihan from the phone in my den. When he came back, he announced that Moynihan was not ready to make such a commitment.

Tisch shook his head in disappointment. There was nothing more to say. My cabal had failed to persuade him. The failure was only temporary, however. Two weeks later, Moynihan called Tisch and told him he had decided to run.

How had I become involved in this Moynihan cabal? To understand that, we need to go back 10 years to the time when I was struggling to find a place in academia.

On December 14, 1966, Edward C. Banfield, the Henry Lee Shattuck Professor of Urban Government at Harvard, had come to Cornell to give a seminar on "Economic Man." Born on a farm in 1916, Banfield studied agriculture at the University of Connecticut and, as a supporter of Franklin Delano Roosevelt's New Deal, went to work for the US Department of Agriculture. He soon came to the attention of Rexford Tugwell, a member of FDR's brain trust. At Tugwell's suggestion, Banfield left the government to get a PhD in government at the University of Chicago and, several years later, became a full professor at Harvard.

I had read his first book, *The Moral Basis of a Backward Society*, which provided me with a new way of looking at amoral politics. I now wanted to meet him, so I signed up for his seminar.

There were about two dozen students from the Cornell government department seated around a rectangular table. Banfield, a lanky man whose protruding jaw and buckteeth gave him an equine look, began the discussion by asking the group for a show of hands of those who had voted in the local elections. Everyone raised his or her hand, except me.

He asked those who raised their hand why they voted. They all gave similar answers about the need to participate in the political process. He turned to me, the lone non-voter. "Why didn't you vote?"

I hesitated, recalling the humiliating result of my thoughtlessly answering a question Nabokov had put me about *Queen of Spades*. I failed then to consider why Nabokov was asking about that particular movie. The lesson for me was that questions could not always be answered without understanding why they were asked.

Since Banfield had made a point in all his books of challenging conventional wisdom, I assumed that he was not asking such an elementary question to make a trite point about civic duty. So I decided to provide him with a more contrarian answer. "Those elections would not be decided by my single vote so it would not have changed the outcome," I ventured. "If I wanted to influence the outcome, my time would be better spent raising money so a candidate could buy media spots."

"What if everyone thought that way?" he shot back, which caused some derisive laughter among my fellow students.

"If everyone else decided not to vote, then I would vote since it would change the outcome."

He didn't call on me again in the seminar.

To my surprise, I received a message that evening from a secretary in the government department saying that Professor Banfield would like me to have coffee with him in the Hilton Statler dining room at 9:00 the next morning.

When I arrived, Banfield was seated with Andrew Hacker, my thesis advisor, finishing his breakfast. He said he had to catch a plane and came right to the point.

"Would you like to come to Harvard in February?"

I would be graduating from Cornell at the end of January. I had considered an academic life, but I had not applied to any graduate schools. "I haven't finished my application," I said.

"That is not a problem," Banfield said. "We can arrange a place for you in the government department."

In leaving Cornell, I would miss my daily routine of placing at least one piece in the common jigsaw puzzle on the table of the Music Room in Willard Straight Hall Student Union, daydreaming over a late-afternoon coffee at the Noyes Lodge on Beebe Lake, and, most of all, the Saturday night gatherings at Andrew Hacker's home, where we watched and commented on 16-millimeter versions of Preston Sturges's *The Lady Eve*, *The Great McGinty*, and *Sullivan's*

*Travels* in the company of professors Allan Bloom, Alison Lurie, Ted Lowi, Walter Berns, Clinton Rossiter, and Alan Altshuler. I was invited to these movie nights not because of my academic standing but because I supplied the 16-millimeter projector. But it was time to move on.

I arrived at Harvard in February 1966 knowing only Banfield. His idea of an intellectual was someone who could see controversial issues in shades of gray, as opposed to a man of action, which included a politician, who saw them in black and white. He believed both types of thinkers were necessary. Soon afterward, he introduced me to two people who would greatly influence my thinking. The first one was his colleague and coauthor, James Q. Wilson. Born in 1931, Wilson attended the University of Redlands in California, where he won the national debate championship, and the University of Chicago, where he became Banfield's first graduate student. After he earned his PhD, Banfield brought Wilson with him to Harvard.

Wilson was a thin, spry, and youthful-looking man with a more formal demeanor than Banfield. His razor-sharp mind was unrelenting in its search for clarity. From that first meeting, I knew I wanted to do my PhD under Wilson.

The second one he introduced me to was Bruce Kovner. He had recently graduated as an undergraduate at Harvard and, like me, was entering the PhD program in American government under the auspices of Banfield. I found almost all the graduate students I met in the government department to be intelligent, but Bruce had an extraordinary kind of intellect that set him apart. Unlike the others, he was able to detach himself from his leanings when analyzing the pros and cons of an issue. Where others tended to play down, if not disregard, evidence when it was hostile to their view, Bruce would seek it out to test the validity of his conclusions. I became fully aware of his intellectual abilities when we taught a summer course in urban politics together. It did not surprise me when, a decade later, he became one of the most successful financial traders of currencies and commodities in history and largely endowed the Juilliard School of Music.

Banfield was true to his word when it came to financing my education. My tuition and other expenses were fully paid for by the Harvard-MIT Joint Center for Urban Studies. The center had been created by both universities in 1959 and funded by a large grant from the Ford Foundation. It had now become a vehicle for Wilson and Banfield to fund their research and, as in my case, their students.

Shortly before I arrived at Harvard, Banfield had brought in Daniel Patrick Moynihan to run the Joint Center. Pat, as everyone called him, personified Banfield's man of action. Born in Tulsa, Oklahoma, in 1927, he grew up in New York City, shining shoes to earn pocket money and working on New York's docks as a longshoreman to earn tuition to the City College of New York. He then chose politics as a profession. With his irrepressible intelligence, insights into human nature, and Irish charm, he rapidly climbed the ladder of Democratic politics. In 1961, he became an assistant secretary of labor in the Kennedy administration. From that vantage point, he encouraged Ralph Nader, then a young lawyer in the Labor Department, to write the book *Unsafe at Any Speed* (for which Moynihan wrote the introduction). After the Kennedy assassination, Moynihan worked briefly as a speechwriter for President Lyndon Johnson before departing for the academic world.

Soon after arriving at the Joint Center, he decided to transform what had been theretofore a dull funding mechanism for a few professors and students in the government department (including myself) into a nationally recognized launchpad for ideas about dealing with urban economic and race issues. His media canny and personal flare quickly made the Joint Center a go-to platform for the media. Within a few months under Moynihan's leadership, the Joint Center was on the cover of *Life* magazine. So was Pat Moynihan.

Pat did not have the analytic abilities of James Q. Wilson, the intellectual depth of Edward Banfield, or the rigor of thought of Bruce Kovner, but he had something else: a pragmatic imagination that he could apply to political issues. There was no better example of this ability than his 1965 report on the African American family. It argued that the welfare payments in Lyndon Johnson's well-intentioned "war on poverty" had the unintended consequence of breaking up families. Though it mired him in controversy, it also created a dialogue that revolutionized the role of government in urban America. If, as Banfield told me, Pat was "a rising star in politics," I wanted to attach my wagon to that star.

Pat also took an interest in me because I was a student of Wilson and Banfield (and officially one of the few fellows at the center). It didn't hurt, in light of his interest in the media, that I was a best-selling author and a *New Yorker* staff writer.

We began having a regular lunch together at the Yard of Ale in Harvard Square. The subject was often the biases of the media. I learned that, among his other virtues, Pat had a refreshingly strong moral backbone, especially when it came to the issue of how men should treat women. I knew he had been a close friend of Sander "Sandy" Vanocur, the NBC correspondent who achieved national fame as the questioner of Kennedy and Nixon in the first televised debate between presidential candidates, but, over a beer at the Yard of Ale, Pat told me that he no longer felt comfortable seeing Vanocur because he had left his wife for another woman. He said he could tolerate extramarital affairs but not wife desertion.

When I passed my oral exams in 1969, he generously hosted a dinner party for me at his home on Frances Avenue in Cambridge to celebrate it. He and his wife Elizabeth invited no fewer than 30 guests. There were the four professors who presided over my oral exam: Ed Banfield, James Q. Wilson, Harvey Mansfield, and Seymour Martin Lipset. He also invited Nathan Glazer and Daniel Bell. Glazer, born in New York City in 1923, had been a sociologist at Berkeley during the chaos of the Free Speech Movement before coming to Harvard. He was also the coauthor of two very important books in my education, *The Lonely Crowd* with David Riesman and *Beyond the Melting Pot* with Moynihan. Bell, also a sociologist at Harvard, had been born in 1919 in New York City and had written the influential book *The End of Ideology*, predicting the demise of the great ideologies that dominated 20th-century politics. Glazer and Bell were also the coeditors of *The Public Interest*, a quarterly for which I wrote.

Besides these, Moynihan asked five friends of mine from New York, including Clay Felker, Milton Glaser, Renata Adler, and Dan and Joanna Rose.

The guests were seated at three tables according to whether they liked their steaks cooked rare, medium, or well done. It was a brilliant system devised by Liz Moynihan to facilitate delivering steaks to guests. The waiter serving those steaks was David Stockman, who less than 11 years later served as President Reagan's all-powerful director of the Office of Management and Budget. At the time, he was a student at Harvard Divinity School who the Moynihans provided with a spare room in return for his occasional service at dinner parties. It was a moment in which everything in my academic life seemed to come together.

In April 1970, Pat came to New York for, as it turned out, the one and only screening of the footage of my *Iliad*. Since I had dined off the story of the disaster so many times, I decided that now, 10 years after I departed for Greece to produce Homer's epic, a time span that appropriately was equal to that of the Greeks' stay in Troy, I should screen it. The venue was the plush Warner Bros. Screening Room in Rockefeller Center. It was provided through the good offices of Daniel Stern, a poet, writer, and ad copywriter who had just become a vice president of Warner Bros. It was shown in unbalanced Technicolor since I did not have the budget to color-correct the scenes.

Of course, Susan Brockman was there. She had been my muse for the entire adventure that had taken me to Greece. The only other person in the audience, other than myself, who had been involved in this flight from reality was Mario Puzo. About a year before the screening, he had published *The Godfather*, which was still at the top of the best-seller list. I found it fitting that his earlier idea of updating *The Brothers Karamazov* into a family war within the Mafia had turned into a commercial success that would change the way the public thought about the Mafia. (He later told me that Marlon Brando would be cast in the film version as *The Godfather*, which I found ironic since he was the very actor who had eluded my efforts to get him to read Puzo's script for my *Iliad* in 1960.)

Moynihan, Banfield, and Kovner came from Harvard to see it. Also in attendance were Clay Felker, who was now the editor of *New York*; Aaron Asher, my editor at Viking; Sterling Lord, my agent; Richard Wald, the vice president of NBC News; Armand Erpf, a Wall Street financier who owned the controlling interest in *New York* magazine; and Raymond Sokolov, the arts editor of *Newsweek*. I invited several colleagues from the *New Yorker*, including Emma Rothschild, Jonathan Schell, Renata Adler, Frank Conroy, and Penelope Gilliatt. What all these attendees had in common was that they had heard some part of my *Iliad* story. The eight hours of footage—mainly retakes—had been reduced to 40 minutes. The room darkened. On-screen, in Cinemascope, Trojan soldiers, some stumbling on their giant shields, rushed between two fiery ships.

Since there was no sound, I narrated (without lyre or other accompaniment) the battle. Aside from the disaster scenes on camera, I told of the disasters off-camera, including the out-of-control chariot, the burning of the region's telephone poles (and the thousand-fold blackout it caused), the shipwrecked LST (for which I was later sued by the Greek general staff), the budget-draining orangeade epidemic among the extras, the obsessive wait for Brando, and the multitude of other inconveniences I visited on the Greeks by following my muse.

When the lights came up, Puzo invited everyone to a celebratory dinner at Elaine's, which, despite complaints about its culinary standards, had become a showbiz hangout. Very little was said about *The Iliad*, which I never showed again. All Moynihan had to say about the film at Elaine's was "I hope it was a learning experience."

It was. I had learned that projects such as moviemaking, which required the cooperation of many other people, were not for me. My moviemaking ambitions were an ego-driven mistake. I needed to find something less entangling. I decided to move forward with my writing career, a career in which I could be the sole author.

Harvard in the late 1960s had no shortage of intellectual surprises. For example, in 1967, there was Graham Allison, a fellow student in the government department who was writing his thesis on strategic decision-making and would later become dean of the John F. Kennedy School of Government. Born in 1940 in Charlotte, North Carolina, he kept, even after graduating Oxford, his folksy southern drawl. He introduced me to Diplomacy, a board game in which seven players are assigned seven countries in pre–World War I Europe and make their strategic decisions. Since there could be only one winner and alliances were necessary to win, the rules permitted players to lie, cheat, and deceive each other. Most of the games were held in the living room of my apartment on Harvard Avenue, and the other players included James Q. Wilson and his wife Roberta; Ed Banfield and his wife Laura; and Paul Weaver, a graduate student doing his thesis under Wilson on the *New York Times*. The negotiations between us went on for days and tied up a good deal of attention of the government department. Graham, who always chose to play France, won most of the games. I was at the time taking Henry Kissinger's seminar, and I unsuccessfully tried to recruit him into the game. "Diplomacy is my favorite game," he said, leaving it ambiguous as to whether he meant the board game or the real game of nations. As he was commuting between Cambridge and Washington, DC, he never came.

Since the game provided me with fascinating insights into the role of deception in geopolitics, I tried to further hone my skills in it by finding players among foreign policy buffs in New York, including James Chace, the editor of *Foreign Affairs*. Chace then organized a game at his home every December 16 for over a decade. Our players were almost always policy wonks in their 30s and 40s, but on one occasion, desperate to find a seventh player, I ill-advisedly recruited the 14-year-old son of my friends Dan and Joanna Rose. Even though I warned the teenager that this was a game which could only be won by misleading and betraying allies, Joey Rose didn't take my betrayal of him kindly. Thirty years later, when he was the commissioner of city planning in New York, he reminded me of that betrayal, telling me it was his first lesson in adult perfidy.

The wild diversity of the political science department at MIT, at least in the 1960s sense of the word, could be found in my office mates in the suite we shared in the Hermann Building. One was the songwriter, satirist, and mathematician Tom Lehrer. Lehrer had been born in 1928 on New York's Upper East Side, entered Harvard as a child prodigy at the age of 15, and after being drafted into the army, wound up working at the National Security Agency, a highly secretive code-breaking agency that had intrigued me since my investigation into the JFK assassination. The other was William Bundy, was a former CIA executive and the assistant secretary of state for East Asian and Pacific affairs during the Vietnam War. Bundy, who had just left the government, could not have come from a more different background than Lehrer or, for that matter, me. He was born in 1917 into a Boston patrician family. His father, Harvey Bundy, was assistant secretary of state under FDR; his younger brother, McGeorge Bundy, was national security advisor to both Presidents Kennedy and Johnson, and his wife Mary was the daughter of Truman's secretary of state Dean Acheson. After attending Yale, where he was a member of Skull and Crossbones, and Harvard Law School and serving a stint in the CIA, he became, along with his brother, one of the architects of the war in Vietnam. As might be expected, our politics sharply differed. I was against the war in Vietnam, Bundy thought it was necessary, and Lehrer was against not only the war but government itself. Despite our differences, I found them to be enjoyable office mates with such bizarre moments as Lehrer hilariously explaining to Bundy how he invented Jell-O shots—gelatin laced with vodka—to evade NSA rules against drinking alcohol.

As a teacher, I found a marked difference between my Harvard and MIT students. The former were socially transactional. Those in my seminar did not hesitate to attempt to negotiate a better grade on their papers. As I enjoy verbal argument, I usually acquiesced in the negotiations to reward their efforts. One student, Tom Werner, even broadened the negotiations to include an idea to collaborate on a TV series based on a Robert Ludlum thriller. (He went on to produce *The Bill Cosby Show*.) On the other hand, MIT students tended to accept their grades as the fate they deserved. They evidenced little interest in engaging in social interaction or negotiations. I did learn from them, however. Unlike their social science counterparts at Harvard, they were the future electrical engineers and computer scientists who would usher in the age of the internet.

There was no shortage of big-time intellectuals at Harvard. One I worked with was David Riesman. Born to a wealthy Jewish family in Philadelphia in 1909, he obtained an undergraduate degree in biochemistry from Harvard College and a law degree from Harvard Law School in 1929, clerked for Supreme Court Justice Louis Brandeis (namesake of Brandeis University), prosecuted criminal cases for District Attorney Thomas E. Dewey (who ran for president in 1948), edited an antinuclear magazine, and taught law at the University of Chicago. His book *The Lonely Crowd* was the best-selling book in sociology in the 20th century, selling over 1.4 million copies. Its astounding success was all the more surprising because it critiqued the middle classes for their social conformity. In doing so, it established the categories of "outer directed," which were people who tuned their actions to those of the herd around them, and "inner directed," who were people whose implanted values acted as a gyroscope in guiding them. Inner directed vs. outer directed became such a hot parlor game in America that *Time* put Riesman on its cover.

In 1970, he took me to lunch at the Faculty Club and persuaded me to be his course assistant for his celebrated undergraduate course, American Character and Social Structure, which was not difficult. The course was ranked as an "Absolute must-take" by the *Harvard Crimson's Unofficial Guide.* Riesman said that even full professors had applied for the course assistant position in past years. And, as if I needed further inducement, course assistants got to attend private biweekly dinners at his house during the semester and for three months preceding it. These dinners, no matter how highly prized by others, turned out to be an onerous burden for me, especially since I often flew to New York on free days.

An even stronger inducement was that another course assistant who would teach with me was my friend Doris Kearns. Doris and I had much in common. We were both born in Brooklyn, attended South Side High School in Rockville Centre on Long Island, and were in the PhD program in government at Harvard. Doris was also an author with a contract to write a biography of Lyndon Baines Johnson, a book that would benefit from the close relationship she had maintained with President Johnson since she was a White House fellow in 1964. (Doris went on to become a Pulitzer Prize–winning historian who married JFK's speechwriter Richard Goodwin.)

Our first dinner was presided over by Riesman and his wife Evie on January 21, 1971. He spent most of the three hours outlining our first task. He wanted Doris and me to establish criteria for winnowing down the herd of student applicants to a number that the lecture hall could seat. Why the precaution? He explained that usually twice as many students applied than could be accommodated. But, as it turned out, not enough students applied to fill half the room.

At the next dinner in February, he asked us to be frank about our assessment of whether *The Lonely Crowd* had held up in the 20 years since he wrote it. *The Lonely Crowd* was one of my favorite titles but not one of my favorite books. Unlike James Q. Wilson, who sought compelling evidence for his theories, Riesman based his concepts about "inner-directed" and "outer-directed" people on anecdotes drawn from his selected interviews. According to my diary entry for that dinner, I had been guarded in my reply, saying only that the fact that it remains the best-selling book by any sociologist in history "speaks for itself."

I also asked what he meant by "individualism reconsidered," the title of his later collection of essays. He said only that he wanted an ironic title. While intrigued by his answer, I was not satisfied with it. Was his title *Individualism Reconsidered* suggesting that there was an alternative of forsaking individualism in favor of the regimentation of herd mentality? While I learned a great deal from Riesman about book publishing as well as sociology, and I enjoyed the collaboration with Doris, I had to resign the Riesman gig to study for my oral PhD exam.

# CHAPTER SIXTEEN

# AROUND THE WORLD
# IN 60 DAYS

By 1973 academic life was wearing thin. The possibility of escaping it came when President Nixon appointed Pat Moynihan as ambassador to India and, in a stroke of good luck, Pat invited me to stay with him and his family at the embassy residence in New Delhi. "Are you up for a round-the-world tour?" he asked.

I was eager for it. "All I need is a ticket."

He had found a novel way to pay for my trip. The State Department had earned a vast sum of Indian rupees from the sale of American wheat to India in the 1950s and 1960s. They were called "PB 484" rupees and could not be exchanged for US dollars, so they had been accumulating in a US government account. Pat discovered that these blocked funds could be used to purchase a business-class air ticket on a US airline, and he proposed using them for my ticket. As a justification, Pat created the "Star Series," in which his chosen invitees would give lectures. So in return for my round-the-world ticket on Pan American Airways, I would give lectures on the state of American journalism in England, Turkey, Iran, India, Sri Lanka, Nepal, Burma, Thailand, Hong Kong, Japan, and Hawaii.

When I asked Pat if I could bring a date, he said jokingly, "Bring two." I had already invited Amanda Burden, the whip-smart daughter of the socialites Babe Paley and Stanley Mortimer and the stepdaughter of William Paley, the founder of CBS. She was studying city planning at Columbia (and would go on to be commissioner of city planning and help bring to fruition the Highline). Because of her classes, she could only accompany me as far as Iran. So I invited her 25-year-old stepsister, Kate Paley, to accompany me on the remaining half of the trip.

Pat and his family had stayed in my apartment in New York while I was in Europe the previous year, so I was more than happy to accept his generous invitation to stay in the embassy residence in New Delhi in December 1973. The plan was for us to tour Rajasthan over Christmas in a private train car he had arranged.

As the PB 484 funds could be used only for airfare, I still had the problem of paying for hotels. My friend Victor Navasky solved it. He threw an extraordinary going-away party for me in his West 67th Street apartment. Victor invited only people I did not know from the 10 countries in which I was stopping. One of these guests was a woman from the Hilton Hotel chain. She gave me a 50 percent discount at Hilton hotels in all the countries I was to visit.

Amanda Burden met me on November 22, 1973, in Istanbul and attended my requisite lecture on media bias to Turkish journalists. Since she was more interested in archeological sites than media, we visited the ruins of ancient Troy—shades of *The Iliad*—as well as Ephesus, Telmessos, and Aspendos.

Next we flew to Tehran, Iran. I had previously met Ardeshir Zahedi, Iran's ambassador to the US, when I was researching the 1953 CIA-led coup in Iran that brought the shah to power and in which his father, General Fazlòllah Zahedi, acted as the CIA's cat's-paw. After I told him about my planned visit, he arranged for us a trip to Shiraz, Isfahan, and Persepolis, complete with bodyguards.

When we got back to Tehran on December 2, Amanda ran into her friend Jack Valenti, Lyndon Johnson's former White House assistant, in the lobby of the Tehran Hilton. He was now the head of the Motion Picture Association of America and had come to Iran for the newly created Tehran International Film Festival. Thanks to Amanda, he invited us to dinner. His other guests were Gregory Peck and his wife, Veronique. Peck, except for his graying hair, looked like he had just stepped out of his role as Atticus Finch in the movie *To Kill a Mockingbird*. He showed a keen interest in our trip to Persepolis but discreetly avoided joining a discussion of the political situation in Iran. Veronique, a former French journalist, was less discreet in speaking about the shah ignoring popular resentment of his regime. Valenti tried to lower the temperature of the conversation by suggesting that the shah's sponsorship of this film festival, the first in Iranian history, was a harbinger of modernization. But Veronique was not convinced, saying, with her enchanting smile, "or of the bubble the shah lives in." At this point, Peck couldn't resist adding that the problem with bubbles is that they burst. His comment proved prescient. Four years later, that bubble burst when the shah was overthrown.

In light of what Veronique discussed at dinner, Amanda and I decided on a further reconnaissance outside of the modern quarters of Tehran. We hired a car and driver from the hotel and set out to visit the ancient city of Qom, a center of Shiʿa scholarship, about 76 miles south of Tehran. The towns we passed through had little connection with modern Tehran; most women were veiled. We never reached Qom, however, because our car broke down. The driver was unable to get parts to repair it for six hours. We got back to Tehran just in time for my scheduled lecture at the embassy.

The next morning, Amanda flew back to New York and I proceeded to India.

Pat was not in New Delhi when I arrived. He had been called back to New York for an emergency meeting concerning Palestine

Liberation Organization (PLO) terrorist threats to US embassies. His wife, Liz, told me I received a telegram from Kate Paley, who said that though her plane had been delayed in Rome, she now was on her way. I had invited her to come on the private train Pat had rented for a tour of Rajasthan.

When Pat returned to the embassy, he said the CIA had intelligence that the PLO was planning to kill or kidnap him. Roosevelt House went into lockdown mode, with Sikh bodyguards and Marines guarding every door.

I had lunch with Pat every day while awaiting Kate's arrival. He was furious at the "minions" in the Nixon administration who were telling him to work to shut down the production of opium in India. "It's idiotic," he said. Although India was the world's largest producer of opium, much of it went to pharmaceutical companies to manufacture codeine, an antitussive. "If they shut down Indian opium, they are going to cause a global coughing crisis."

It was a role reversal for Pat. When he served in the Nixon White House two years earlier, he had advocated overriding ambassadors and using the threat of military action to suppress opium. I realized that Pat, a chameleon, adapted his views to coincide with his position. In other words, he was a political animal.

He also liked an afternoon beer after lunch in the embassy garden. I noticed it made him much more talkative. After one lunch, he talked about Nixon's advisors John Ehrlichman, Egil Krogh, and H.R. "Bob" Haldeman, who he called "The Mormons." They were actually Christian Scientists, as he knew, but they had become jokingly known by their enemies as the Mormon gang. "The Mormons now think a heroin epidemic is about to explode, but they know nothing." He explained that when he joined the Nixon administration, there was a concern that drugs and street crime were linked. He suggested to Nixon that the link theory could be tested by temporarily disrupting the supply of foreign drugs into the United States. What he had not foreseen is that "the Mormons" would expand his idea into policy. "I was as surprised as anyone when they turned my suggestion into the war on heroin."

Terrorism continued to interrupt my plans for India. For one thing, Kate's plane was delayed in Rome for three days because of a PLO attack at the Rome airport. While waiting for her, I traveled to Madras, Bombay, Calcutta, and Colombo. In each city, the State Department arranged for me to give lectures on the state of American journalism. When I got back to Delhi, Kate was waiting, frazzled and upset by her airport ordeal. She was even more upset by the lockdown at the embassy. She was also shocked that Pat had taken it upon himself to send a cable to her father, William Paley, saying that Kate was in good hands with me. What Pat didn't know was that she had not spoken to her father for over a year and had not told him about her trip to India with me.

For another, security concerns caused Pat to cancel the Christmas train tour of Rajasthan. Instead, we went to Fatehpur Sikri, the deserted 16th-century capital of the empire, which was about a four-hour ride by car. Ruth Prawer Jhabvala and her husband Cyrus Jhabvala, who were friends of Pat, joined us. Ruth, a prize-winning novelist and screenwriter, was a diminutive woman who had lost some 40 relatives in the Holocaust. She had been living in India since 1951. Cyrus, a Parsi architect, headed the School of Architecture in Delhi. He guided us through the dead city, pointing out that its founding emperor, Akbar, had chosen a combination of Islamic, Hindu, and Christian architecture to reflect the different religions of his three wives. The city was a victim of an environmental crisis. Sixteen years after it was built, its wells ran dry and it had to be abandoned. I was fascinated with Ruth and Cyrus's insights into this ancient ghost town, but Kate, still jet-lagged by her long flight, became increasingly disturbed by the constant intrusion of aggressive hawkers and beggars. She also wanted to see the Taj Mahal, so we drove to Agra, where we spent the next two days. We returned to Delhi for Christmas with the Moynihan family.

On December 29, Kate and I went to Tiger Top, a game park in neighboring Nepal. After riding a well-trained elephant through the jungle, we flew to Kathmandu for New Year's Eve. At a Tibetan-style restaurant we ran into an old Cornell classmate of mine, Lhendup "Lennie" Dorji. Although I did not know it at Cornell, Lennie was a prince of Bhutan whose sister was married to the king. Now in exile in Nepal, he supported himself by trafficking in antique Enfield rifles. He invited us to a New Year's Eve party in a casino, where most of his Bhutanese and Tibetan guests were high on marijuana.

One of the most educational aspects of this voyage was meeting with four American ambassadors—Moynihan in India, William Cargo in Nepal, William Macomber in Turkey, and Richard Helms in Iran. The officials from the State Department and the US Information Agency who met me at every airport sped me through customs and briefed me on the political situation in each country I visited. In each city, the embassy hosted a small dinner party at which I met local journalists who proved helpful later in my career. The trip also convinced me that three days in a country was sufficient for sightseeing.

My round-the-world trip ended in Los Angeles in February 1974. I had been appointed the regents' professor of government at UCLA and had to teach classes four days a week on American politics. Many of my students commuted to campus and worried more about finding parking spaces than keeping up with the rapidly changing political system. Professor Charles Nixon (no relation to President Nixon), the chairman of the political science department, invited me to his home for dinner a few weeks after I arrived. The invitation was accompanied with a marked-up freeway map and a page of convoluted instructions on how to get from UCLA to his home and where to find parking for my rented car. When I got lost en route, I decided that I belonged in Manhattan, with its subway lines and easily hailed taxis. I did not renew my teaching contract and that summer moved to New York.

# CHAPTER SEVENTEEN

# AMATEUR POLITICS

Pat Moynihan left India in December 1974 and returned to teaching at Harvard. In India we had discussed jointly writing a textbook entitled *The Limits of Government* for Jason Epstein, our mutual editor at Random House. Epstein (no relation) seemed keen on publishing it, but we never got past the introductory chapter before, on June 30, 1975, President Gerald Ford appointed Pat as the US ambassador to the UN. He was happy to leave academic life, moving into the elegant suite of rooms in the Waldorf Tower in New York that is the residence of the UN ambassador.

Although my penthouse cabal attempt to prod him to do so in February 1976 failed, Pat decided on his own to run for the Senate that April. Excited by the idea of a man of Pat's brilliant intellect in the Senate, I again took on the task of lining up financial support for him in the Hamptons, where I had rented a home on Georgica Pond.

One of the most promising contributors was my next-door neighbor on West End Road in East Hampton, Steven J. Ross. He was the chairman of Warner Communications, a conglomerate that included Atlantic Records as well as Warner Bros. Studio. In light of his role in the entertainment industry, Ross was in a position to raise money. In some ways, he arose from similar circumstances as Moynihan. Like Pat, Ross had an incredible rags-to-riches success story. He was born on April 5, 1927, in Brooklyn, New York, to immigrant parents. When he was a child, his father lost all his money during the Great Depression. He changed the family name from Rechnitz to Ross in hopes of finding work with a less Jewish name, but he never did. Unable to afford college, Ross went to work at his uncle's store in lower Manhattan. He worked as a stockman in the garment district, tried his hand at performing gigs as a magician at bar mitzvahs and weddings, and, at the age of 24, got a job as a funeral director at the Riverside Funeral Chapel, owned by Edward Rosenthal. After marrying Rosenthal's daughter, Carol, he turned Rosenthal's highly profitable chain of funeral homes into a mini-conglomerate by buying companies that rented cars, operated parking lots, cleaned offices, and constructed buildings. He took the company public, using its stock to buy a host of entertainment companies, including the Warner Bros.–Seven Arts studio, the Ashley-Famous talent agency, Atlantic Records, and DC Comics. By 1981, Warner Communications, as he had renamed the conglomerate, also owned MTV, Nickelodeon, and other cable networks and dominated a large part of the entertainment business. Unlike Pat, Ross never completed college, rarely read books, and had no claim to being an intellectual. Even so, I thought the chemistry between them would work.

I met Ross when he began dating my friend Amanda Burden, who had accompanied me to Turkey and Iran. Since he lived next door I saw a good deal of him. So, in May 1976, after Pat decided to run, I broached the topic with Ross. He responded, "He's great. He should be president."

"I agree," I said. "But he's running for the Senate this year."

"So we'll first make him senator. What does he need?" Ross offered not only to raise money for him but also to recruit Frank Sinatra and Barbra Streisand to perform at his fundraisers. I had no reason to doubt that he could deliver on both stars.

"How should we proceed?" I asked.

"Let's meet." He suggested Pat come to his home in East Hampton for dinner on Saturday, June 19.

I reported that conversation to Pat and suggested they meet. He replied, "Why not take a trip to the Hamptons?"

The plan was for Pat and Liz to stay at my house over the weekend and go next door to Ross's house for dinner on Saturday night. I also invited Arthur Klebanoff, who was Pat's lawyer; his wife Susan, a professional fundraiser; and Richard Blumenthal, one of Banfield's former students at Harvard, who was now assisting Pat in the campaign. (Blumenthal would himself be elected senator from Connecticut in 2011.)

But things did not go as planned. I had failed to warn Pat that Steve Ross despite all his uncanny successes in business, was dangerously insecure about his intellectual standing. Unlike Pat, who earned a PhD, Steve had dropped out of Paul Smith's College. Because of this insecurity, Steve went to great lengths to impress others with his intellectual powers. A few months earlier Steve asked me to come over for a game of Scrabble, a game Amanda and I occasionally played to kill time. It struck me as an odd invitation because Steve had never before played with us. When I arrived, he and Amanda were already seated around the board. We each drew seven tiles, with Steve going first. Before I even looked at my tiles, Steve laid down *zygomat*, an obscure seven-letter word that gave him one of the highest scores possible on an opening move. With that coup, he declared himself the winner and excused himself from the balance of the game because he said he had a conference call.

Amanda quickly figured out that Steve had cheated. She had seen him take the Scrabble set to his bedroom the night before. He was a former professional magician, and she assumed he had pocketed the seven tiles for *zygomat* and, with sleight of hand, switched them for the seven tiles he actually picked. To prove her hypothesis, she counted the tiles and found that exactly seven were missing, which presumably were still in his pocket.

I asked why Steve would go to such extraordinary lengths to appear to be a Scrabble whiz. Amanda said Steve had to demonstrate that he was smarter than both of us at everything.

Amanda had even caught Steve cheating in a game with her seven-year-old daughter, Belle. The game was Mastermind, in which one player tries to guess the color of the other player's pegs, which were concealed behind a rack. According to Amanda, Steve would distract Belle and then peek. "Steve always needs an edge." (Twenty years later, Belle told me she could see Steve peeking but pretended to be impressed at his game-playing skills.)

Unfortunately, I did not mention any of Steve's cheating tricks to Pat.

Promptly at 7:00 p.m., our party, including Pat, Liz, Arthur and Susan Klebanoff, and Blumenthal, proceeded through the gap in the hedges that separated the houses. Pat, not appreciative of the faux casualness of the Hamptons, was dressed in an elegant business suit and tie. Steve and Amanda, both dressed in white, were waiting for us at a candlelit table at the pool. Behind the pool was Georgica Pond.

Steve was fulsome, almost sycophantic, in his praise of Pat, telling him he was "the greatest American of his generation." He wanted to hold a fundraiser for Pat at his home on the July 4 weekend that "would raise zillions." He said that he admired his speeches at the UN, quoting word-for-word a passage from a 1975 speech in which Pat had denounced a UN effort to equate racism with Zionism. I could see Steve had done his homework, which, in retrospect, should have set off alarm bells. I could also see by his rapid consumption of a drink that this flattery made Pat uncomfortable. So did Steve's constant stroking of Amanda, whom he had been dating for just over a year. Pat, though hardly a prude, did not like public displays of affection.

As dinner progressed, Steve reclined so far into Amanda's shoulder that it looked like they were seated in the same chair. While Pat tried to cut his lamb chops, Steve asked rapid-fire questions about the status of various New York State bonds. Seeing that he had clearly prepared these questions as part of an agenda, I changed the subject back to Israel and the UN. Steve persisted, however, in asking technical questions about bonds until Pat, whose face was getting redder by the minute, answered condescendingly, "The US Senate deals with national and foreign issues, not the relative merits of local bonds."

Steve was not about to forgo his *zygomat* moment of besting Pat in front of Amanda. He had prepared his "gotcha" on an obscure New York City–backed sewage treatment bond. "Yes, I just want to know hypothetically how you would deal with the covenants in this municipal bond in the event of bankruptcy."

Pat finished his glass of wine in one long gulp. "That is a subject to be discussed in the future, and hopefully by someone else." He rose to his full six-feet-four height, took Liz by the hand, and said, "It has been a long day for us, sir." In a matter of five seconds, he was out the door and heading for the gap in the hedges that separated our houses. I shrugged, said goodnight, and followed my houseguests through the hedge.

Steve was apoplectic, I learned from Amanda the next morning. "Moynihan made Steve look like an idiot," she said. "Steve is talking about going to war." Not only would there be no Frank Sinatra, Barbra Streisand, and rollout of stars, but Steve had decided to give the July 4 fundraiser for Bella Abzug, Pat's chief rival in the Democratic primary. She added that I would be invited.

As it turned out, Pat did not need Sinatra, Streisand, or the "zillion-dollar" fundraiser. He was by far the best candidate. He easily won the Democratic primary and defeated Republican James Buckley in the general election. Pat was sworn in on January 3, 1977, as the junior senator from New York.

Two weeks later, I witnessed an incident that demonstrated to me Pat's superbly fine-tuned judgment in walking out of Steve Ross's dinner in East Hampton. Steve had invited me to Las Vegas to belatedly celebrate Amanda's birthday. Aside from Amanda and me, he also invited Ken Rosen and Jay Emmett (his top executives at Warner Communications), their wives, and William vanden Heuvel, who about to be the US ambassador to the European office of the United Nations in Geneva, along with his fiancée, Melinda Pierce. During the flight on the Warner Gulfstream, Steve revealed that he had a prodigious memory that gave him unbeatable card-counting skills. Since no casino in Las Vegas would allow him, with his known skills, to play blackjack, he played in disguise. He then invited us to invest $1,000 in his stealthy playing. "No need to give me money," he said, explaining that he rarely lost, but there was one ironclad rule: none of us could leave the Frank Sinatra suite at Caesars Palace in which we would all be staying. In the eight-bedroom suite with a 40-foot-square white-carpeted living room, with a white piano in the center, we watched a Clint Eastwood movie on a giant TV. After Steve left, Milton "Mickey" Rudin, Frank Sinatra's lawyer, joined us. In no more than 45 minutes, Steve returned, hugged Amanda, and said dramatically. "It was hard, baby." He then began disgorging chips from his pockets, handfuls of hundred- and thousand-dollar chips that came from various casinos on the Strip. From the size of the stacks he put on the glass coffee table, I reckoned there was over a quarter-million dollars in casino chips. He next handed each of us precisely $7,000 in chips as a return on our investment. Steve said he couldn't cash the remaining $200,000 or so of chips or the casinos would figure out he was using his card-counting ability, so he asked some of his guests to cash them in neighboring casinos on the Strip. That evening all the chips were converted to cash, which Steve put in his attaché case.

It seemed impossible to me that Steve had won this windfall by card counting. As far as I know, that technique, though it provides a statistical edge over the dealer, yields a slow return over many hours of play. Yet Steve claimed to have won a quarter-million dollars in less than 45 minutes at different casinos. Nor was it the first time. Amanda told me that Steve had performed this same trick, with the same results, on their three previous trips to Las Vegas. My suspicion was that Steve might be getting the chips as a payoff from the casinos. If so, he was using his guests to unwittingly launder these payoffs.

As part of my continuing education into the political realm, I made almost weekly trips to Washington in 1977. One reason was that I wanted to see how Pat, who had never before held an elected office, would adjust to his new political life. It turned out that he took to the Senate as a fish to water. As a man of action, he dealt with his colleagues' wheeling and dealing, his constituents' complaints, and the demands of the media with a skill set that combined the winning charm of an Irish bartender with the erudition of a university professor.

The Moynihans had moved into a modest townhouse with a small backyard in the Capitol Hill area, a location from which he could easily walk to the Senate. Liz brilliantly decorated the house from artifacts she had bought in India and hyperrealistic sculptures done by Tim, their oldest son. One such lifelike sculpture of a Jeeves-like butler stood in the vestibule by the front door. Its positioning caused me some embarrassment when I first dined there. This was a highly enjoyable dinner in which Pat described his recent meeting with Jimmy Carter, the new president. He expressed concern that Carter's overweening sense of righteousness could affect his judgment on choosing between unpleasant political realities. It was again the conundrum we danced around so often at Harvard: Could a president put his private morality above the well-being of the people?

By dessert, Pat's bleary eyes suggested he was growing tired. Unlike in New York, dinners tended to end early in Washington. Shortly before 10:00, Liz called a taxi to take me back to my hotel. Out of politeness, Pat and Liz sat with me while I waited for it to arrive. After a half hour or so, Pat hardly could keep his eyes open. Liz impatiently called the taxi service. After some back-and-forth, we learned that the driver had arrived promptly at 10:00 p.m., but rather than ringing the bell, he had left a message with the "butler" that he would be waiting in his car for me. Tim's sculpture had totally fooled him and made me a guest who had stayed too long.

Another reason that brought me to Washington was the opportunity to lunch at the White House, a building I had not yet seen from the inside. This chance came about because Rick Hertzberg, a former colleague of mine from the *New Yorker*, had become President Carter's speechwriter. Rick, who had been one of the most insightful writers at the *New Yorker*, knew how curious I was to see the White House in action and had invited me to come for lunch in the White House cafeteria whenever I was in the District. I took him up on his generous offer. Members of his speech-writing team, including journalists Chris Matthew and Jonathan Alter, often joined us for lunch in the "navy mess," as the White House cafeteria on the ground floor of the West Wing was called because the navy ran it. Rick had a beeper, then considered an ultra-hi-tech piece of equipment. Everyone looked up when it suddenly went off, anticipating some crisis had arisen for which President Carter urgently needed appropriate words. On one such occasion in April 1980, we had gone to Mama Ayesha's Palestinian restaurant for dinner when the beeper sounded. Jumping out of his seat, Rick rushed to the nearest pay phone. Saying only "gotta go," he raced back to the White House. He returned in time for the baklava dessert, saying that he had to write something for the president. Soon afterward, President Carter was on television telling the public, presumably with the help of Rick's elegantly crafted words, that the secret effort to rescue 52 American hostages from Iran, called Operation Eagle Claw, had disastrously failed.

When Carter was away, Rick gave me guided tours of the West Wing, including the Oval Office and Situation Room. I have always considered it helpful to see the appurtenances of presidential power in its three-dimensional form. What struck me about the White House was how physically small these rooms were. Rick left the White House with Carter in 1981, and when he got married, I was his best man.

I also had a practical reason for my frequent trips to DC in the mid-1970s. I learned that the Church Committee, formerly known as the United States Senate Select Committee to Study Governmental Operations Concerning Intelligence Activities, had discovered CIA files bearing on an issue that had obsessed me for five years. The material linked the CIA and the international oil cartel to the overthrow of the elected government in Iran in 1953. I had no problem gaining access to these files. My cousin Jerome Levinson was the chief counsel and staff director of the committee, demonstrating that a family member could be a great asset. Every time the committee discovered a new piece of that puzzle, I rushed to Washington to see it. In that story of a coup d'état, the CIA key operative was the elusive grandson of former president Theodore Roosevelt, Kermit "Kim" Roosevelt. He had no immediate interest in the mid-1970s, however, in a meeting to tell a journalist how he had changed the face of the Middle East.

# CHAPTER EIGHTEEN

# MEETING KIM ROOSEVELT

Finally, in 1978, I met with Kim Roosevelt. He could claim the distinction of being a true kingmaker, having put both Abdel Nasser in Egypt and the shah of Iran back in power. What made the meeting I had long sought so odd was that Roosevelt was also a fictive character in a novel I had recently written.

This novel came about because, thanks to the recommendation of Clay Felker, the movie studio 20th Century Fox had optioned the film rights to an article I had written for *New York* magazine that concerned the shah of Iran. The producer was Michael Gruskoff, who had just produced *Young Frankenstein* with Mel Brooks. When we had our script conference, he told me he wanted the movie to be about how America had put the shah on the throne of Iran. As part of the deal, I would write a thriller on the subject based on my article.

"I've never written a novel," I told him.

"Just find a realistic hero and invent everything else. It'll write itself."

Since the money he offered was attractive, I discussed the proposed novel with Ned Chase, my very supportive editor at G.P. Putnam. He loved the idea, especially since it already had a movie studio option, and he commissioned me to write my first novel. It would be entitled *Cartel*.

Now I needed to find a CIA officer on whom to model the fictive hero. In Washington, I went to see Ambassador Loy Henderson. He had been part of the original team of Russian experts at the State Department that also included George Kennan and Charles "Chip" Bohlen. Since he had gone on to be the US Ambassador in Tehran at the time of the CIA coup in 1953, he was in a position to find the hero I needed. "Who made it happen?" I asked.

"Kim Roosevelt is your man," Henderson answered with a wry smile. He explained that the operation was code-named Ajax, and it was the first time the CIA had succeeded in overthrowing a democratically elected government. It effectively put the CIA in the regime change business. Ajax replaced the regime of Prime Minister Mohammad Mosaddegh, the French-educated politician who had moved to nationalize the oil concession of the Anglo-Iranian Oil Company, with the 32-year-old pro-American shah, Reza Pahlavi, who had not yet been crowned.

I asked how Kim Roosevelt came into the picture.

"Like gangbusters." Henderson further explained that in 1953, Ajax couldn't get off the ground because the gun-shy shah was afraid to challenge Mosaddegh, who had immense popular support. The CIA was about to abort it and ordered Roosevelt, the CIA's 37-year-old "ground operational planner" for Ajax, to leave Iran. Roosevelt simply ignored those orders and went directly to the shah. "The naïf shah was so impressed by Roosevelt's name and powers of persuasion that he decided to go along with the plan." As a consequence, and after a good deal of machinations, the coup took place.

A CIA agent who ignored orders from superiors to act as a rogue kingmaker could be the perfect Hollywood movie hero. So I decided to write the book around a fictional version of Roosevelt.

I had just read Edgar Doctorow's dazzling 1975 novel *Ragtime*, which had mixed real characters such as J.P. Morgan, Harry Houdini, Evelyn Nesbit, and Henry Ford with fictional ones to create an illusion of verisimilitude. I asked Doctorow at a dinner in East Hampton how he made these real-life characters so believable. He said that the trick was deliberately avoiding knowing anything more about them other than a few rudimentary facts available in the encyclopedia. The key was to reinvent them following the requisites of the plot. I followed his advice. Aside from the facts I had gleaned from the Church Committee documents and my single interview with Henderson, I avoided further research for the novel. Instead, I invented out of whole cloth the fictional versions of Roosevelt, Mosaddegh, the shah, and other real characters. It took me just over a year to write since I had to meet the deadline the movie studio had insisted on.

Even though Fox decided not to make the movie, Putnam published *Cartel* in November 1978. Despite the fact that I clearly had not mastered the art of writing a thriller, it received generous reviews in the *New York Times Book Review*, saying, "Epstein makes fantasy out of reality in this flamboyant suspense novel." Actually, as far as I was aware, it was mainly fantasy.

Soon after the *Times* review, I found a message from Kim Roosevelt on my answering machine. Initially, I feared he intended to sue me for using a fictionalized version of him, but how could I not call back a character that has jumped out of one's own novel? He said he wanted to talk to me about Operation Ajax. He acknowledged that he had staged the coup in Iran that had put the shah back in power and onto what Roosevelt called the "Peacock Throne." In fact, it was a replica of the real Peacock Throne, which was destroyed in Delhi in 1737. In any case, Roosevelt did change history in the Middle East, and I wanted to hear how his version differed from the one I had invented. Hence our meeting in a lounge at the Washington, DC, airport.

With a roundish face, thinning hair, and horn-rimmed glasses, and supported by a cane, he looked far less robust than the king-maker in my novel. After a few minutes of introductory back-and-forth, he came straight to the point. He wanted to write a nonfiction memoir about the Ajax operation but, as his memory was vague, he needed help. Would I be interested in helping him? He suggested I could ghost it for him.

I had never, and would never, ghostwrite a book. Yet I was curious to hear more about how my book diverged from his reality, and its protagonist was offering to tell me. I asked in my most humble voice, as if speaking to a book reviewer, "What did you think of my novel?"

"You got a couple of details wrong." He gave by way of example my Kim Roosevelt character cooking a pig on a spit at a barbecue for General Zahedi, whose troops at Roosevelt's direction then took over the Iranian Parliament and arrested Prime Minister Mosaddegh. "It was a goat on the spit, not a pig. Muslims don't eat pork."

He was of course right. It was one of many absurd scenes in my novel. The pig-on-the-spit was the product of my imagination based loosely on a barbecue I had on my terrace in Manhattan (where my guests did eat pork). Was he was now saying that my invented scene coincided with a real goat barbecue he organized for Zahedi in Iran?

When he finished his critique of *Cartel*, I asked him about the actual 1953 coup. After all, according to Henderson, he was at the center of it. "What really happened?"

"I thought you caught the flavor of Ajax pretty well in your book."

Rather than pointing out that my novel was a product of my uninformed imagination, I asked him more about the actual mechanisms of Ajax. All his answers seemed to be taken straight out of *Cartel*.

I tried to prod him about the day-to-day chronology of Ajax.

Evading the questions, he answered that these events took place 25 years ago and were now all blurred together.

Since a British oil company was at the heart of the dispute, I asked something that should have not been part of the blur. "You must recall how you coordinated Ajax with British intelligence in Tehran?"

"I don't," he said with a blank stare. "As I told you, I have a bit of a memory problem."

I saw no point in pressing him further. Whatever his memory problem was, it explained why he had approached me to ghost-write his memoir of Ajax. I had made him a hero in *Cartel*, and he probably assumed I had researched his role instead of taking Doctorow's novel-writing advice and inventing it.

After I told him I was hard at work on another book, we parted on good terms.

I never heard from Roosevelt again, but in August 1979, he published a nonfiction book, *Countercoup: The Struggle for the Control of Iran*. It was different from my novel in many details, but there were enough similar scenes in it to make me wonder if Oscar Wilde was right when he said, "Life imitates Art far more than Art imitates Life." Roosevelt's art was further confirmed for me four decades later in Ray Takeyh's history *The Last Shah*, in which he depicts Roosevelt as a self-promoter whose account "is debunked by the declassified record." Even so, through his talent for self-inflation, he managed to falsely cast himself in the public's mind as the architect of the coup.

Here I am (left) driving my horse and buggy onto campus with Wright T. "Lefty" Lewis (right) in 1954.

*The Iliad* is filming in Greece.

Susan Brockman is pictured on the set of *The Iliad.*

I am shown researching *The Iliad* at Minos's palace in Knossos, Crete, in 1959.

The Warren Commission was (from left to right) Gerald Ford, Hale Boggs, Richard Russell, Chief Justice Earl Warren, John Sherman Cooper, John McCloy, Allen Dulles, and J. Lee Rankin, pictured in 1964.

A 1992 Town Hall debate featured (from left to right) Oliver Stone, Nora Ephron, me, Norman Mailer, and Victor Navasky.

Daniel Patrick Moynihan (right), then the US ambassador to India, and I have lunch in the garden of Roosevelt House, the embassy residence in New Delhi, in 1973.

My neighbor Amanda Burden in East Hampton, 1977.

Housemates in East Hampton in 1981 (from left to right): Clay Felker, Jerzy Kosinski, Carol Lynley, David Frost, and me.

Jimmy Goldsmith (center), David Tang (right), and I cruise around Hong Kong on Tang's yacht in 1990.

Jean Pigozzi, courtesy of the Pigozzi Collection

Jimmy Goldsmith (left front) and Jean Pigozzi (right front) on the tender to the yacht in the Mediterranean Sea, 1988. In rear are Louise White and Gian Carlo Bussei.

President Nixon arrives at Jimmy Goldsmith's estate in Mexico and is greeted by Jimmy (left), his son Jethro (with toy camera), and me (right), 1992.

Michael Endicott

On the lower steps of Jimmy Goldsmith's home in Mexico, 1992: me (left), President Nixon (center), former Secretary of the Treasury William Simon. On the upper step: Jimmy (left), Robert Abplanalp (center), and Bebe Rebozo (right).

En route to Inner Mongolia on Jimmy Goldsmith's plane. I (left) am next to Sonserai Lee, and Laure Boulay is seated in front, 1990.

In Bhutan in 1991 Jimmy Goldsmith (right) and I (left) visit my college friend Prince Lenny Dorji (center), the brother-in-law of the king of Bhutan.

On our visit to Las Alamandas, the estate of Jimmy's daughter Isabel Goldsmith, Isabel (left front) leads President Nixon (center), Jimmy (right), former Secretary of the Treasury William Simon (left rear), and me (center rear) to the beach for a swim in 1992.

President Nixon (left) poses for a photo by Jimmy's son Jethro Goldsmith (right) while I, from seven steps above, direct Jethro, 1992.

I (right center) attend a lunch in London to celebrate the transfer of Leonardo da Vinci's codex to Armand Hammer. Hammer is seated at the far end of the table. His wife Frances Hammer is seated between me and Sir John Foster, the barrister who negotiated the deal.

Susana Duncan (center) and I (left) celebrate her birthday over chocolate soufflés at the Knickerbocker Club in 2018.

Oliver Stone (right) and I dine at Palma restaurant in New York in 2015 to discuss my upcoming trip to Moscow to investigate the case of Edward Snowden, the NSA contractor who defected to Moscow in 2013.

Viewing Hong Kong from Victoria Peak in 2015. After Vladimir Putin's shocking revelation in a press conference that former NSA contractor Edward Snowden had been in contact with Russian officials in Hong Kong shortly before he defected to Moscow in June 2013, Hong Kong became a focus of my investigation into how America lost its secret.

I am at the New York Film Festival in 2017 with Ena Talakic (left) and Ines Talakic (right) for the showing of their film *Hall of Mirrors*.

# CHAPTER NINETEEN

# MY DOUBLE LIFE

Academic life was good to me. From 1969 to 1973, I was an assistant professor in MIT's political science department, which was as much a learning as a teaching experience. My undergraduate students, though far grubbier in appearance than those I taught at Harvard, were mainly engineers-in-training who understood far more than I did when it came to computer science and its potential to change society.

I taught two days a week at MIT and commuted to New York to work in my office at the *New Yorker*, where I was a staff writer. The commute itself was fairly easy since the American Airline shuttle in those days was only $50 round-trip and, unlike the security lines of today, I just joined the queue and walked directly onto the plane. If one plane was full, another plane rolled up on the runway. It took less than two hours door-to-door.

I found New York far more interesting than Boston but also socially challenging. Ever since Clay Felker arranged the publication of my first book, *Inquest*, he had assisted much of my career in journalism. He also became a close friend. We rented houses together, along with David Frost, in East Hampton. His girlfriend (and later wife), the writer Gail Sheehy came out to these houses only every other weekend, as she spent her alternate weekends with her young daughter, Maura Sheehy. Clay, to my amazement, filled the gap on these alternate weekends with a constantly changing stream of other female guests. He frequently dined with and acted as a mentor to three women who were senior in age to him: Dorothy Schiff, who then owned the *New York Post*; Katharine Graham, who owned the *Washington Post*; and Pamela Harriman, a power broker in the Democratic Party who had been married to Randolph Churchill (the son of Winston Churchill), Leland Hayward (producer of *The Sound of Music*), and W. Averell Harriman (former governor of New York). If Clay seemed entranced by powerful women, they seemed enamored of his crusading editor image.

In 1967, when the *Herald Tribune* ceased publication, Clay bought the rights to its *New York* section and launched *New York* as a stand-alone magazine. It was one of the first of the city magazines and enormously successful. The Wall Street financier Armand Erpf, a major investor in *New York*, began inviting Clay, Gail, and me up for weekends at his estate in Arkville, New York, where he had built a walled labyrinth with a sculpture of the Minotaur at its center. When I invited Susan Brockman to one of these weekends, we got lost in the labyrinth for more than two hours, perhaps reflecting the confusion in my life.

Between teaching at MIT and my trips with Clay, I lived a double life, which sorely tested the limits of commuting. At one point, for example, Clay called me in Cambridge at 5:45 p.m. telling me that Barbra Streisand's escort for a dinner party had been stuck in London. The dinner party, given by her agent, Irwin Winkler, at his Manhattan residence, was at 8:00 p.m. Could I substitute for the stranded man? Although I had classes to teach the next day, I was not about to turn down a date with Streisand. So I was on the 7:00 p.m. and made it to Winkler's home shortly after 8:00. Clay's usual crowd was there: Tom Wolfe, Jimmy Breslin, Peter Maas, and Barbara Goldsmith, as well as Winkler and his producing partner Bob Chartoff. Clay and Pam Tiffin with Barbra in tow arrived almost an hour late. Arriving late, as I would learn later, was considered permissible for Hollywood stars.

Once she made her round of hugs, waves, and air kisses, we went into the dining room. There were place cards for everyone. Since I was Barbra's nominal escort, I was, in the fashion of splitting up couples, seated at the opposite end of the table from her. After we finished the second course, Barbra, taking advantage of another star privilege, left before dessert, saying she had "an early call." As I result, I never had a chance to speak to my "date." That was the way New York dinner parties worked in the 1960s. People seemed more interested in being seen in illustrious company than speaking to any of the guests.

A few days later, I had a private lunch with Tom Wolfe at the Isle of Capri on Third Avenue and Sixty-First Street. Born in Richmond, Virginia, in 1930, Wolfe went to Washington and Lee University, where he so excelled as a star pitcher that the New York Giants recruited him as a professional baseball player. Instead, he enrolled in Yale University's American studies program and, after getting his PhD, became in 1962 a reporter for Clay Felker on the New York section at the *Herald Tribune*. At the time, Clay had instituted a form of first-person reporting, and it is often said that he made Wolfe. But the opposite is true. By bringing to stories a level of cultural anthropology not before seen in newspaper journalism, they created what would be called "New Journalism." A tall, blond, boyish-looking man, Wolfe arrived dressed much the same as he was at the Streisand dinner, in a three-piece white suit, white shirt, spats, and white shoes. A razor-sharp observer of America's consumer culture of brands, he had decided a brand was also necessary for journalists and branded himself with this white outfit. He had chosen the Isle of Capri not for the food but because the grotto-like downstairs was usually nearly empty at lunch time, which meant conversations were not drowned out by background noise.

After I told Wolfe that I have kept a typed diary since college, he said in his soft southern voice that my diaries might come in handy if I ever decided to write a memoir. I said that since I had omitted a great deal, the title would have to be "The Memoir of a Forgetful Journalist." He then told me, in a more serious tone, that a memoir to be true would have to describe the writer's most painful humiliations, as Jean-Jacques Rosseau did in his *Confessions*. He said that would not be easy because a human brain is not wired to relive painful moments. To test Wolfe's proposition, I later tried to recount one but, as he predicted, it was too traumatic.

Since few other writers branded themselves by their attire, one difficulty I ran into among the profusion of incredibly talented writers at the *New Yorker* was that, although I knew them by their work and names, I often did not recognize them in person. The most embarrassing incident proceeding from this gap came at a party given by Penelope Gilliatt, the *New Yorker*'s film critic, at Mike Nichols's apartment at the Beresford. Nichols had let her use his apartment while he was away scouting locations for his upcoming film *The Day of the Dolphin*. When I arrived, she led me into the spacious living room in which about a dozen people were gathered. The only one I immediately recognized was my friend Frank Conroy, the author of *Stop-Time*. He was at the far end of the room admiring a strategically placed quasar telescope at the window pointed at Central Park. I walked over and asked him about the other people in the room. He asked, "Do you know Ved?"

"No." I assumed he meant Ved Mehta, the Indian-born writer on the staff of the *New Yorker*. I enormously admired Mehta's precise interviews and vivid descriptions of Oxford philosophers that were published in the *New Yorker*. What made them even more impressive was that he was blind, having lost his sight at the age of three.

"Let me introduce you." Frank led me to a short, Indian-looking man. "Ved, this is Ed," he said, and then rushed off to speak to his wife, Patty Conroy, who had just entered the room. I was left standing with Ved.

I was wearing a white and blue pinstriped shirt, which, to my amazement, Ved complimented and then asked if I had bought it in London, which I had. Since he couldn't possibly see the stripes in my shirt, or the Turnbull & Asser styling, I assumed he had made an intuitive guess. I had heard from one of his assistants at the magazine about his uncanny ability to flawlessly negotiate the corridors and offices of the magazine without a cane and his almost magical way of figuring out who people were and what they were wearing. As our conversation continued, I noticed that each time he reached into the dish of mixed nuts on the table, he unerringly picked out a single cashew nut. I stared at his hands as they moved toward the dish, wondering how his fingers possibly could sense the difference between macadamia nuts, peanuts, and cashew nuts before even touching them. I was so intrigued by his accuracy in nut selection that I decided to test it by extending the fingers of my hand between him and the path to the nuts. To my incredulity, my barrier did not impede him. He steered his hand around it. I repeated the test but got the same results. Could it be that he was sighted?

Before I could further test the issue, Patty Conroy, Frank's wife, came rushing up and pulled me away. When we were out of Ved's hearing range, she asked in a stern voice, "What are you doing?"

"I think Ved Mehta can see," I replied.

"That's not Ved Mehta. That's V.S. Naipaul." I told her that her husband had introduced him as "Ved." She explained that Frank always called Naipaul by his nickname, "Ved." So ended the mystery of the cashew nuts.

I later learned that such confusions were reoccurring phenomena among the tangle of new writers in Manhattan. Several years later, another misidentification occurred when I arrived at Clay Felker's East 57th Street apartment. He was seated at the round table in his two-story living room with a man in his 40s who I had not met before. Getting up to introduce us, Clay simply said, "You know Nick Pileggi?"

We shook hands. I had not met Pileggi, but I knew that he wrote about the Mafia and was the cousin of the writer Gay Talese. So I asked him, "How is Gay?"

He looked at me quizzically before answering, "You would know better than me."

I next asked about his investigation into the Mafia, and, looking oddly at me, he replied again with another question. "Isn't that what you do?"

It was only then that Clay realized the source of our confusion. He had mistakenly introduced Nick Thimmesch, a columnist for the *Los Angeles Times*, as Nick Pileggi. As a result, we each had thought the other person was Pileggi.

•  •  •

In January 1973, Alice Mason, a well-connected real estate agent, found me a two-story penthouse on East Eighty-Sixth Street. It was a 1929 rent-controlled building, with rent of only $650 a month, which was a fraction of the equivalent rent in a non-rent-controlled one. It also came with free electricity. The upper and lower terraces, which had views of the East River, the Hudson River, and Central Park, were large enough to accommodate 100 or so people. I decided to have urban barbecues when the weather permitted.

The first dinner was for my new friend Stanley Milgram, a short, stocky social psychologist with a well-groomed beard. His work was highly controversial. Indeed, his experiment on obedience at Yale a few years earlier had caused an intellectual firestorm. Social psychology experiments were not unlike practical jokes in which the victim is thrust into a totally contrived situation. In Milgram's Yale experiments, subjects were recruited by newspaper ads for employment in what they thought was a legitimate laboratory doing a study in learning. In reality, the lab was part of a massive confidence game in which everyone in the lab, except the subjects, were actors hired to dupe them. Each subject was given the task of administering increasingly higher electric shocks when the actor pretending to be the "learner" made mistakes. The subjects were further instructed to ignore the "learner's" objections. The disturbing part of the experiment, especially for those who believed that individuals would not easily bend their will to authority figures, was that most of the subjects continued to administer the shocks that were ordered even after the learners feigned pain and screamed for them to stop. The implication was that torture would not be difficult to implement.

Milgram had contacted me on a very different project concerning the extent to which people would allow another person's voice in their head to dictate their actions. He had read the *New Yorker* excerpt from my thesis and wanted to know if I had come across this issue in my research on network television and, in particular, on the performance of TV anchormen.

I had observed many instances of on-air correspondents repeating the exact words fed to them by their behind-the-scenes producers like ventriloquists' dummies. "Would they qualify?"

He explained that he was in the early stages of developing an experiment based on "Cyranoids."

"Cyranoids?" I interrupted.

He had coined the word from the 1898 play *Cyrano de Bergerac*. In that play, the hero Cyrano assumes he is not physically attractive enough to woo a beauty named Roxane, so he gets a handsome cadet to stand in for him under her window. He then covertly whispers into the cadet's ear the words that will win her. The result is that Roxane falls in love with the body of one man and the mind of another. The fusion, according to Milgram, creates an illusion in which Roxane is unable to separate the person mouthing the words from the one creating them.

Finding his "Cyranoid" concept extremely intriguing, I asked how I could help.

He said he had been finding Cyranoids among hostage negotiators who repeated the words covertly whispered to them through a tiny FM receiver behind their ear by others and who stopped thinking for themselves. He asked me whether TV anchormen who repeated words whispered to them through their earpiece might also be Cyranoids.

I realized that the Cyranoid illusion could have consequences in TV news, just as it had with Cyrano in the famous play. If audiences believed that the words coming out of the mouth of on-air news personalities were the product of their mental abilities, it confused reality. The job of the writers producing the words, like the job of Cyrano, was to remain in the deep background. The same Cyranoid illusion might also be produced by politicians reading words on a teleprompter written by a speechwriter.

Milgram's most impressive quality was his provocative mind. It fascinated me. We had several lunches in the cafeteria at CUNY, where Milgram taught, in which he told me other inventive ideas he planned to test through experiments. I thought these ideas might make a great piece for the new science section of *New York* magazine. Clay had just appointed Susana Duncan, a brilliant Cambridge-educated anthropologist, as its editor. Since Susana had an astounding ability to diagnose entangled issues—she later went on to be a superb doctor—I invited her to meet Milgram and his insightful wife Sasha. I of course invited Clay, since he was interested in getting an article for *New York*, and Milton Glaser, Clay's partner in *New York* magazine and his longtime guru when it came to innovative ideas. Milton was also a true genius in graphic design, having created, among other things, the city's "I heart NY" logo. Milton brought his wife Shirley, an artist in her own right, who gifted me a set of pop art ties she created—and which I still wear.

Since I did not know how to cook, I recruited Susana to help me cook my first terrace dinner. She had extremely innovative ideas about cuisine. She grilled three types of fish stuffed inside each other: sardines inside a trout inside a flounder. As the result of an olive-oil-fed conflagration on my outdoor barbecue, only the charred remains of the sardines survived. Even so, everyone pretended to enjoy the burnt fish. One reason was that the guests, especially Susana, Clay, and Milton, were fascinated with Milgram's revelations about his work. He told us how we all carry personal maps by which we orient ourselves. After dinner, Susana commissioned him to write a cover story on cognitive maps of New York City, and Milton said he would personally orchestrate the artwork for it.

Milgram never fully finished his Cyranoid project. He died prematurely of a heart attack in 1984. His death left unanswered the question of how much of what appears to be a solo performance of a politician is produced by a Cyrano. A few years later I thought of this question while watching the speechwriter Rick Hertzberg play Cyrano by feeding President Carter his lines to explain the failure of the hostage rescue in Iran. It was also used in the film *Broadcast News*, in which a dumb but telegenic anchorman (played by William Hurt) rose to the top of network news by mouthing word-for-word what was covertly fed to his in-ear receiver by his producer (played by Holly Hunter) and he tells her, "It was amazing having you inside my head."

I continued my terrace dinners for the next four decades, though I had to cut back on the culinary scale. Instead of three fishes stuffed inside each other, I served less risky precooked sausages from the nearby Schaller & Weber charcuterie. Even so, the dinners became enough of a media legend for Michael Wolff, who I didn't know then, to write an article in 1999 for *New York* magazine entitled "Dinner Party Hacks," saying, "At any particular point over the past two decades at Epstein's (rent-stabilized) duplex penthouse (one of Epstein's notable accomplishments, says a friend, is the irrigation system he's built on his terrace), you might have seen Katrina Vanden Heuvel and Victor Navasky, who run *The Nation*, Christopher Hitchens, Rick Hertzberg, Michael Kinsley, Alexander Cockburn, Clay Felker, Anthony Haden-Guest, Anna Wintour, Carly Simon, Mort Zuckerman, Jeffrey Steingarten, Amanda Burden, Charlie Rose, Tina Brown and Harry Evans, Caroline Kennedy, Renata Adler, Candace Bushnell, various movie stars of the moment, and often, before he died last year, the British billionaire takeover artist Sir James Goldsmith."

Wolff's description, alas, was not entirely accurate. My fabled "irrigation system" was actually just a leaky garden hose, and I had fallen out with a number of the people he mentioned. Even so, I invited Wolff and his wife Victoria Floetle to all my future terrace dinners. My last sausage grilling before the arrival of COVID-19 was to celebrate the arrival of Barry Humphries and his wife Lizzie Spender in New York. Barry, an actor, author, and art collector, had invented the satirical character Dame Edna, who he played in one-man shows around the world. Lizzie, the daughter of poet laureate Stephen Spender, was an actress, writer, and extraordinary chef. Barry, Lizzie, and I had given joint barbecues since 1999. Because of the mixing of his friends and mine, it was also one of my most eclectic gatherings. The other guests included the newspaper publisher Rupert Murdoch and his wife Jerry Hall, Tom Wolfe, who came with his wife Sheila Berger and daughter Alexandra, the former editor and doctor Susana Duncan, the actor Griffin Dunne, the television host Dick Cavett, the opera singer Sasha Lazard, the foreign correspondent Bartle Bull, the Columbia professor Clémence Boulouque, the financier Grant Winthrop, the supermodel Claudia Mason, the theater critic Max McGuinness, the actress Lacey Dorn, and the journalist Mario Platero.

Despite the renown of these rooftop barbecues, I never learned how to cook anything but precooked German sausages.

# CHAPTER TWENTY

# FORGETTING OBAMA

W hereas my rooftop barbecues achieved some renown in New York, they were nothing compared to those thrown by Tina Brown and her husband, Harry Evans. I had first met Tina at a party given by journalist William Shawcross in London in November 1974. At the time, she had just turned 21 and had recently graduated St. Anne's College at Oxford, where she had edited Oxford's unfortunately named literary magazine *Isis* and also won the Sunday Times National Student Drama Award for her play *Under the Bamboo Tree*, which was performed at the Edinburgh Festival. Her immense talent was reflected in her meteoric career in journalism. By 1979, she had brilliantly resuscitated the nearly extinct magazine the *Tatler* in London. In 1984, she was appointed editor-in-chief of Condé Nast's newly revived *Vanity Fair*. In 1992, because of her success at *Vanity Fair*, she was appointed the first female editor-in-chief of the *New Yorker*.

Tina's husband Harry Evans, who was knighted in 2004 for his services to journalism, also had a remarkable career. Born in 1928 in Eccles, England, Harry became editor-in-chief of the regional daily the Northern Echo at the age of 33 and turned into such an investigative powerhouse that he was hired by the *Sunday Times* in 1966 to build its "Insight Team" into a world-class investigative unit. The following year he became editor-in-chief of the *Sunday Times* and later *Times of London*. His Insight Team's exposure in the mid-1960s of Kim Philby's role as a Soviet spy in infiltrating British intelligence had served as a model and inspiration for my own investigations into the corruption of intelligence services, and I offered the *Sunday Times* the worldwide serialization rights to my book *Legend*, which Harry bought in 1977. Both he and Tina became lifelong friends, and I was always honored to attend their book parties, which were among New York's most memorable and best attended literary occasions. For these events, the furniture in their Sutton Place apartment would be loaded into a rented van and driven around Manhattan to make space for the guests.

In March 2003, Tina and Harry gave a book party for *The Clinton Wars*, a book by Sidney Blumenthal, who was Clinton's former White House advisor and, before that, Tina's Washington editor at the *New Yorker*. I found it particularly memorable because it was the first time I had met President Bill Clinton. I recall also that it was a warm night and that most of the 80 or so guests migrated out to the courtyard.

Some five years later, in 2008, the day after Barack Obama won the Democratic nomination for president, I received an email from Katie Rosman, then a reporter for the *Wall Street Journal*, asking about an exchange I had with her and Obama in 2003 when he was serving in the Illinois Senate. I wrote back that she must be mistaken since I had not even heard of Obama in 2003, and I never had met him then or afterward. She must have the wrong person, I said.

She was insistent, however, that we had both met Obama at Tina Brown's 2003 party, where I had a heated discussion with him. At that point, I did remember talking to Katie at Tina's party. She was young, witty, pretty, and insightful. She said she was a freelance writer looking for a career in journalism. Since I had kept a diary, I checked the entry for that night. It mentioned many of the guests at the party, including Zandy Forbes, my date, who arrived on the late side, and Katie Rosman. I recalled that as Katie knew very few people in the room, I introduced her to some of them. But I had absolutely no memory of introducing her to, seeing her with, or chatting with Obama. And my diary made no mention of him.

In our back-and-forth, Katie said Obama was standing with Vernon Jordan, whom I also did not know and did not recall ever meeting. She went on to say that she was so impressed with our conversation with Obama that immediately after Tina's party, she pitched the idea of doing a piece on him to an editor at the *New York Times Magazine*, but it was rejected on the grounds that a story about an unknown Chicago politician did not belong in the *New York Times*.

At that point, since she was so sure such a meeting had really occurred, I decided I should investigate my memory lapse.

I first called my friend Sid Blumenthal, who spoke while walking his dog, Pepper, in a park in Washington. Since he was a keen political observer with a superb memory, I assumed he would know. I asked him if Obama had been at his book party. He answered, "If he was there, I would have seen him." He also checked with his wife Jackie, who had headed the White House Fellows Program under Clinton. She too had no memory of Obama at the party.

I called both Tina Brown and her husband, Harry Evans. They did not recall seeing Obama at their home that night. I also called Tina's assistant, Kara Simonetti, who put together the guest list. She said Obama was not on it. I asked six other people who attended the party. None of them remembered seeing Obama. One guest even suggested jokingly that government agents might have induced the mass amnesia, as in the movie *Men in Black*.

I reported back to Katie that no one at the party, except her, recalled seeing the future president there and that she may have conflated two different events. She offered to send me the reply she got from the *Times* editor, but she didn't. With that, I temporarily ended my investigation. Even so, I still wondered whether I could have completely forgotten the only meeting I ever had with Barack Obama.

It was not until June 3, 2013, that I got another chance to solve the mystery. The occasion was a celebration of the 90th birthday of Henry Kissinger in the grand ballroom of the St. Regis New York. And it was memorable. A mariachi band played as some 300 guests entered the room. During dinner almost all the living secretaries of state, from George Shultz to John Kerry, toasted Kissinger's accomplishments, as did former French president Giscard d'Estaing and other world leaders. Bill Clinton delivered the final toast.

While others listened to Clinton, my attention turned to a guest seated at the next table, Vernon Jordan. I recalled that Katie had claimed Jordan was standing next to Obama at Blumenthal's book party five years earlier. Could he help me resolve the mystery?

When I approached Jordan, he was talking with Robert Kraft, the owner of the New England Patriots, who had presented Kissinger earlier in the party an official Patriots jersey with the number 90 on the front and the name Kissinger on the back. I waited for them to finish their conversation and then said to Jordan, "I have an odd question for you."

Jordan eyed me with a who-the-hell-are-you look. As a Clinton confidant and quintessential Washington insider, he had been one of the three witnesses called at the impeachment trial of Bill Clinton. (Sid Blumenthal and Monica Lewinsky were the other two.)

"By any chance were you at Tina Brown's book party for Sid Blumenthal?" I meekly asked.

"Yeah, I was there," he answered. "I brought Obama as my plus one. I thought he would enjoy seeing a New York party."

So ended my investigation. Both the previous and the future president of the United States were at Tina's 2003 party.

I had truly forgotten seeing Barack Obama, but, as far as I could determine, so had everyone else at Tina's party. Up until then, I believed I had a good memory. There is an obvious problem with such a conceit. One remembers everything *except* what he or she forgets. That exception in this case included an encounter with a future president. Nietzsche no doubt was on to something when he wrote, in *The Use and Abuse of History*, "Life in any true sense is impossible without forgetfulness."

# PART FOUR

# REVERSING RECEIVED WISDOM

# CHAPTER TWENTY-ONE

# NEWS FROM NOWHERE

I f I had to choose the best period of my life, it would be the eight years between 1966 and 1974 I spent getting my PhD at Harvard. The changes I experienced were not only in my education. The entire world changed in unexpected ways.

In the government department, what interested me most was the intellectual lens that Professor James Q. Wilson was using to study decision-making in a political context. The lens was somewhat prosaically called "organization theory." It held that over time an organization shaped the decisions made by the individuals in it. In doing so, it provided a means of challenging interpretations of events based on a Manichaean view of good versus evil leaders.

Wilson proposed I do my thesis under him using organization theory to study television networks. The question I was to answer was: Why did television produce a different picture of reality than other news media?

Wilson's approach made perfect sense to me. After all, network television news is a product manufactured by an organization, not by individuals. Its content is not entirely determined by news events themselves or even, for that matter, by the personal biases of reporters and news personnel. In 1969, there were only three television networks: NBC, CBS, and ABC. Each network, to survive in a competitive media world, had to meet certain requisites. Each had to satisfy economic demands, such as keeping the cost of its news production within budgetary limitations to avoid unacceptable losses; political strictures, such as keeping its reporting within the criteria of fairness then defined by the Federal Communications Commission to avoid its stations losing licenses; and social needs, such as maintaining morale among its employees to prevent the defection of its key personnel. And while at one level a newsperson chose and prepared individual stories, at another level the organization chose the newsperson. Those who were able to adapt to the networks' values were retained and promoted. Those who were not able to accept those values were weeded out and shunted aside. From this perspective, it was the organization, not the individuals, that determined the pictures of society represented on national television.

The first hurdle was getting real access to television networks. Initially, all the networks were unresponsive to my request to sit in their newsrooms. Like all news organizations, they preferred to keep secret what went on behind the curtain. As I had done so often in the past, I again turned to Clay Felker. For reasons I never fully understood, people found it difficult, if not impossible, to say no to Clay. Perhaps it was the unvarnished directness with which he asked a favor. In any case, he prevailed on his friend Dick Wald to let me do "an anthropological study," as he put it, of NBC News. To my surprise, Wald's boss, Reuven Frank, the president of NBC News, also agreed. After that, the other two networks, ABC and CBS, followed suit.

I began by spending four months in the NBC offices at 30 Rockefeller Plaza in New York. Each day I was able to sit in its newsroom assignment desk, go out with news crews, and then go to the editing room to see how the story was cut into the news. I also interviewed reporters, producers, writers, and executives and used the office Xerox machine to copy memos and other documents from the file cabinets. In those days, there were no PR monitors who attended these interviews.

I next went to Washington to see how the network's news bureaus selected political stories. During this research, I stayed at the Georgetown home of Katharine Graham, the owner of the *Washington Post* and the CBS-affiliated TV station in Washington. I had met her through Clay Felker in New York and, after I told her about my television news project, she extended the invitation. She also had me chauffeured in her limousine to her television station to interview her executive, but this proved more embarrassing than useful. Far more helpful was her shrewd insight into the convoluted relationship between the owner of television, who is responsible not only for the media's economic survival but also for keeping the government from challenging its license, and the news executive.

I found that television news was akin to a roulette game in which the croupier was on the level but the table itself was not. The tilted table in this case wasn't the news reporter; it was the entire organization that produced the news. Even though the *New Yorker* had never before excerpted an unpublished PhD thesis, William Shawn decided the topic of network news merited it. William Whitworth, who went on to edit the *Atlantic*, did a brilliant job of boiling it down and it appeared in the March 3, 1973 issue under the title "The Selection of Reality." The artist Saul Steinberg illustrated it with a cartoon of reality in a television viewer's head. When I offered to buy the original drawing for the illustration from Steinberg, he told me he only bartered his art with *New Yorker* writers for some object for which he had an immediate need.

What did he need?

He answered with "an electric pencil sharpener." So I rushed out to a nearby hardware store and bought the best electric pencil sharpener I could find. After trading it to Steinberg for his drawing, I had the art framed (and it still hangs in my apartment).

Random House then published my PhD in 1974 under the title *News from Nowhere: Television and the News.* The problem was that the technology of television—including the advent of the video recorder, the cable network, and the remote control—was changing more rapidly than I anticipated, leading Michael J. Robinson, a professor of politics at Catholic University, to point out in an article with the intriguing title "Beyond Edward Jay Epstein":

> Virtually all academic research concerning television news has shown the influence of [two] contemporary "institutions"—the Vanderbilt Archive, from which most of us get our data about television news, and Edward Jay Epstein, from whom most of us have borrowed a theory of television news. Our problem in 1978 is that one of these institutions—Edward Jay Epstein—has so thoroughly dominated professional thinking about television that social scientists have "overlearned" the thesis in *News from Nowhere.*

He was right. Television news had changed, but I had provided a new way of looking at news organizations that went beyond the personality explanations that remained the bedrock of journalism.

# CHAPTER TWENTY-TWO

# THE BLACK PANTHERS

In 1970, while teaching at MIT and writing my thesis, I joined the staff of the *New Yorker*. Although I was still living in Cambridge, I was given an office on the 18th floor of the office building on Forty-Third Street. The magazine's editor, William Shawn, also asked me to do long-form investigative reporting. Not only was the *New Yorker* arguably the most respected magazine in America, but it also paid its writers up to $25,000 an article (equivalent to $100,000 in 2019). After accepting the offer, I gave a great deal of thought to what sort of investigative reporting I should do. I knew that much of it involved "advancing the story" by re-reporting what was already in the clip file, which was largely on spools of microfilm in those days, and then obtaining new quotes that effectively updated what had been previously reported. That was not what I believed worthwhile. My idea was to hold in abeyance the palimpsest of cumulative reporting called the clip file, go back to square one, and report the story de novo. Shawn offered me the opportunity to do so by assigning me to investigate the allegations of a conspiracy by the Nixon administration to murder the entire leadership of the Black Panthers, a group of militants opposing the government oppression of Blacks. The *New York Times*, *Washington Post*, *Los Angeles Times*, and other newspapers had reported as fact that the police had killed 28 Panthers. Shawn told me to find out whether the murder of 28 Panthers by the police was, as he put it, "part of a pattern of genocide."

I traced the number 28 to Charles R. Garry, the chief counsel and spokesman for the Black Panther Party, in December 1969. I interviewed Garry for the *New Yorker.* It turned out that he had provided the now-famous number to reporters as an educated guess because it seemed to him like a "safe number."

"But how many were killed by police?" I asked.

He said the number was 20. He would provide me with a list of these "documented" cases. The list arrived, but it had only 19 names, and none of the cases were documented.

I set out to document each and every one of the putative deaths. I hired researchers from Harvard Law School to dig out the court records of all the alleged murders. As it turned out, one of the "deceased" Black Panthers on Garry's list was still very much alive. That left 18 dead Black Panthers. Of them, eight had been killed not by police but by other militants, storekeepers (during attempted robberies), or their wives. So 10 Black Panthers had been killed by law enforcement. Of those 10, six of the Black Panthers were killed by seriously wounded policemen who clearly had reason to believe that their own lives were in jeopardy from suspects in burglaries and robberies, and, according to the evidence, these police had no way of knowing that they had been shot by Black Panthers. That left four questionable deaths in shoot-outs, and all of them were with local, not federal, police.

While "four deaths, two deaths, even a single death must be the subject of the most serious concern," I wrote, I concluded that false numbers bandied about in the press had only confused the issue of police violence with a conspiracy theory about government genocide.

My article, "The Panthers and the Press: A Pattern of Genocide?," appeared in the *New Yorker* in February 1971. It caused, to put it mildly, an uproar in the media. On March 1, David Frost devoted an entire prime-time hour of his *David Frost Show* on CBS to a debate between me and Charles Garry, the lawyer representing the Black Panther Party.

Afterward, to their credit, many newspapers, including the *Washington Post* and the *Los Angeles Times,* who had lazily repeated the false numbers of Black Panther deaths, printed editorial apologies to their readers. Pat Moynihan wrote to President Nixon just before the article appeared. "For the past six months a young friend of mine, Edward Jay Epstein, has been writing a story for the *New Yorker* about the 'plot' to 'genocide' the Panthers." He speculated further, "He was given the assignment in the expectation that he would demonstrate the existence of such a plot. (He is the author of *Inquest,* a devastating account of how the Warren Commission did not do its job.) They did not reckon on their man."

David Frost was also generous after the debate. He offered me the use of a white-stucco-fronted townhouse on Egerton Crescent in London while he was finishing his television shows in America. I spent two weeks there enjoying his home, and especially the slot-racing track he had installed in the basement. David himself returned on the Concorde on weekends, as did his elegant and clever girlfriend Caroline Cushing, who organized a couple of fabulous dinner parties there. But there was also a downside to directly challenging an established story in the press. As I was to learn, journalists have long memories.

# CHAPTER TWENTY-THREE

# NIXON'S WAR ON DRUGS

A principal obstacle to investigative journalism is obtaining access to the source material. In the private sector, nondisclosure agreements, fiduciary laws, and corporate protection of documents block access. Unlike a government investigator, a reporter cannot obtain search warrants, subpoena records, or compel a witness to testify. In the public sector, access is blocked by government classification of documents, privacy laws, and a virtual wall of communication officers who are tasked with the job of keeping information from reporters. More often than not, what purports to be a "leak," or accidental disclosure, is a deliberate disclosure aimed at manipulating the facts. If so, such deliberate disclosures were more like "plants" than "leaks." I sought a way of breaking through these barriers to do the kind of reporting that I believed to be worthwhile. The way came in 1972 when my mentor James Q. Wilson was appointed chairman of President Nixon's new National Advisory Commission on Drug Abuse Prevention and given access to all the government records on the war on drugs. At the time, Wilson was also supervising my PhD thesis and had become a personal friend. We had lunch at the Harvard Faculty Club, where we discussed his new commission. I asked him why it was so difficult to solve the heroin problem when politicians of both parties accepted the assumption that heroin was a cause of urban crime and that a reduction in heroin use would reduce crime. "Can't the government act when everyone agrees with a policy?"

Wilson answered that as plausible as such a link between heroin and crime sounded to the public and politicians, it had not yet been factually established by the government.

He had reviewed all the material, both secret and public, that our government possessed. No one who knew him doubted his razor-sharp powers of analysis when it came to empirical data. Could it be that Nixon's entire war on drugs was predicated on an unproven premise?

I asked to see the studies.

"Come to Washington," he answered.

So, on January 21, 1973, I went to his office in Washington—a townhouse in the new Executive Office Building—to read the existing research. The most impressive analysis was a secret report the White House had commissioned from a RAND-type think tank called the Institute for Defense Analyses (IDA). To my surprise, it concluded that the statistics that government press officers gave to the public had been badly distorted to support a rationale for the war on drugs. It found, among other things, that estimates of the number of crimes committed by drug addicts had been exaggerated by a factor of 500 times in some cases. It also found that the very number of drug addicts proceeded from faulty assumptions and were, at best, educated guesses. Further, it undercut the international effort to cut off heroin supplies by presenting evidence that most addicts were not addicted to a single drug, such as heroin, but could switch to barbiturates or alcohol if their supply was interrupted or the price rose. When, for example, an East Coast dock strike in the 1960s drove up the price of heroin, addicts simply found another drug. I understood why this report had been kept under wraps. It vitiated the logic of the programs aimed at curtailing a heroin epidemic. Even if all opium supplies were destroyed, addicts would move to other drugs.

I decided to investigate how the White House had dealt with this hostile data. Nixon's point man in the war on drugs was Egil "Bud" Krogh Jr., a 36-year-old assistant to Nixon's powerful domestic affairs advisor, John Ehrlichman. Krogh, who had been an Eagle Scout in Seattle before joining the White House staff, was assigned to the notorious "plumbers" who had broken into the offices of the psychiatrist of whistleblower Daniel Ellsberg. After these break-ins were exposed by the Watergate investigation, Krogh served six months in prison. When I called him, he was an unemployed ex-convict struggling to pay his family's expenses. He told me he had taken his White House files home with him and that they contained day-to-day memoranda on the progress of what he called the "obsessed and sometimes crazy war on drugs."

"Crazy in what way?" I asked.

"In ways you wouldn't believe," he answered. "Nothing was off the table." By way of example, he handed me a memo he had written in 1970 describing Nixon's attempt to recruit Elvis Presley. "Elvis showed up at the northwest gate of the White House with velvet pants and his silk shirt opened to his waist." The memo continued, "He wanted to tell the president how strongly he felt [about the drug problem] because he loved his country." When Nixon thanked him, Presley "said he'd also like to have a BNDD badge, because he collected badges." In return, he offered Nixon the gift of a .44 Colt automatic pistol with bullets. Krogh said it was "the most bizarre meeting I'd ever seen."

Presley next told Nixon, according to the memo, "Mr. President, I believe in what you are doing, I love my country. I love my family, I think law enforcement is great." Nixon, not one to miss a political opportunity, suggested that Presley put an anti-drug theme in his songs. Presley responded by showing the president his badge collection and again asked for a BNDD (Bureau of Narcotics and

Dangerous Drugs) badge. Krogh noted, "The president shook his head in disbelief and Presley ended the interview by suggesting that they keep this meeting secret. Nixon responded, 'Absolutely! Don't tell anybody; preserve your credibility at all cost.'"

Since Krogh needed money to pay bills and I needed his file on the drug program for the book I was planning, I offered him $2,000 for these files as well as an interview in which he would comment on the memoranda in these files. The interview would appear in *The Public Interest*, a magazine edited by my good friend Irving Kristol (who would reimburse me the $2,000).

The reason I wanted his file was that I had learned in my work on the Warren Commission that contemporaneous memoranda were far more valuable to understanding a complex issue than the retrospective memories expressed in even the most candid interviews with people involved in the issue. I had no compunction in paying for an archive of memoranda, especially since it was not in the public domain. Just as news organizations commonly pay for archival TV footage as well as other copyrighted material in books, I see no reason that authors should not pay for archival documents that will help them get closer to the truth.

Krogh and I began meeting for breakfast regularly in the fall of 1974. To further familiarize me with his role in the drug program, he gave me 10 cases of files, internal documents, notes written for the president's attention, analyses of the drug problem, domestic counsel issue papers, and correspondence. The "Krogh File," as I called it, was not complete. These were only the files that he had brought home to work on. The government had seized the rest of his files when he became involved in the Watergate affair; they were not available even to him. But the Krogh File provided me with a means of getting others in the government to talk to me. After all, when I could cite their positions from documents I had in hand, they had an incentive to set the record straight by granting me an interview.

Still, I now had a view of how the White House manipulated the data on the war on drugs. There were, for example, the drafts of President Nixon's June 17, 1971, speech and the comments on it by various staff assistants. The speechwriters had tried to specify the number of addicts in America (300,000), the nature of heroin addiction (a fatal, irreversible disease), and the amount of crime that could be attributed to heroin addiction ($10 billion per year).

As the war of memos and counter-memos proceeded in the drafting of the speech, it became painfully clear that the government had not established any of these facts. Various estimates had put the number of addicts between 50,000 and 600,000, but without any consensus as to the correct number there was considerable doubt about the nature of heroin addiction (whether addicts could be detoxified or had to be maintained on heroin for the rest of their lives); and no agency had any firm idea of how much crime was committed by addicts (although $10 billion was an obvious exaggeration).

One early draft of the speech claimed that all organized crime in the world was based on heroin trafficking, but that again proved to be a completely unsubstantiated claim and was deleted from the final draft. As non-facts were winnowed out, and as speechwriters glossed over the glaring gaps in the state of the knowledge about drugs, it became clear that the crusade was based on very little hard information. After John Ingersoll, the former director of the Bureau of Narcotics and Dangerous Drugs, told White House staff members that the BNDD lacked statistics, Nixon publicly humiliated him in a cabinet meeting televised by ABC, asking him questions that Krogh had predetermined Ingersoll could not answer.

The Krogh File revealed a very dark side to the drug war. One document referred to a "$100 million clandestine law enforcement fund" that would be used for assassinations of drug traffickers abroad. As I learned from Krogh, "clandestine law enforcement" was a euphemism for assassination. No one was willing to tell me how this money was used.

Another dubious project that emerged was biological warfare. The Department of Agriculture had been assigned the task of developing a weevil called the "screwworm," which would devour poppies throughout the world. Krogh's files contained a memo to President Nixon about the insect under development. Nixon asked if the "screwworm" would destroy only poppies. The answer was that it was not "host-specific," which meant it would also destroy rice crops in Asia. That project was prudently canceled.

I believe it is necessary for an investigative reporter to "walk the battlefield." My first stop was Afyon, Turkey, where, with the able assistance of my friend Susana Duncan, I followed the opium trail. In Ankara, I spoke with William Macomber, the US ambassador, who provided me with a full briefing of the opium business in Turkey.

My next stop was France. The main target of the war on heroin was the laboratory network that converted the opium base into heroin in Marseille. I first met with Arthur Watson, the former ambassador to France, whose father had founded the fabled IBM Corporation. While he was ambassador, he developed a drinking problem, which was widely reported in the media after a sexual harassment incident with a flight attendant on a transatlantic flight. Before resigning, he was one of Nixon's principal crusaders in the drug war and was among a number of those crusaders who drank heavily but railed against less conventional addictions.

Over lunch, Watson became tipsy after drinking a carafe of burgundy. He told me that he piloted his own private plane and, together with his anti-heroin team, flew back and forth from Paris to Marseille, hunting heroin labs. During one flight, Watson recalled, a French official in Marseille gave them a packet of heroin to fly back to police officials in Paris. He joked with his team about the predicament that might arise if the plane crashed on the return flight and heroin was discovered on their persons.

Watson put me in touch with Edgar Piret, a science attaché in the US embassy. Piret, a former university professor, had, according to Watson, devised a "sniffer" to locate heroin labs in Marseille. When we met in Paris, Piret gave me the usual briefing on heroin interdiction, describing the routes from Turkey to Marseille and then to America. When I said I was more interested in the sniffer that he had invented, he looked at me with horror.

"That's highly classified information … Only about 20 people in the world know about the sniffer." He then warned me that if I published information about it, I would destroy the entire "sniffing operation." I told him I had heard that the sniffer had already been dismantled and returned to the United States. He looked sad for a moment, as if recollecting a deceased pet, then said someday it might be revived and that it was best not to give out the modus operandi. He then reached into his desk and produced photographic albums with hundreds of nostalgic pictures of himself and Ambassador Watson in Marseille. He had gone there every weekend with the "team" to chart out the smoke plumes and the wind streams that various odors might take. He said designing the sniffer had been "an unusual adventure."

Just as I was leaving, I mentioned the efforts to detect heroin in the sewers of Marseille. The horror returned to his face. "No one knows about that … perhaps only three people in the world." To reassure him, I told him that Ambassador Watson had mentioned it to me. As I walked him to his car in the embassy parking lot, he again tried to swear me to secrecy.

Although I began by tracking the efforts to deal with a drug emergency, I found a new conspiracy developing concerning the Watergate cover-up in 1973. A legitimate political enterprise merged with a shadowy enterprise setting up a secret White House team to assist Nixon. It became unclear whether I was following two separate undertakings that converged by coincidence or a single conspiracy.

The cast of characters in the drug war was the same as those involved in the Watergate break-in. It included John Caulfield, a liaison on drugs, who had proposed the privately financed White House detective agency; Krogh, who superintended the drug program while heading the "special investigative unit" that broke into offices on behalf of the White House; G. Gordon Liddy, an employee of the newly created Office of National Narcotics Intelligence (ONNI), who supervised the Watergate break-in; and E. Howard Hunt, who was on the payroll of the Domestic Council as a consultant on drug interdiction and also participated in the Watergate break-in. William Sullivan, the former FBI deputy chief, and Lucian Conein, who ran assassination programs for the CIA, had also been transferred to ONNI. I was able to establish that, while being paid out of drug funds, these men (all of whom I spoke to) were organizing covert operations to which no one in the government, except for the Domestic Council staff in the White House, were privy. This use of the drug program seemed to be more than a simple coincidence.

I went to see Henry E. Petersen, the assistant attorney general. I gave him my list of these five newly appointed advisors to the drug program who were involved in extracurricular illicit activities for the White House and asked him point-blank: Was the drug program camouflage for a team of White House political operatives?

"I would say that at minimum there was a political motive behind it," he replied.

"If they were acting in concert under the directions of the White House staff, wouldn't that be a conspiracy to evade congressional oversight?"

"That question could better be answered by Krogh," he said with a mischievous smile.

When I told Krogh that Petersen suggested there was a political motive behind the formation of this drug task force, Krogh replied, "Mr. Petersen's right in saying that there was a political motive behind it, as there was a political motive behind practically everything that was undertaken, in addition to a substantive desire to reduce a problem area." Krogh added that Attorney General John Mitchell, who was also involved in the Watergate cover-up, knew about this political motive but did not "realize the extent of the plan."

I flew back to Cambridge in 1975 to discuss the Krogh File with James Q. Wilson. After reading it, he said, "Even the best intentions can go haywire in a government bureaucracy." That was no doubt true, but I proposed that there was an intelligent design behind the transfer of seven top operatives to a newly created narcotics office and that it was not coincidental they took part in Watergate and other illegal activities.

"By 'intelligent design,' do you mean a high-level conspiracy?"

I answered affirmatively. A conspiracy would fit all the actions described in the Krogh File. It would explain why, even though his staff knew differently, Nixon maintained that heroin caused crime and that international actions would solve the problem. It would also account for how the plumbers and other operatives could operate on the government payroll without attracting attention.

Wilson did not buy my conspiracy theory. "I prefer the idea of an out-of-control bureaucracy," he said. "Government agencies do not always act rationally."

Either explanation worked, but my job as an author was to choose the one that best fit my view of the world.

G.P. Putnam and Sons published the result of that choice as *Agency of Fear* in 1977. My editor, Edward "Ned" Chase, was a brilliant, if quirky, 13th-generation New Yorker. At one point, in September 1975, he asked me if could give his son Chevy, who then was working as a delivery boy for a liquor store, a job as a researcher. I agreed to hire him, but before he could begin, Chevy Chase got a better offer from *Saturday Night Live*.

# CHAPTER TWENTY-FOUR

# THE DSK TIMELINE

Timelines have always been an important part of my investigations because they show the missing gaps in the chronology of a crime. In July 2016, I began building one for the events surrounding the arrest of Dominique Strauss-Kahn. DSK, as he was called in France, was not a minor criminal. Less than two months earlier, he was head of the International Monetary Fund (IMF), one of the world's most powerful financial institutions, and planned to run for the presidency of France against Nicolas Sarkozy. In May DSK was already more than 20 points ahead of Sarkozy in the polls. Then, on May 14, he was arrested at JFK airport, as he was about to board a plane for Paris, and charged with sexually assaulting Nafissatou Diallo, a maid at the Sofitel in New York City. At the Rikers Island jail, DSK was put on suicide watch and, after given bail, he was put under strict house arrest. He had no choice but to resign from the IMF and abandon his bid to become president of France.

I was not interested in the crime for which he had been arrested. DNA evidence left little doubt that had been guilty of vile sexual aggression against Diallo. My interest was in another alleged crime that same day: the theft of DSK's Blackberry phone. He had used it two hours before his encounter with the maid to call his wife, and the police found it was not in his room after the incident. Indeed, the reason the NYPD was able to find and arrest him was that he kept calling the hotel, by then a crime scene, to ask the manager if his lost Blackberry had been located. How could the head of the IMF lose his phone shortly before, during, or immediately after committing an alleged sex crime? Blackberry phones, after all, are not really inanimate objects. In this age of surveillance, in which movements are constantly tracked to produce valuable location data, Blackberry phones ping one or more cell towers every three seconds to find the nearest one. Also, his hotel monitored the activities of people via CCTV cameras in the lobby and the electronic locks in rooms.

I proposed the idea of investigating DSK's missing phone to Bob Silvers, the founding coeditor of the *New York Review of Books*. Ever since I had first met him nearly a half century earlier, I knew him to be an editor with an almost insatiable curiosity about complex mysteries with international ramifications. On July 4, 1966, just after my book *Inquest* was published, Bob invited me to dine at Sun Luck Imperial, an elegant Chinese restaurant in the Imperial House on East Sixty-Ninth Street. He was a serious-looking man in his late 30s dressed in a well-cut navy-blue suit. He articulated with such precision that I thought he might be British (but, as I learned afterward, he grew up in the same town on Long Island as I had). Over a Peking duck, he wanted to know whether it was possible that someone had impersonated Oswald in visiting the Russian and Cuban embassies in Mexico City seven weeks before the assassination. He suggested a "Two Oswald Theory" in which a CIA conspirator impersonated the real Oswald to frame him and throw the blame on Russia. I suggested a meeting with Wesley Liebeler, the lawyer who investigated this area for the Warren Commission. So our next meeting included Liebeler. Bob, though he spoke in a soft, polite voice, was relentless in his interrogation of Liebeler.

He later published philosophy professor Richard Popkin's "The Two Oswalds," which Popkin, under the guise of a review of my book, presented his conspiracy theory about a double for Oswald. While I thought very little of Popkin's logic, I was impressed by Bob's determination to publish a controversial theory. We became friends afterward and he attended many of my rooftop barbecues, always wearing a dark suit.

Now, 50 years later, over dinner in a Japanese brasserie, I pointed out that a police search using the most sophisticated methods had failed to find the phone. He asked if an unknown party took it. I told him that seemed likely, and finding the person who took the phone during the events leading to DSK's arrest and downfall in French politics could be of interest to his readers. He agreed and commissioned me to investigate this mystery.

The prosecutors, meanwhile, had discovered that Diallo, DSK's accuser, had perjured herself in her Grand Jury testimony, including statements concerning the alleged crime. They had no choice but to drop all charges against DSK, who returned to France.

I spoke to DSK's lawyers, Zuckerman Spaeder; the detective firm it hired, Guidepost Solutions; and prosecutors in the DA's office. I assumed the prosecutors had obtained with a search warrant the Sofitel's CCTV, phone, and electronic key card data for the day of the crime, which is the standard operating procedure. They then had turned it over, as required by law, to DSK's lawyers. And his legal team, headed by William W. Taylor III, provided it to investigators at Guidepost International for analysis. As my question about the missing phone was of interest to all these parties, I managed to obtain a great deal of non-public data, including the hotel's electronic key card records for DSK's room as well as other rooms on his floor, the cell phone records of the hotel's security team, police tapes of the 911 call, and CCTV footage from cameras both inside and outside the hotel. With this data, I began constructing my timeline.

The key card records painted a temporal map of the activities in DSK's suite. DSK had arrived at 7:13 p.m. on May 13. Afterward, they show only five people entering the suite. One was DSK, who had gone out for dinner and reentered the suite at 1:53 a.m. As the lobby CCTV cameras showed, he was with a blond woman, who left two hours later. Four other people entered the room on May 14: Haquem, a room service waiter, who used his key at 12:05 p.m.; the maid Diallo, who used her key three times between 12:06 p.m. and 12:16 p.m.; the head housekeeper Markozina, who used her key at 12:38 p.m. to enter the room with Diallo; and head engineer Yearwood, who used his key twice, once at 12:45 p.m. and once at 12:51 p.m.

The key records further show that Diallo entered room 2820 directly across the hall on May 14 before the arrival of the police four different times. This raised questions in my mind. Why had Diallo repeatedly gone into both DSK's suite and the room across the hall, and why had Yearwood entered the suite twice?

Cell phone records showed that Yearwood had been called by the hotel's head of security, who, it turned out, was in touch with the head office of Accor, the French hotel chain in Paris that owned the Sofitel.

There was little doubt that the French Ministry of the Interior, under whose authority the French intelligence operates, was keeping an eye on DSK. Indeed, according to a December 2011 article in *Le Monde* entitled "What Sarkozy Knew About DSK," the DSK dossier extended back to 2006, when President Sarkozy was the minister of the Interior. Such surveillance did not require teams of agents lurking in the background. In 2011, it could be done through his cell phone. A cell phone can provide not only his GPS location data; its microphone can also be turned on remotely to monitor his conversations. On the day DSK was arrested (and his phone went missing), he had scheduled a stop at the airport in Paris so that his security team could take apart and examine his cell phone.

He was that certain it had been compromised. There was also a special group within the intelligence service that was reporting on DSK directly to the Élysée Palace in the spring of 2011, according to the well-sourced book *The President's Spy* by Didier Hassoux, Christophe Labbé, and Olivia Recasens. Intelligence could not be unaware, even from press reports, that DSK was an uninhibited womanizer. So if Sarkozy's staff in the Élysée Palace were privy to the French surveillance of DSK in New York, it likely would have been aware of the unfolding situation at the French-owned Sofitel that could knock DSK out of competition for the French presidency.

Even though DSK had not spoken to any journalist about the case, he agreed to see me on April 13, 2012. We met in the restaurant at the Pavillon de la Reine on the Place des Vosges in Paris. He arrived looking remarkably fit, dressed in a dark suit and an open-necked blue shirt that showed off his tan. He spoke perfect English. He said that if he had come out of the shower a minute later, the maid would have gone, the encounter would not have happened, and he would have flown to Berlin to meet German chancellor Angela Merkel. With a sad smile, he said, "Timing can undo the best of plans."

I then asked DSK, "Did the Élysée Palace intervene?" He answered that he believed Sarkozy supporters had used their connections to add fuel to the fire to destroy him but added that he had no proof. Neither did I.

In analyzing the data provided by the DA's investigation and the telecommunications providers, I hired a white hat hacker who traced the telemetric data through nearby cell phone towers to the Sofitel hotel before and after the alleged sexual encounter. But since the telemetric location was only accurate to about 80 feet, it could not be established which room on the floor it was in before the signals abruptly stopped pinging to the cell phone towers at 1:30 p.m. The analysis suggested that someone had moved it to another room (since it was not found in DSK's suite) and disabled it. But who? According to the key card records, there were only three suspects who had access to the room after DSK left—Diallo, Markozina, and Yearwood—but only Diallo and Yearwood were in the room alone. Did either of them take DSK's phone?

I now needed to know for my timeline what happened between Diallo and Yearwood in the hour and a half before the police were called. The maid had spent most of this time, much of it with Yearwood, in a security station on the ground floor of the Sofitel, which was monitored by CCTV cameras. On November 9, after some resistance, I persuaded DSK's lawyers to let me view the CCTV footage in the offices of Zuckerman Spaeder. A technician ran the 90-minute tape for me three times. I could see the maid, a tall woman, having a heated discussion with Yearwood and a security guard; then, after about 35 minutes, a third hotel employee placed the 911 call to the police. As soon as the call was made, Yearwood and the guard disappeared through a door leading to a loading dock. "Is there a CCTV camera in the loading dock?" I asked.

The technician quickly found the footage and played it. It showed the two security officers doing a victory dance with high fives. I asked the technician to replay this footage for Shawn Naunton, one of the lawyers working on the case.

"Clearly they are celebrating something," Naunton said coolly.

The victory dance, when published in the *New York Review of Books*, became in itself headline news in many countries and was shown on television around the world. The phone was never found or accounted for. When I discussed it with DSK in Paris, he said, "Someone stole my phone but I don't know who or why." Again, neither did I.

The DSK case had an unexpected consequence for me. In the midst of the furor over the victory dance, which was shown and analyzed repeatedly in newscasts around the world, I received word from Kyiv that Leonid Kuchma, the former president of Ukraine, urgently wanted to see me about a murder in which he was now implicated. Born in 1938 and trained by the Soviet Union as a rocket engineer, Kuchma became Ukraine's first prime minister in 1992 after it separated from the Soviet Union and its president between 1994 and 2005. The murder that concerned him, and which he wanted me to investigate, involved the decapitation of Ukrainian journalist Georgiy Gongadze in 2000 and its connection with the suspicious deaths of a half dozen people involved in the investigation. What made the matter urgent was that Ukrainian prosecutors had in 2011 charged Kuchma with involvement in the murder because he could be heard asking one of his ministers to deal with the journalist on a cassette tape surreptitiously recorded in his office shortly before the murder.

When I arrived in Kyiv on December 11, 2011, I first had lunch in an all-glass house with Kuchma's son-in-law Victor Pinchuk, an oligarch with political connections in Washington, DC, who told me that Kuchma wanted me to do the same type of reconstruction I did on the DSK case. I then went to see Kuchma, who told me he believed that the cassette tape had been forged by the Russians or some other intelligence intent on destabilizing his country. While I found Kuchma's theory intriguing, I could find no evidence to substantiate it. A few months later, the charges against him were thrown out by the high court on the grounds that the tape and other evidence against him had been illegally obtained, leaving open the question of whether they were genuine, and Kuchma went on in 2014 to become one of the principal Ukrainian negotiators with Russia in the effort to avoid the Russian invasion.

# CHAPTER TWENTY-FIVE

# THE ZIA CRASH

Very few events are more thoroughly investigated than an airplane crash. After all, the fortunes of the airline, the airplane manufacturer, airplane insurers, and government agencies all rely on the forensic determination of what caused the crash. This rule especially applies to crashes in which government leaders are killed.

On August 17, 1988, President Mohammad Zia-ul-Haq of Pakistan; General Akhtar Abdur Rehman Khan, the chairman of the joint chiefs of staff; nine top Pakistan generals, Arnold Raphel, the US ambassador to Pakistan; and Brigadier General Herbert M. Wassom, the chief American military attaché in Pakistan, were all killed when Pak-1, a Pakistan Air Force C-130 plane, crashed in eastern Pakistan. Because the crash altered the face of politics in Pakistan in a way in which no simple coup d'état could have, the investigation, led by American forensic investigators, became a matter of concern for the United States. The State Department leaked a story to the *New York Times* that the plane had crashed because of a "malfunction" rather than sabotage. To find out what was behind the leak, I went to my friend Pat Moynihan, who was on the Senate Intelligence Committee and had a longtime interest in the Indian subcontinent.

"This may be the hottest hot potato in Washington," Moynihan said. "To call it sabotage is to set in motion a whodunit to which no one knows the answer." As Moynihan no doubt knew, such an answer only intensified my interest.

In late January 1989, I spent a week in Washington setting up six appointments with government officials in Pakistan, including Sahabzada Yaqub Khan, the highly articulate foreign minister. I discussed my planned trip to Pakistan during a dinner with Elizabeth "Lally" Weymouth, the daughter of *Washington Post* owner Katharine Graham and a close friend of Foreign Minister Yaqub Khan. After I told her I had obtained the still-secret 365-page investigative report done by the US Air Force, Lally's interest perked up. "Does it say it was murder?"

I told her the report ruled out all the mechanical malfunctions that could cause a C-130 to fall from the sky but not a criminal act or sabotage. "So it could be murder," I said.

"So you are going to say it was a conspiracy," she said, looking at me with an accusatory hard-cocked eye.

"Let's say I am trying to keep an open mind," I said, not entirely convincingly.

"Ha," Lally replied.

I flew to Islamabad on February 15, checked into the Holiday Inn, and began calling my appointments. All six, including Yaqub Khan, canceled for unstated reasons. Their secretaries simply said they would be unavailable. I suspected Lally had tipped off her friend Yaqub Khan in Pakistan. If so, it was my fault for not being more discreet, a virtue I unfortunately completely lack.

In any case, I was stranded in Islamabad with literally no government officials willing to see me—not even a press officer. *Vanity Fair* had paid all my expenses. I couldn't return to New York and tell its editor, Tina Brown, I had not managed to get a single interview. I needed to improvise a plan B.

I had first learned the importance of improvising when I was six years old. We lived then in a beachfront house on the Rockaway peninsula in Queens. When food rationing was announced at the start of World War II, my father stocked the basement storeroom with enough canned goods to last for three years. What he had not reckoned on was a near hurricane that flooded the storeroom. By the time the water receded, the labels had been washed off all the cans. As a result, we didn't know whether we would be eating spinach, peas, or pineapple when we opened those cans. Even as a child, I didn't enjoy such culinary surprises. Since I had little else to amuse me in those days—there was no television in the early 1940s—I stared at the anonymous cans, seeking patterns among them. Seeing that they were not identical, I sorted them into piles by size, weight, edge marking, and other attributes. With a bit of trial-and-error openings, the patterns provided a fairly good means of predicting the contents. I now needed a similar triumph in Pakistan.

I made it a practice to keep a chronological journal of my interviews and contacts in an investigation on blue 3x5 cards. I turned one after another over as if I was playing a game of solitaire. Halfway through the deck, I saw that one member of Pat Moynihan's staff on the Senate Intelligence Committee had suggested off the record that I interview the children of the victims of the crash. He even wrote down the name and number of one of the children. At the time it seemed like a far-fetched and outlandish suggestion. How could I ask a grieving child about something as technically complex as a plane crash investigation? I had hoped to find forensic experts, pathologists, military intelligence officers, and top government officials, but now all those possible connections had been blocked by the government.

Without any adults to call, I reluctantly dialed the number of the first child on the list: Haroon Khan in Lahore.

There was a long, confusing delay at the other end. Finally, Haroon came on the line. He did not have the voice of a child. He said he was the 32-year-old son of General Akhtar Abdur Rehman Khan. His father, who had died on the plane, had been one of the most powerful men in Pakistan. He had founded and run the ISI, Pakistan's intelligence service and, at the time of the crash, was Zia's second in command. I told him briefly about the conclusions of the secret air force report that I had obtained. "You must come to Lahore immediately," he said. "You might not be safe in Islamabad."

That afternoon I flew to Lahore. Haroon, a well-built man with sharp, wolflike eyes, was waiting for me at the airport. He had a large mobile phone in his hand and was flanked by several large bodyguards. He told me it would be best if I stayed at his family's compound and led me to his waiting convoy of SUVs.

The walled compound had several houses on it and a half-dozen armed guards. He explained that the public phone system could not be trusted but he still retained his father's military phone operator, who had been with the family since his father ran the ISI (part of the military). Even better, he could use the military communication system to contact anyone in Pakistan's military or intelligence services. I was now back in business.

Haroon told me that all the bodies of the victims had been buried before any autopsies could be performed on them, the army had seized most of the evidence, and no one in the government would talk about the crash. He said the children of the victims, including his family and that of Zia's, believed it was a massive cover-up, which was why had written to the Moynihan staffer on the Senate Intelligence Committee.

After I suggested to Haroon that his radio operator could be useful in finding other planes in the area, the operator, calling people at control towers, found that there were three other planes in the area tuned to the same channel as Pak-1 the day of the crash. One was the turbojet carrying General Aslam Beg, the army's vice chief of staff, which was waiting on the runway at the airport to take off; the second was Pak 379, the backup C-130 that stood ready in case anything went wrong with Pak-1; and the third was a Cessna security plane that took off before Pak-1 to scout for terrorists.

Haroon's operator, to my amazement, also managed to locate the pilots of each of these planes. All the pilots were well acquainted with the flight crew of Pak-1 and its procedures, and they had been able to listen to the conversation between Pak-1 and the control tower. They each independently described the same sequence of events.

First Pak-1 reported its estimated time of arrival in the capital. Then, when the control tower asked its position, it failed to respond. At the same time, the pilot of Pak 379 was trying unsuccessfully to get in touch with Pak-1 to verify its arrival time. All they heard from Pak-1 was "stand by," but no message followed. When this silence persisted, the control tower got progressively more frantic in its efforts to contact Zia's chief pilot, Wing Commander Mash'hood Hassan. Three or four minutes passed. Then, a faint voice in Pak-1 called out "Mash'hood, Mash'hood." One of the pilots overhearing this conversation recognized the voice. It was Zia's military secretary, Brigadier Najib Ahmed, who apparently, from the weakness of his voice, was in the back of the flight deck (where a door connected the cockpit to the VIP capsule). If the radio was switched on and was picking up background sounds, it was the next best thing to a cockpit flight recorder. Under these circumstances, the long silence between "stand by" and the faint calls to Mash'hood, like the dog that didn't bark, was the relevant fact. Why wouldn't Mash'hood or the three other members of the flight crew have responded to the calls if they were in trouble?

The pilots aboard the other planes, who were fully familiar with Mash'hood and the procedures he was trained in, explained that if Pak-1's crew was conscious and in trouble they would not in any circumstances have remained silent during this time. If there had been difficulties with controls, Mash'hood instantly would have given the emergency "Mayday" signal so help would be dispatched to the scene. Even if he had for some reason chosen not to communicate with the control tower, Mash'hood would have been heard shouting orders to his crew to prepare for an emergency landing. And if there had been an attempt at a hijacking in the cockpit or scuffle between the pilots, it would also have been overheard.

Since both the pilot and copilot were known to be loyal to Zia, the only plausible explanation I could find for their lack of response on the tape was that they had been rendered incapable of answering—or of flying the plane. Since there was no sound of an explosion or gunshot on the tape, I concluded that it was likely that a container of nerve gas or other quick-acting poison had been released in the cockpit. I didn't know how it was smuggled into the cockpit, or by whom, but I had no doubt that it was part of a plot to facilitate a regime change in Pakistan.

In April 1995, more than five years after my article on the crash was published in *Vanity Fair*, Imran Khan, the cricket star and future prime minister of Pakistan, invited me to lunch at Laurent, a restaurant in Paris. He wanted to know more about the reconstruction of the plane crash I did from the tapes and what my conclusions were.

I told him I saw no other possibility than that the pilot and copilot had been immobilized by a bomb or poison gas canister planted in the cockpit. And in light of the cover-up that followed, I thought it likely that the orders had come from the highest level.

"So there was a conspiracy?" he asked.

I nodded.

Imran thought carefully for a moment and asked if I had a view of who could organize such a coup.

I said among the possibilities were Zia's rivals in the military, the Pakistan Peoples Party (PPP), a political opposition party angered by Zia's execution of Zulfikar Ali Bhutto, and the Soviet KGB, concerned about Zia's role in Afghanistan.

"You left out the CIA," he said pointedly.

I replied that the American ambassador was aboard the plane, and it was difficult for me to believe the CIA would kill the US ambassador. I thought this answer would satisfy him, but it didn't.

"It had the means and motive," he said and elaborated on his theory about the CIA and US machinations in Pakistan. He had such a singular focus I did not interrupt him. I was indeed intrigued by his deep-seated conspiratorial view about America's role in Pakistan

In April 2022, when Imran was prime minister of Pakistan, he used the same American conspiracy theory to explain the no-confidence vote in him by parliament that led to his downfall.

PART FIVE

# THE GOLDSMITH DETOUR

# CHAPTER TWENTY-SIX

# BEING EARLY

I was invited to come at 8:00 p.m. on November 29, 1984, for dinner at the home of Taki Theodoracopulos. Taki was a Greek shipping heir married to Princess Alexandra Schoenburg from the Hapsburg royal family. He not only lived a playboy's life but also wrote, appropriately, the High Life column for the London-based *Spectator*. It was the first time I had been invited to his home. Unable to escape my childhood fear of being late for an appointment, I arrived at his Upper East Side townhouse at 7:30 p.m. As it was far too early to ring the bell, I walked around and around the block, my usual remedy for pathological earliness. It was a walk that would greatly change my life.

After my third circle, a tall, bald man in a pinstriped suit passed me. I saw that he was also circling the block. When he stopped to look at his watch. I caught up with him and asked if was going to Taki's home. He laughed. "Yes, I'm Jimmy Goldsmith. Let's circle together."

I had of course heard of Sir James Goldsmith. He was born in February 1933 in Paris. His father, Frank Goldsmith, had been a Conservative member of the British Parliament and owned the Hotel Scribe in Paris, and his mother, Marcelle Mouiller, was French. A gambler at heart, Jimmy quit Eton at the age of 16 after winning 8,000 pounds on a single horse race and began speculating on the London Stock Exchange. From there, he went on to buying companies, including the retail chain Mothercare in Britain, the French weekly *L'Express* in France, and the Grand Union supermarkets in the United States. When he was 20, he eloped to Scotland with Isabel Patino, the 17-year-old daughter of Antenor Patino, the Bolivian ambassador to London. She died in childbirth bearing his daughter Isabel, his first of eight children. He then married Ginette Lery in Paris and subsequently took as his mistress Lady Annabel Birley, for whom Annabel's Club in London was named. After he married Lady Annabel, Laure Boulay de La Meurthe, a French journalist whose ancestors included the pretender to the French throne, became his constant mistress. Defending this wife/ mistress practice, he repeated Sacha Guitry's quip: "When a man marries his mistress, he creates a job vacancy." He didn't believe in abandoning his wives, maintaining a luxurious home in Paris with Ginette, with whom he had two children, homes in England and Spain with Annabel, with whom he had three children, and a townhouse in New York with Laure, with whom he would have two children.

He was decidedly an unconventional man, as I learned during these laps around the block. As I struggled to keep up with his rapid stride, he railed first against the *New York Times*, which he called "subversive"; next against the corruption of British government, even though it had awarded him his knighthood in return for his campaign contributions; then against the Wachtell Lipton law firm for assisting "entrenched corpocracies"; and finally against the KGB for infiltrating French newspapers, even though he owned *L'Express*. As he spoke, his face reddened with fury.

After our fifth lap, seeing we were still 10 minutes early, he suggested a drink. We went to a nearby restaurant on Lexington Avenue, and while standing at the bar, he said the only reason he was going to Taki's dinner was because Taki's wife Alexandra had been the love of his life a decade ago in Paris. By the time we got to Taki's house, at precisely 8:00 p.m., I knew we would be friends.

Soon afterward, Jimmy and I had dinner at Raga, an upscale Indian restaurant in Rockefeller Center. Even though I arrived 10 minutes early, Jimmy, casually dressed in a blue cashmere pullover and slacks, was already seated pasha-style in a booth and ordering trolleys of Indian dishes from a turbaned waiter. Next to him was Laure Boulay de La Meurthe, a French woman in her late 20s with inquisitive eyes and a quick wit. They had fallen in love at a ball in Paris six years earlier and, despite his still being married to Annabel, she was now his constant companion.

As I slid into the booth, Jimmy was talking to Laure about his plans to relaunch *L'Express* with separate sections, including one called Style, which Laure would edit. A moment later, six trolleys of tandoori dishes arrived.

Bringing me into the conversation, he asked, "Any thoughts about relaunching *L'Express*?"

"None at all," I answered.

"Then what do you know about?" he asked, lighting up a long cigar.

I was just beginning my book on the KGB and the CIA, so I answered with a smile, "I know something about the order of battle of the Russian intelligence service, its penetration of Western intelligence services, its disinformation operation, and its manipulations of currencies."

Laure said with a laugh, "My father believes the French republic is infiltrated by KGB moles."

"It likely was in the 1960s," I answered.

"And how do you know that?" Jimmy asked, puffing on his cigar.

"A French intelligence officer named Philippe de Vosjoli told me that when I interviewed him for my book." I added, "He is the only French officer to defect to the CIA and was handled personally by James Jesus Angleton."

Jimmy's eyes widened. The name Angleton had piqued his attention.

"Could I speak to Angleton about it?"

"Whenever it suits you," I replied, confident I could arrange the meeting. Angleton was a Francophile who I knew would want to hear Jimmy's conspiracy theories about the French government.

"Tuesday?" Jimmy asked.

"There is an Eastern shuttle to Washington every hour," I suggested.

"We have our own shuttle," Laure said, referring to Jimmy's private Gulfstream.

At this point, the waiter politely asked Jimmy to extinguish his cigar. Jimmy, relighting it, told him that Raga's tandoori ovens produced more pollution than a hundred of his cigars. The standoff ended when Jimmy stood up, pushed the food trolleys out of his way, and left.

Promptly at 10:00 a.m. on the following Tuesday, Mr. Peck, Jimmy's chauffeur, picked me up. Jimmy, who was staying at the Carlyle Hotel, was in the car. We drove to Teterboro Airport and onto the tarmac to Jimmy's BAC jet. By noon, we were at the restaurant at the Madison Hotel in Washington, where I had arranged for Angleton to meet us for lunch. We were half an hour early.

Angleton, wearing a light gray suit, looked frailer than I remembered. He began by asking Jimmy if President François Mitterrand could govern effectively now that his party had lost its majority. He had done some homework on Jimmy, who, with *L'Express*, was deeply involved in French politics and intrigues.

Jimmy answered that Mitterrand has always done whatever it takes to survive. "There are those in France who even believe he made a deal with the KGB," he said as he sampled the Montrachet Grand Cru. "Do you think the French government can be trusted?"

"I wouldn't know," Angleton answered cautiously. "I retired 10 years ago."

"But Ed tells me you had a defector from France—"

"Ancient history," Angleton interrupted. He explained that he had been the liaison with SDECE, the French intelligence service, in the early 1960s and his counterpart was a French officer.

"De Vosjoli?" Jimmy interrupted.

Angleton nodded and continued. He described how de Vosjoli had come to him with a "shopping list" of questions about US missiles for the French government. Normally, Angleton would pass such a request on to the Department of Defense, but he had seen de Vosjoli's list of questions a year earlier. It had been given to him by the defector Anatoliy Golitsyn as a list of targets that the KGB planned to obtain via espionage. So Angleton told de Vosjoli that whoever had drawn up this list was likely a KGB mole in French intelligence. De Vosjoli, upon making some inquiries, reported back to Angleton that the questions had been passed down from the head of the intelligence service. Shortly after, de Vosjoli was told that he had been targeted for assassination by his own service when he returned from America.

"I arranged for him to defect to save his life," Angleton concluded.

Jimmy pointed out that in 1962, Mitterrand, as the minister of the Interior, was responsible for SDECE. "Could Mitterrand have known?"

Angleton did not answer. After a telling pause and enigmatic smile, he changed the subject to one of his great passions, fly-fishing. His slow but eloquent description of the intellectual operation used to lure salmon to the bait gradually mesmerized Jimmy. Fly-fishing was a deception based on trial-and-error feedback.

When we flew back to New York after lunch, Jimmy asked, "Was he talking about fishing?" It was not a question I could answer, as Angleton often used fly-fishing as a metaphor for espionage.

A week later, I called Jimmy at his new townhouse on Eightieth Street. Laure told me Jimmy had gone to Barbados and wouldn't be returning until January. She was staying in New York for Christmas, so I invited her to my Christmas dinner and asked about Jimmy's absence. "I would rather spend half my time with an interesting man than all my time with an uninteresting one," she said.

The next time I saw Jimmy was on January 12, 1985. We had lunch at Maxwell's Plum. Jimmy had just returned from London, where he had dinner with Margaret Thatcher. He reported that Thatcher told him President Reagan had done everything wrong economically and she had done everything right, but he had succeeded in restoring American culture while she had failed at that in Britain. Jimmy said he replied, "You can make economic changes, but you can't change a nation's culture—and culturally, England is dead." Jimmy would later host President Reagan at his estate in Mexico.

Jimmy also held a series of well-cast dinners at his townhouse. He generally invited people whose politics coincided with his own. The attendees on March 14, 1985, for example, included Jeane Kirkpatrick, the US ambassador to the UN; Norman Podhoretz, the editor of *Commentary*; Bob Bartley, the editor of the *Wall Street Journal*; and Rupert Murdoch, the fast-rising newspaper mogul. I had previously met Murdoch through Clay Felker in 1977 when Clay tried to induce Murdoch to buy out the *New York* magazine shareholders who were resisting his expansion plans. Murdoch, after quietly listening to Clay's proposal, said in an almost chilling voice, "I don't buy part of a magazine. I buy it all." And he did.

Jimmy had his chef prepare a dinner of peppered sausages from Spain, wild salmon from Iceland, and rack of lamb. He also served Lafite Rothschild from his wine cellar. According to my diary, the conversation was wide-ranging. Ambassador Kirkpatrick described how Colonel Bo Hi Pak, of Sun Myung Moon's Unification Church, tried to recruit her as a Moonie by telling her she was "the chosen person" and offered her the editorship of the Unification Church–owned *Washington Times*. Jimmy laughed, saying the newspaper was losing $80 million and the money was coming from the South Korean government.

Murdoch was not given to participating in conversational banter, but his steel-trap mind was activated by statements that he considered to be nonsense. When Bartley raised his pet theory that America should go on the gold standard by pegging the dollar to the price of gold, Murdoch snapped back, "It is interesting that the editor of the *Wall Street Journal*, which is dedicated to a free market determining prices, believes that the most important price of all, that of the dollar, should be fixed by the government." Bartley gave no answer. (Years later, Murdoch bought the *Wall Street Journal*.)

A few weeks later, Jimmy proved very helpful in getting me into the inner sanctum of the so-called High-Yield Bond Conference in Beverly Hills. This was where Mike Milken, the recognized king of junk bonds, gathered the takeover raiders he financed, including Carl Icahn, Ron Perelman, Boone Pickens, Ivan Boesky, Irwin Jacobs, Asher Edelman, and Oscar Wyatt. I wanted to go because I was writing a monthly column for *Manhattan, Inc.* called Wall Street Babylon. Even though Milken forbid any journalist from attending, Goldsmith not only introduced me to Milken but also took me to the party, which would become infamous, thanks partly to my writing about it, as the "Predator's Ball." It was held in Bungalow 8, a pink double bungalow at the Beverly Hills Hotel. Drexel Burnham Lambert, the sponsor of the conference, used that particular bungalow because it had direct street access and a private pool. The party's organizer, Donald Engel, who worked for Milken, invited about 20 attractive young women he curated from his roster of starlets, models, and what he called "Hollywood players." I heard him say to one 26-year-old actress at the pool the morning of the party, "You will meet the richest men in the world tonight."

When I arrived with Jimmy and Joe Flom, a senior partner from Skadden, Arps, Slate, Meagher & Flom, many of the model types that I had seen at the swimming pool that afternoon were now huddled together, like pigeons waiting to be released for trap shooting. Most were dressed to kill. Initially, there were only a few men at the cocktail hour, which began at 6:00 p.m. Milken himself made it a point not to attend these annual parties. But gradually, his junk bond clients, all in dark suits, threaded their way through the crowd of women. Their discussions of poison pills, golden handcuffs, and stripped equities seemed to leave the young women confused, if not agog. Boone Pickens left after one drink. Rupert Murdoch, who had just returned from China and was looking tired, left almost as quickly.

Jimmy joked to me, "If in Moscow, we would call this a honey trap." He turned to Flom and suggested the party was becoming dangerous. Flom, whose judgment Jimmy prized, nodded. And they left. I remained a little longer. As Jimmy told me later, "Those guys have no idea of how to run a revolution."

The next morning my then girlfriend Hillary Johnson joined me for breakfast in the Polo Lounge. I was telling her about the party when a short man with gray hair and a fulsome smile popped up in the adjacent booth and said, "Sorry, couldn't help overhearing you were at the party last night?"

He then joined us in the booth, introduced himself as the film producer Elliott Kastner, ordered a half grapefruit, and said he was expecting a call from Marlon Brando.

"You know Brando?" I asked, thinking back to the days when I tried, without success, to show him the script for my *Iliad*.

"I want to make a movie with him about a corporate pirate. Bungalow 8 might make a great setting. Would you like to write it?" he asked.

I told him I did not write movies. He said, "Not until now. I want to commission you to write *Bungalow 8*."

Three half grapefruits later, he called Ziggy Zeigler, a long-established Hollywood agent, who brokered the deal. I wondered if this was a typical breakfast in the Polo Lounge. I wrote a short treatment of *Bungalow 8* but Kastner never made it into a movie.

I flew back the next day with Jimmy. En route to New York, we watched the movie *Day of the Jackal*, appropriately about a presidential assassin.

# CHAPTER TWENTY-SEVEN

# A WORLD OF HIS OWN

By 1986, for reasons I would only grasp 11 years later, Jimmy Goldsmith became so disenchanted with the world he lived in in New York, London, and Paris, he decided to build his own. He bought a 10,000-acre tract in a tropical rainforest on Mexico's Pacific coast between Acapulco and Puerto Vallarta, hiring hundreds of workers to build roads, lay sewage pipes, and construct villas. Money was no object since he could buy Mexican pesos at a huge discount through a US financial gimmick called Brady bonds. Its centerpiece, his personal Xanadu called La Loma, was a domed Moorish-style structure nearly the size of the White House with its own cloister. To furnish it, he chartered a jumbo DC-10 to fly back and forth to India, where it was loaded with tons of tiles, latticed woodwork, furniture, and giant silk pillows. For his ex-wife Ginette, he built a four-bedroom round house for her on the beach a few miles away. His 25-year-old daughter, Alix, was given a five-bedroom guesthouse. And he constructed six lavish villas for his guests. He then expanded it to encompass lagoons with crocodiles, savannahs with antelope and zebras, beaches with a protected turtle preserve, and a landing strip. To make it autarkic, he added an organic farm to provide fruits, vegetables, livestock for milk, and artesian wells for his own version of bottled water.

To run it, serve his guests, and guard its perimeter, he hired some 300 employees. This was his kingdom by the sea, Cuixmala, and anyone who violated his rules or gave offense to him, as Virgin Atlantic tycoon Sir Richard Branson found out in 1992, would have their bags packed for them and taken to the airport by his security detail.

On my first of 10 Christmas vacations there, I met such extraordinary associates of his as John Aspinall, Jimmy's oldest and closest friend. Born in India in 1926, "Aspers," as Jimmy called him, began life as a bookie at British racetracks, which was the only gambling allowed at the time under the laws of the United Kingdom. With his profits, Aspinall hosted illegal chemin de fer games in flats he rented in London, which were attended by dukes and princes. When gambling was legalized in 1960, these were turned into the Clairmont Club and other casinos, in which Jimmy was a partner. I met Jacob Rothschild, who would become the next Lord Rothschild. Born in 1936, he received a first at Christ Church College in Oxford and now headed the powerful Rothschild Investment Trust. There was also Henry Keswick, born in 1938 in Shanghai, who was, as chairman of Jardine Matheson Holdings, the taipan of Hong Kong. And Selim Zilkha, born in 1927 to a Jewish banking family in Baghdad, who founded Mothercare. Despite their difference in backgrounds, they all shared a high appreciation of Jimmy's brilliance and were investors in his adventurous corporate takeover. But, as became apparent at one extended breakfast on his terrace, they didn't always agree with his ethics. For example, when Jimmy explained to the gathering that he planned non-recourse loans to partly finance his next corporate raid because if it failed he would not be obligated to repay them, Rothschild, who prided himself on a having an ethical standard that superseded a technical legal obligation, replied, "I'd pay it back anyway." Aspinall, on the other hand, who based his ethics on animal behavior in his private zoos, argued that Jimmy should be more predatory in "weeding out the weak." In the end, Jimmy's views always prevail—at least in his kingdom by the sea.

Jimmy also found that private planes were another form of private kingdom where he could exercise power. Tom Wolfe, in his essay "The Ultimate Power: Seeing 'Em Jump," asserted that one reason the super-rich own private jets was to experience "a magical moment" in watching the pilots, and their guests, jump like puppets on a string when they abruptly change the flight plan. Jimmy was no different, as I learned in 1985 aboard the Boeing 737 that served as his airborne yacht.

He had rented the airliner to take Laure and their one-year-old daughter, Charlotte, on a month-long global tour to celebrate the completion of his takeover of Crown Zellerbach. Aside from me, he also invited Jean Pigozzi, a 32-year-old Harvard-educated photographer, who had inherited a sizable fortune from his father, Henri Pigozzi, the founder of Simca Automobiles; Pigozzi's lively girlfriend, Evan Seidel, a recent graduate of Middlebury College; Guy de Baguenault, Jimmy's backgammon-playing friend from Paris; Alexander de Noyes, an aristocrat friend of Laure's from Argentina; and Patricia Charnelet, a TV journalist who Jimmy liked to describe as the "Dan Rather of France." Jimmy's plan was that we would zigzag around the globe according to his whims, as it was his plane, and end up at Carnival in Rio. As we flew across the Pacific headed for Bora Bora, I was reading one of my files when Jimmy, standing behind me, screamed at me, "Get it off my plane, now!" I thought the "it" might refer to me until Pigozzi, pointing to the rubber band on my tray, whispered, "Get rid of the rubber band." I did and the crisis passed. It turned Jimmy had a phobic fear of rubber.

We stayed our first night at the Hotel Bora Bora in a bungalow constructed on stilts in a lagoon. Each bungalow had a glass floor through which to watch the aquatic life below. My only lasting memory of the Hotel Bora Bora is swimming at dusk in my snorkel mask and having a tourist in another bungalow, who apparently mistook me for a manta ray, throw fish food toward me.

After refueling at Easter Island, we flew back across the Pacific to Santiago, Chile, to go on a horse-riding expedition to the glaciers on the southern tip of Chile. Unfortunately, that plan was aborted when Jimmy's taxi driver got lost attempting to find a restaurant the first night. Jimmy was furious and, having had enough of Chile, decided that rather than go to the glacier, we were leaving for Argentina. The change in plan was so abrupt that the flight crew didn't have time to retrieve their uniforms from the cleaners and had to fly in the colorful beach clothes they had bought in Bora Bora.

When we arrived in Buenos Aires that afternoon, Gilberte Beaux met us at the airport. Madame Beaux, as Jimmy called her, began as a shorthand typist after World War II and had become one of the most powerful corporate executives in France when Jimmy allied himself with her in 1967. She now ran Jimmy's entire business empire in Europe. She had recently bought an island between two rivers in northern Argentina, which had a 20,000-acre cattle ranch on it, and she wanted Jimmy to be her 50-50 partner in the ranch. Madame Beaux described it over lunch as a "paradise of wild birds." She invited us to visit the ranch the following week and stay overnight in the guesthouses. After showing us around Buenos Aires for three days, she went to her island to prepare for our arrival.

As Jimmy's Boeing 737 was too large to land on the airstrip at the ranch, we flew to the airport in Mendoza, where Madame Beaux had chartered two single-engine planes flown by bush pilots. These were fairly primitive prop planes in which the pilot estimated the remaining fuel from a stick that floated in the gas tank. As only half our party would fit in both of them, we needed to be ferried to the ranch in two shifts. While Jimmy, Laure, Patricia, and Guy boarded the planes, Pigozzi, Evan, and I remained aboard the 737 watching a video of *Chariots of Fire*. In an hour, both planes returned with all the passengers still aboard. Jimmy got out first and, looking discombobulated, made a "zero" sign with his thumb and forefinger, pointing to the pilot.

"He has zero intelligence," was the message. "These idiots couldn't find the ranch," Jimmy shouted. "They nearly ran out of gas. Forget the damn ranch. We are leaving immediately for Brazil."

We landed in Rio de Janeiro on February 7. A fleet of SUVs waited to take us to the Caesar Park Hotel in Ipanema. The hotel opened onto a spectacularly beautiful beach. Jimmy's advance man in Brazil had arranged for us to attend what he called "the A-list parties" in the Carnival celebration. That evening we went to a black-tie event on Sugarloaf Mountain in which the women wore low-cut gowns and the men sported large bodyguards with earpieces. Jimmy's bodyguard told me that kidnapping had become an industry in Brazil.

The main event for Carnival took place in the Sambadrome on Tuesday, February 11. Jimmy had rented a VIP box directly above where the judges choose the winning samba troupe. Even though it was a sweltering night, the box came with a chef, a butler, and barrels full of cracked ice. We could watch from our comfortable perch or join the celebrants below, many of whom were ripping off their shirts and other garments to get in the spirit of the night as samba troupes, outfitted in vivid colors, paraded into the Sambadrome.

Pigozzi, seated directly behind me, made a video, often turning the camera in the direction I was looking. Although I was unaware of the video at the time, it was an actual record of what I had seen. He gave me the video on eight DVDs 20 years later and, watching them, I saw how they differed from my two-decade-old memory of Carnival, further demonstrating the aptness of Marcel Proust's observation that "Remembrance of things past is not necessarily the remembrance of things as they were."

Even with Jimmy's spontaneous flight changes, I met extraordinary people, saw new and exotic places, and had a great time, visiting 29 countries in all with Jimmy from 1985 to 1996. As Oscar Wilde said, "I can resist everything but temptation." These trips allowed me to be the proverbial fly on the wall, including at meetings with power brokers. In Benahavís, Spain, we met with the Saudi arms dealer Adnan Khashoggi, who demonstrated to us his own version of Monopoly (in which all the squares in it were named for properties he owned). In Hohhot, Inner Mongolia, we celebrated with the governor in a giant yurt the release of eight feral Przewalski's horses into the grasslands of central Asia, which Jimmy's friend John Aspinall provided from his private zoos. In Shanghai, China, Huang Ju, a top member of the Politburo Standing Committee and later the first-ranked vice premier of China, took us in a private boat to see the Pudong development on the east bank of the Huangpu River to entice Jimmy to invest in it. In Hanoi, Vietnam, we, along with Sir David Tang, met members of the Communist Politburo to win approval for Jimmy's purchase of the city's rundown Grand Hotel. In the Kingdom of Bhutan, we were hosted by Prince Lhendup Dorji, the second-eldest son of the hereditary prime minister and the brother-in-law of the king (as well as a Cornell classmate of mine); in Israel, Bibi Netanyahu, then the deputy prime minister, took us for a two-hour walk along Jerusalem's walls while describing the machinations of Israeli politics; and in Lahore, Pakistan, I witnessed a leading politician, who would later be Pakistan's prime minister, unsuccessfully attempt to extract a bribe from Jimmy Goldsmith, saying repeatedly, "Just tell me what you want and you will get it." To be sure, it was a detour, but it was worth it.

# CHAPTER TWENTY-EIGHT

# NIXON'S VACATION

In early 1992, Jimmy attended a monthly "stag dinner" at the home of former president Richard Nixon in Saddle River, New Jersey. Other guests included Rupert Murdoch, the owner of News Corporation; William Simon, the former Treasury secretary; Adnan Khashoggi, the Saudi arms dealer; Brent Scowcroft, Bush's national security advisor; and Prince Bandar bin Sultan, the Saudi ambassador to the United States. When Jimmy described to me how Nixon impressively acted as a rapporteur in keeping the conversation focused on geopolitical issues, I said I had always regretted not meeting Nixon, who I had written extensively about in my book *Agency of Fear.*

"It's not too late," he said. He was planning to invite Nixon to Cuixmala, his private retreat in Mexico, for a week. Would I like to come?

Despite his ultimate disgrace in the Watergate scandal, I still considered Nixon to be one of the most intriguing presidents in history. Every previous president since the end of the Second World War—Harry Truman, Dwight D. Eisenhower, John F. Kennedy, and Lyndon Baines Johnson—had attempted to isolate China, a country with one-quarter of the world's population, by not recognizing it. Going against this entrenched policy, which required using stealth to cut out much of the US government, Nixon opened up rela-tions with China, which, for better or worse, changed forever the geopolitical and economic world. Since I have always had a deep curiosity about how the world works, there was no way I could forgo this opportunity to be a fly on the wall on Nixon's vacation.

Soon after I accepted the invitation, I received a phone call from Edith, Jimmy's secretary in Paris. Could I be at Jimmy's home in Mexico on January 10, 1992? she asked.

I wanted to know who would be there.

She answered, "You, Jimmy, and President Nixon."

On January 9, I flew to Mexico.

What was bringing Nixon to Mexico, Jimmy later told me, was the Nixon Library in Yorba Linda, California. The US government had financed all other presidential libraries, but Nixon did not want that intrusive arrangement, so he needed to raise money for it. Former Treasury secretary Bill Simon, a billionaire in his own right, was its chairman, and Bebe Rebozo and Bob Abplanalp were its other two trustees. Simon, Rebozo, and Abplanalp had almost single-handedly subsidized Nixon's presidential library up to now, but they needed more financial backing. Nixon had asked Jimmy for help with this at the last stag dinner, and Jimmy invited him to Mexico to discuss it.

## DAY ONE

On the morning of January 10, heavy rain flooded the anti-scorpion moats around the palatial La Loma. Unable to go outside in the torrent, Jimmy and I passed the time waiting for Nixon by watch-ing Yul Brynner's *The King and I* in his screening room. Jimmy suddenly paused the movie.

"The rain is a very bad omen," he said.

"It's just El Niño," I said, trying to relax him. I knew Jimmy believed in omens.

He began pacing in a circle. At each turn, he cited other omens that day. A coral snake had been found coiled at the base of the table where he had breakfast, he saw scorpions crossing the moat on leaves, and the price of gold (a commodity in which he was heavily invested) had dropped.

"This is a bad time," he said. "I am going to cancel Nixon."

To my horror, he picked up the phone. Since I had come all the way to Mexico to meet Nixon, I tried to dissuade him. "Nixon is already on your plane," I said. "You can't abort his trip while he is in midair."

"I'll tell him the plane had engine trouble."

Fortunately, he couldn't get a dial tone. It was another bad omen. He began pounding the phone against the desk until it broke. He went to another phone, but the line was dead. Rainstorms often knocked out the single phone line in Cuixmala. The only other phone that might work was 30 miles away at the supermarket, which Jimmy had bought just to have a reliable phone.

"Screw it," he said, putting down the phone. An hour later, the rain had stopped and the phone was working again. The pilot called to say the plane would be landing in an hour. Jimmy decided to meet the plane on horseback, mainly to impress Nixon.

I went to the landing strip in a jeep with Jimmy's bodyguards. Just as the plane was preparing to land, Jimmy arrived and dismounted from his horse. He was wearing rumpled white cotton slacks, a blue polo shirt, and, loosely slung over his shoulders, a cashmere sweater. Nixon was the first off the plane. Even though he had just celebrated his 79th birthday, he had a sprightly spring to his step. Next came Bill Simon, who was helped down the stairway by Mike Endicott, Nixon's Secret Service bodyguard until Nixon, unlike any other former president, elected to give up his Secret Service protection because he did not want to live his life under constant surveillance. The last two men off the plane were Charles "Bebe" Rebozo, the Cuban American banker from Florida who had helped Nixon launch his political career 40 years earlier, and Robert Abplanalp, the multimillionaire inventor of aerosol valves for shaving cream, which had been blamed for damaging the ozone layer around the earth.

The five men looked somber as they walked toward the waiting convoys of SUVs on the landing strip. Nixon wore a dark blue suit, rep tie, and white shirt. Simon wore a sports jacket and a tie. Rebozo, although he was the same age as Nixon, looked much older. He wore a rumpled blazer and a tie that exactly matched Nixon's. Abplanalp wore a brown suit. Endicott was the only member of the group without a tie.

Jimmy introduced me to Nixon, who looked at me askance. I learned later that he had not expected a journalist to be with Jimmy. To break the ice, I told him that I had been a student of Pat Moynihan, who was Nixon's Domestic Counselor in 1970.

"Pat must have been a great teacher," he said with a flicker of a smile. What immediately impressed me about Nixon was the clarity of his voice and the firmness of his handshake.

After finishing the round of introductions, Nixon and his party got into the waiting convoy of SUVs. Jimmy gave his horse to a waiting groom and followed with me in a jeep. It was a 20-minute drive to the Moorish-style palace, called La Loma, of which Jimmy and his son were the only occupants.

When we reached the house, 20 servants in their pink Cuixmala uniforms were lined up to greet us.

I had many questions for the only president to ever resign. I had always been curious about his rapid rise to power. He certainly did not follow the usual script of American politics. Whereas other American presidents could point to their "humble origins" with some sort of romantic pride—or even describe their family summer home as a "log cabin" as FDR did—Nixon came from a seriously impoverished background. His family moved to California at the turn of the century after his father had been frostbitten working in an open streetcar in Columbus, Ohio. Nixon's mother was forced to work as a scrubwoman in a sanatorium in Arizona to pay for the treatment of Richard's brother Harold, who suffered from tuberculosis. At the age of 10, Richard was sent to work as a farm laborer to help his family. In the depths of the Great Depression, the only job the 14-year-old could get was as a barker for a fortune wheel in the Slippery Gulch Rodeo. He used the pennies he earned to attend Whittier College, a small Quaker school, and won a scholarship to law school at Duke University. When World War II broke out, he joined the navy as a junior officer, assisting in liquidating contracts for, among other people, Howard Hughes, whose celebrated "Spruce Goose" flying boat, then the largest airplane ever built, project for the navy had to be liquidated. After Nixon left the navy in 1945, he had no money, no family connections, no civilian suit. He wore his navy uniform to job interviews. Despite his poverty, he rose in politics. In seven years, he not only won a US Senate seat, but he became General Dwight D. Eisenhower's vice president. Since he had no visible wealth, I wanted to know what personal quality, political skill, or perhaps secret backer accounted for his rapid rise to power.

After drinks on the terrace of La Loma, Nixon and his party were driven in minivans to their individual guest villas. Nixon was given Casa Borrado, a fully staffed five-bedroom house originally built and named for the estate's general manager (whom Jimmy had fired in 1988). It was about three miles away. Nixon's guests and I were put in five one-bedroom villas—each decorated like a maharaja's bungalow, with silks and artifacts flown in from Rajasthan—that ringed the hilltop across from La Loma. Each of our villas was protected against scorpions by a moat. Jimmy had become obsessed with this danger after his son Jethro had been badly stung by one two months earlier.

We assembled at 8:00 that evening in the circular library at La Loma for margaritas before dinner. Rebozo, spry and bouncy, and Abplanalp, obese and slow-moving, were the first to arrive. I asked Rebozo how he met Nixon. Rebozo said he met Nixon in 1946—when Nixon was attempting to find a job as a lawyer.

Simon arrived next. While waiting for his drink, he perused the titles of books in the library. The books were divided into five sections by topic: American politics, espionage, Mexican history, biography, and gossip, each section represented one of Jimmy's main current interests. Above each section was a stone bust of a Roman emperor.

Nixon was the last to arrive. He was accompanied by Jimmy's Mexican bodyguard, Ignatius. To my surprise, Nixon was conversing with him in Spanish, which he spoke fluently. (Ignatius later told me Nixon once asked him what sort of future his children would have in Mexico.)

Dinner was served in the courtyard under the Moorish dome. Jimmy employed an Indian chef, an Italian chef, and a Vietnamese chef. It was his idea of cultural diversity. Their cuisine was put on separate buffet tables. Nixon, inspecting the Vietnamese table, said it reminded him of a trip he and Rebozo had made to Thailand. To my surprise, Nixon had a wicked sense of humor. He joked about how Rebozo indulged himself in a Siamese double massage and "fell in love" with both his masseuses. He added he only vicariously partook in "Bebe's excesses." Nixon chose the blander Italian cuisine.

At dinner, it became clear to me that Nixon had an extraordinary ability to establish a rapport with others in a small group. It was from neither the charisma through which politicians win audiences nor the skill of telling anecdotes. Instead, Nixon listened and responded in a way that made others feel they were included in the conversation. For example, Jimmy had briefly mentioned during drinks in the library that I was researching a book on the KGB. Later in the evening, Jimmy asked Nixon about the efficiency of intelligence services in Russia, mentioning that I had just obtained the KGB files on Armand Hammer, a oil tycoon who spent his early years in Russia. Nixon, who had known Hammer, prefaced his reply with "As I am sure Ed would understand from his investigation of Hammer," thereby bringing me into the discussion. He also seemed perfectly willing to defer to others at the table. When Jimmy asked him if he thought the economy might collapse, he said modestly, "I wish I was better informed on the business cycle. Bill, do you think we are headed for collapse?" His deep bass voice added a sense of weight to what he was saying, even if he was merely complimenting Jimmy on his choice of wine. Jimmy had had many other impressive dinner guests at Cuixmala, including Henry Kissinger, Jacob Rothschild, and Ronald Reagan, but none demonstrated Nixon's ability to make others in a group feel that they were part of the discussion. His talent at creating this sort of rapport with others at small dinners might have accounted for his amazing comeback after he lost both the presidential election to JFK in 1960 and the California gubernatorial race to Pat Brown in 1962. While the media had written his political obituary in 1962, he demonstrated that obituary was premature. In 1968, he was elected the 37th president of the United States. Perhaps what political commentators had not fully reckoned on when counting him out was that he would win the support of tens of thousands of local Republican politicians through small gatherings.

When the conversation turned to British politics, Jimmy expressed his loathing for Prime Minister John Major, whom he described as "a circus clown." He said Major had "destroyed the pound" by lowering the interest rate in a misguided effort to relieve unemployment. "How can a leader be so stupid?" he asked Nixon.

"Sounds like he let himself get gulled by economic advisors and their Phillips curve." Nixon turned to Simon. "You once pointed out that economists use fancy-sounding theories to make themselves sound smarter. Correct me if I am wrong, Jimmy. As I understand it, the Phillips curve is an economist's graph showing that as inflation is pumped up, unemployment goes down."

Jimmy nodded, visibly impressed. I was surprised that Nixon not only grasped such an arcane theory as the Phillips curve but that he could succinctly explain it in a few words.

"Maybe that theory works in the short run," Nixon continued, "but as you just pointed out with Major's fiasco, it can also undermine a nation's economy."

"Exactly," Jimmy said. "Economists know how to measure, not how to value."

"For what it's worth, John Major reminds me of that character Chance the gardener in the movie *Being There*," Nixon said with a chuckle. He was referring to the 1979 movie in which Peter Sellers plays Chance, a mentally diminished gardener. "Chance thought he could change unpleasant things in real life by pointing his TV remote control at them—and clicking."

During dinner, the El Niño rain started again, presenting a potential catastrophe for Jimmy's guests. Nixon, Rebozo, Abplanalp, and Simon, all of whom had had recent problems with their backs, somehow had to get back to their guesthouses. The only means of exiting La Loma was to descend a flight of 30 marble steps, with no banister for support. In the rain, each step had become as slippery as ice. So, one by one, Jimmy's bodyguards, like Sherpas going down Mount Everest, accompanied first Nixon, then Simon, then Rebozo, and finally Abplanalp down the stairs, while pink-clad servants held large umbrellas over their heads.

I stayed to talk to Jimmy about the evening, but he flipped on the satellite TV. On it was American figure skating star Kristi Yamaguchi on winning the semifinals of the world championship. Without taking his eyes off the twirling skater on-screen, he asked what I thought about the former president.

"He was different from what I expected."

"And different from your book?" he asked with his teasing smile.

"That too," I admitted. Entirely from descriptions by journalists, I had depicted Nixon in *Agency of Fear* as a thuggish, socially awkward man who was ill at ease in the company of other people. But that was decidedly not the Nixon at the dinner table tonight.

On returning to my villa, I wrote in my diary, "How could I have gotten Nixon so wrong in *Agency of Fear?*"

## DAY TWO

Jimmy did not provide the bungalows with cooking facilities because he wanted all his guests, even former presidents, to take all their meals at La Loma. Breakfast was served under a giant palapa. The palapa concept, first made popular by the British socialite Gloria Guinness in Acapulco, was meant to create an open-sided outdoor living room. Even grand houses in Mexico usually have only one palapa, but Jimmy ordered his architect, Robert Couturier, to build three: one for breakfast, one for lunch, and one for dinner. The breakfast palapa, a 40-foot cone made of sisal and palm fronds, was supported by four petrified tree trunks and overlooked a tropical lagoon that had slithering crocodiles, white egrets, and pink flamingos.

The round table under the sisal cone could seat 12 people. In its center was a built-in lazy Susan with serving plates full of chunks of pineapple, oranges, berries, melons, and local fruits. Servants behind each chair provided whatever else anyone ordered. There were also a dozen copies of the *New York Times* and the *Wall Street Journal*, which a courier traveled seven hours on a bus to obtain every day.

When I arrived at 9:00 a.m., Nixon, Simon, and Jimmy were already there. They were all casually dressed in polo shirts and slacks. Jethro, Jimmy's three-year-old son, was seated on his father's lap, demonstrating to Nixon the toy camera he had gotten for Christmas. Two of the missing guests, Rebozo and Abplanalp, had sent word that they were recovering from last night's slippery trip to their villas. And Mike Endicott had gone off to check the security of the property.

I sat next to Simon and listened to Nixon's take on the coming 1992 election. He was pessimistic about the prospects of the Republicans. He said matter-of-factly that George Bush would lose his bid for a second term because "no Republican can carry California with the Cold War over." Simon, a staunch conservative, disagreed. He said the Democrats were better than Republicans at partisan politics but insisted Bush could win if the economy improved. "That could change the equation, Bill," Nixon replied. "But as far as I can see, Bush has run out of options on the economy." (As it turned out, Nixon proved correct and Bush lost.)

"What about Pat Buchanan?" I asked. Buchanan was challenging Bush for the nomination. "The polls show him ahead in New Hampshire."

"He may get 40 percent of the vote in New Hampshire," Nixon answered, "but it doesn't matter. Pat is an isolationist—and a pretty nasty one at that—and no isolationist will get the Republican nomination again, ever."

Jimmy, who had given a dinner for Buchanan in Paris, was taken aback. "Pat sees the dangers of globalism. That is not necessarily a bad thing."

"That may be so, Jimmy," Nixon answered politely without giving an inch. "But let's face it. The real danger is believing that America can dodge its role in the world. There is no exit for us. The Soviet Union is over and, whether we like it or not, we are now everyone's 911 call."

What struck me about Nixon was that he left himself out of his analysis. Even though he had won the vice presidency and presidency twice, winning more electoral votes than any other Republican in history, and even though Bush and Buchanan had both served under him, he analyzed the situation as if he was a detached observer. Unlike other politicians I knew, Nixon did not draw on personal anecdotes or inside information. He chose not to use such rhetorical trump cards as "Mao confided in me" or "I learned from my daily CIA briefing" to make his point. He spoke as if he were an outsider relying only on icy-cold objectivity. I had not expected to find that sort of detachment in Nixon. Years earlier, when I was still at Harvard, I asked Moynihan why he had worked for Nixon at the height of the Watergate scandal in 1973. He answered, "He's not the man you see on TV."

At 11:30 a.m., we were still at breakfast. Jimmy, seeing the sun peeking through cloudy skies, suggested we take a walk on his beach.

The beach in front of the house stretched for about one mile, bounded on the south by the Cuixmala River and on the north by jagged rocks that protruded into the ocean. Although the white dunes extended to the ocean, its beach fell off so precipitously that the powerful undertow made it too dangerous to go swimming. After Jimmy bought the property for $800,000 in 1987, he planned to invest another $2 million in dumping thousands of tons of boulders in the sea to make his beach swimmable. But he discovered another problem. Sharks were so abundant along with his property that one couldn't walk along the beach without seeing the fins of these predators.

Unable to discourage the sharks, Jimmy bought an enclosed beach about an hour away by jeep and surrounded it with shark nets. The El Niño rains, however, washed away the access to that beach just before Nixon arrived. Since we could not swim, Jimmy suggested a leisurely walk along the beach to view the turtles, which he saved from birds and kept in pens.

As we walked, Jimmy told Nixon his theory about Robert Maxwell, the British media mogul who had vanished from his boat during a pension fund scandal three months earlier. Jimmy's lawyer, Sam Pisar, who had been on the phone with Maxwell just hours before he died, had piqued Jimmy's interest in the case. Jimmy said that he put the odds at 90 percent suicide and 10 percent murder.

"How could he be murdered on his own boat?" I asked.

"You have a good novel there, Ed," Nixon replied.

As we walked, Jimmy pointed out a guardhouse overlooking the beach. He had gifted it, and the barracks behind it, to the Mexican army. It was not entirely an act of charity. Jimmy assumed that the 300 or so troops quartered there would provide another layer of protection. Such precautions were necessary since the area was rife with kidnappers, and Jimmy and his guests were likely targets.

Near the guardhouse were hundreds of baby turtles protected by wire netting. They would remain in these pens until it was determined it was safe for them to make their run for the sea. Nixon, who showed great interest in this project, asked how many turtles would survive if left on their own. Jimmy said without his protection only one in 100,000 turtles would survive the bird attacks.

"So you are not against social engineering," Nixon joked.

"It has its place." Jimmy laughed.

At this moment, Jimmy's car arrived, driven by Ignatius. Jimmy was driving back since the sun was too hot. Simon joined him in the car. Nixon, who was enjoying the beach, said he would walk back with Mike Endicott and me.

On the way back, Endicott brought up the JFK assassination, saying he had read my book *Legend: The Secret Life of Lee Harvey Oswald.*

Nixon said, "The Warren Commission said Oswald first planned to shoot me. Is that true, Ed?"

"That is what his Russian wife testified," I said, adding, "She did not always testify truthfully."

"Was Oswald the shooter?" Nixon asked.

"Yes," I answered. "The Warren Commission was right about that, but I do not think the Warren Commission precluded the possibility that someone encouraged him to do it."

"That is a question that may never be answered," Nixon said.

Endicott asked about Oliver Stone's film *JFK*, which had been released three weeks earlier. He said that during his years in the Secret Service he had ridden in dozens of presidential processions, and what impressed him about the film was the verisimilitude.

Nixon asked, "Should I see it?"

I answered that Stone was very skilled at creating the illusion of accuracy, but he had corrupted history in this film by mixing in fact-based scenes with ones that he invented.

Nixon asked, "Don't journalists also do that?"

Before I could answer, Nixon pointed to the fins of two sharks just a few yards away from the beach.

We assembled for a late lunch at the swimming pool under a smaller palapa. The main course was a huge prehistoric-looking fish. The Vietnamese chef sliced it with the precision of a pathologist performing a forensic autopsy. Nixon, who didn't seem to like the fish, asked Jimmy about the economy.

"It's gone, dead," Jimmy replied. "The deficit will soon exceed savings, the rise in the stock market is a joke."

Simon, who had made close to a billion dollars investing in private equities since leaving office, was more optimistic. He said, "My view is that we are just turning the corner." Nixon listened quietly, turning his head like a spectator at a tennis match, back and forth from Jimmy to Simon, as they argued about whether the economy was dead or alive. Nixon was not someone to verbally jaywalk.

It began to rain heavily before we finished the fish, trapping us in the palapa. The waiters were totally soaked by the time they served coffee, followed by a 50-year-old cognac.

The rain infuriated Jimmy. As if issuing an ultimatum to an unseen force, he said, "If El Niño doesn't stop, I am going to level this damn place and move to France. I don't want to die in a rainy jungle."

"Isn't the politically correct term a rainforest?" Simon joked.

To relieve the tension, Simon told a curious story, apropos of dying in a rainy jungle. The subject was the death of the reclusive billionaire Howard Hughes, one of Nixon's early backers. It occurred when Simon was secretary of the Treasury under President Gerald Ford in April 1976. He got a phone call from Adnan Khashoggi, the Saudi financier, who was his close friend.

"Khashoggi is my neighbor in Spain," Jimmy interrupted. "What did he have to do with Howard Hughes?"

"He told me it was a matter of national security that I take a call from Frank Morse." Morse, who was Hughes's as well as Khashoggi's lawyer, called him as soon as Khashoggi hung up. He told Simon that Hughes had been living under the alias John Conover in the penthouse of the Acapulco Princess Hotel. "That's just west of here, Jimmy?"

"About 300 miles," Jimmy answered.

"He said that Hughes was dead, although no one knew it yet," Simon continued. According to Simon, Hughes's body had to be smuggled back to Texas on a private plane or Mexico might make huge death tax claims against the Hughes Medical Institute. It was a matter of national security because the institute owned the Hughes Aerospace Corporation, one of America's largest defense contractors.

"You mean Mexico could hold a corpse for ransom?" Jimmy asked apprehensively.

"I decided it best not to find out," Simon said. He ordered the US Customs Service, which was part of his Treasury Department, to allow the private plane carrying Hughes's body to fly uninspected to Houston, so it could be claimed he died while flying over US territory. "I am not sure it was legal, but I acted."

Nixon said, "I'm glad you did that. He did me a couple of favors."

"You knew Hughes?" I asked Nixon.

Jimmy could see that I was about to ask Nixon more about the "favors" and stopped me, saying, "On that note, I am going to take my afternoon siesta." The servants, holding umbrellas, escorted us to the waiting cars.

Dinner was in the library since the rain had intensified. Abplanalp and Rebozo opted to have dinner in their bungalows because they didn't want to walk the drenched path. Jimmy accommodated them, having the servants deliver them their meal on trays.

At dinner, I worked up my courage and asked Nixon about his involvement in the Hiss case, which he had brought to prominence as a senator. I had met Alger Hiss in 1973 through his son Tony Hiss, who worked with me at the *New Yorker*. Alger and I had lunch together on two occasions, and I found he had an unusual perspective about the politics in the Roosevelt era, but I was not about to tell Nixon, who had helped put him in prison for perjury, about Hiss's insights. Instead, I only said I had interviewed him after he got out of prison.

"What about?" Nixon asked, his interest piqued.

"I was doing a book on spies." I asked him how he learned about Hiss's activities.

He said his source about Hiss was none other than J. Edgar Hoover. Hoover told him in the late 1940s the FBI had evidence that Hiss was only the tip of the iceberg. The iceberg was a plot by the Comintern (the Communist International) to take over US foreign policy in the mid-1930s. Hoover further said Undersecretary of State Adolph Berle had brought it to his attention when FDR was president, but the Democrats elected not to pursue the Hiss allegations.

"Did he tell you why?" I asked.

"Russia was our ally then, and FDR wanted to build the alliance."

"What about Hoover?" Jimmy asked. "Why didn't he open an investigation?"

"Hoover had a pretty good nose for which way the wind was blowing," Nixon replied. "He was more interested in preserving his power than catching spies."

"So you thought Hiss was a spy?" I was unable to suppress the doubts I had in the tone in my voice. Ever since I had heard Hannah Arendt discuss the Hiss case at Cornell, I did not believe Hiss ever wittingly spied for Russia.

"Hoover thought that. The only thing clear to me at that point was that Hiss was perjuring himself when he said he did not know Whittaker Chambers," Nixon said.

"What do you think now?" Jimmy asked.

"Now that the Cold War is over, I would like to see the Russian intelligence files on Hiss," Nixon replied.

"That might be possible," I said. I was attempting to get the Russian intelligence files from the 1920s on Armand Hammer for the book I was writing. I said had paid a research company, East View Publications, to get them. Supposedly, they had connections with archivists in Russia.

"How much?" asked Simon, who liked to know the going price of everything.

"$30,000."

"It will be worth it if it shows he worked for the KGB," Nixon said. "All I know about Hammer is that he did exactly what he said he was going to do." Nixon added that he considered delivering on one's promise a great virtue.

I had many more questions to ask him about Hammer, who I knew had supplied part of the cash for the Watergate cover-up. Nixon, however, had pushed himself up from the table and was getting ready to leave. Jimmy, locking arms with him, walked him to the waiting SUV.

## DAY THREE

The heavy rains resumed the next day. The telephone lines were again down. Even the TV satellite connection was not working. Unable to watch CNN, Jimmy said fatalistically, "We are completely cut off."

There were no indoor activities at Cuixmala and that morning Nixon did not show up for breakfast. As a diversion, I took Mike Endicott for a tour of the property in a jeep. Endicott, who had headed both Kissinger's and Nixon's Secret Service details, had learned to be a keen observer of any anomalies in behavior. He said, "The job of a Secret Service man is not to miss anything."

"The Secret Service missed a great deal in the JFK assassination, including the assassin," I said, steering the conversation back to a subject in which I still had a great interest.

Endicott said he had two friends in the detail that guarded JFK on November 22, both of whom believed the official version.

"What about Nixon? Does he believe the official version?" I asked.

"Nixon never believes official versions. You should ask him about the *Warren Report*."

Since Endicott was an amateur photographer, I stopped the jeep on the so-called African plain. Jimmy had stocked this part of the estate with wildlife he imported from Africa, including herds of zebra, eland, red deer, and oryx. Endicott left the jeep to photograph two baby zebras. We next set off to see the crocodiles in the lagoons.

I took this opportunity to ask him about Nixon's conspiracy theory about Howard Hughes. "Does Nixon believe the story about smuggling Howard Hughes's body out of Mexico to be true?"

"Yes," Endicott answered. "So do I. I was operations supervisor for Vice President Nelson Rockefeller's security and heard that Hughes's body was being brought to Texas."

"What about the favors that Nixon spoke of?"

"Yesterday was the first time I heard Nixon mention them. All I can say is Nixon knew Howard Hughes."

After the tour, Endicott and I returned to La Loma, where everyone had by now gathered. The rain had turned to a drizzle, allowing us to dine in the large palapa overlooking the sea.

To cheer everyone up, Jimmy served a very expensive bottle of Petrus. Nixon carefully savored it and then said to Abplanalp, "We should have a wine like this on Walker's Cay, Bob."

Toward the end of dinner, Jimmy asked Nixon about leadership. "Who would be on top of your list?"

"Jack Kennedy," Nixon said. "Whatever you thought of his politics, he was a natural leader. He knew how to use rhetoric in private as well as public."

I asked Nixon why he thought rhetoric was important in politics.

"As I recall, some Greek philosophers defined rhetoric as the ability to see the available words for persuading people. Isn't that what politics is all about?"

I nodded, realizing that the philosopher he was paraphrasing was none other than Aristotle. I wondered whether he had read Aristotle's book on rhetoric, but I didn't get a chance to ask. He politely excused himself and left.

## DAY FOUR

A walkie-talkie system linked up all the houses, cars, guards, and plane pilots at Cuixmala. It suddenly began crackling at 11:00 the next morning. I could hear frantic orders to the pilots, who were quartered in small houses on the estate. A moment later, I received a message to take a bathing suit and go to the landing strip.

Nixon and his party were already there. Jimmy, out for his morning ride, rode up on horseback just as the twin-engine Otter was touching down. He said that since it was not raining at Las Alamandas, we were going there for a swim. Isabel Goldsmith, Jimmy's 38-year-old daughter, had inherited Las Alamandas from Don Antenor Patino, her Bolivian grandfather. The immense property was about 50 miles from Cuixmala and had exquisite white sand beaches and less dangerous currents. She had built five cottages, which she rented out to such Hollywood stars as Robert De

Niro, Penny Marshall, Robin Williams, and Christopher Walken, all of whom had been there as paying guests the previous Christmas. Since the actors insisted on indoor exercise machines, Isabel furnished an entire bungalow with treadmills for them.

The flight there took only 15 minutes. There were a few goats on the edge of the airstrip. Nixon asked Jimmy jokingly whether they were scapegoats.

Isabel met us there wearing a white blouse, blue skirt, and a flower in her flowing black hair. To my surprise, Nixon took an instant liking to her. She linked her arm with his and walked him to the waiting vans, which took us to the beach, where her servants offered strawberry daiquiris.

While the others were drinking, Nixon strode into the surf in his black bathing suit. I caught up with him as he bucked the waves. Finally, I was alone with him. Taking Endicott's advice, I asked him how the past 20 years had changed his view of Watergate.

He answered my question with his own: "Have you read Ehrlichman's novel?"

John Ehrlichman had been Nixon's chief White House advisor. After the Watergate scandal, he had written a novel, *The Company*, in which the top executives in the CIA feared Nixon would acquire a secret report describing illicit CIA activities involving Cuba. To prevent this, they both instigated and manipulated the Watergate break-in to bring down Nixon. I told Nixon I had read the novel with great interest and asked, "Was it all fiction?"

"Who knows," Nixon answered, his deep voice resounding above the crashing waves. "Ehrlichman did have some interesting material to work with. The guys who led the Cubans into the Watergate, Hunt and McCord, both worked for the CIA. McCord also inexplicably left the tape on the door, which gave them away to the police."

"And a CIA front provided the early stories to the *Washington Post*," I said to further the Ehrlichman theory.

"Ehrlichman thought it could all be a setup—or, at least, that it would make a good read," Nixon said.

"A CIA setup?"

"Ehrlichman believed the CIA had an active agent among the burglars."

Was Ehrlichman referring to either John McCord or Howard Hunt? I asked.

"No, Ehrlichman said it was one of the Cubans," Nixon answered. "He said the CIA briefed him, but it refused to provide his file because it would compromise their agent. Ehrlichman spun his theory from this."

I assumed that he was telling me these details because he gave credence to at least part of Ehrlichman's theory. "Do you have a theory about this?"

"I am still working on it," he said, stepping away into another wave. On the beach, a ringing bell signaled that lunch was ready.

The table on the terrace was strewn with bouquets of red bougainvillea to match the floral sarong that Isabel had changed into. She placed herself between Nixon, on her right, and her father on her left. She had a copy of Nixon's book, *Seize the Moment*, which he autographed for her. Referring to a passage in the book, she asked, "Was Gorbachev sincere in wanting to reform Russia?"

"I think he was sincere," Nixon answered. "But, if your goal is wrong, sincerity is not a virtue. Gorbachev's goal was saving Socialism."

When Jimmy asked him a question about the failure of Communism, he prefaced his answer by saying, "As Isabel correctly pointed out ... " After lunch, Isabel took him for a walk on the beach. Jimmy, looking perplexed, said to me, "I had understood that women made him uncomfortable."

"Apparently not," I answered.

When we returned to Cuixmala that afternoon, Jimmy had a private meeting in his office with Nixon and Abplanalp, who was the president of the Nixon Library, to discuss his contribution. Abplanalp wanted Jimmy to commit himself to an initial donation.

As the El Niño had finally abated, I offered the other guests, Rebozo and Simon, a tour of the lagoons in one of the electric-powered boats designed for that purpose. I was by now a veteran of taking Jimmy's guests on this sunset reconnaissance for crocodiles, having guided Henry Kissinger, Rupert Murdoch, Robert De Niro, Ivana Lowell, and Alfred Taubman on previous lagoon trips. The boatman also knew the crocodile haunts by heart. Because of the recent rains, no crocodiles were visible. There was, however, an abundance of pink flamingos and other wading birds, which took off with great whooshes of air as the boat approached them.

It was the first real chance I had to speak with Rebozo, who was Nixon's oldest friend. He told me he had personally spent $700,000 defending himself in government investigations stemming from his friendship with Nixon, "but I've never regretted a penny of it." The investigation had cost Nixon $3 million and wiped out his savings. Simon added that, unlike other presidents, Nixon had turned down million-dollar speaking fees from foreign countries, preferring to support himself with the books he writes.

Dinner that night was on the beach. Jimmy had giant silk pillows, which he had brought back from India on a chartered DC-10, strewn on the sand next to 10-foot-high blazing bonfires. To add to the festive atmosphere, a Mexican band of seven troubadours played music while dozens of servants in pink uniforms delivered drinks. The buffet table, as usual, was manned by the three chefs.

Nixon did his best to look comfortable, squirming on his pasha-sized pillow while cutting his lamb chops. Simon, unable to balance himself, sat cross-legged like an Indian yogi. Rebozo, Abplanalp, and Endicott sat on a single pillow. I, concerned about my back, preferred standing. Jimmy, much more at ease, reclined in front of us like a true pasha. He asked about the expulsion of Iraq from Kuwait.

"Did Bush succeed?"

"It was a failure," Simon answered. "We didn't get rid of Saddam."

Jimmy had become obsessed with this subject. "We should have gone for the jugular. Saddam will come back to haunt us."

Nixon was more circumspect. "Bush gets credit for masterfully orchestrating the alliance against Iraq, and for not getting us in a quagmire. Maybe he should have gone further, but, as I understand it, our allies, the Saudis, said no. The Saudis may have a good reason for not wanting to break up Iraq. But that may not have been good reasons for us. I really don't know."

I was impressed that Nixon, after analyzing a complex strategic decision, could say, "I don't know."

The beach party ended with seven troubadours serenading seven men who only wanted to discuss politics. We were back in our bungalows by 10:00 p.m.

## DAY FIVE

Early the next morning someone was screaming "Help." I looked for the source. The six guest villas were connected by a vine-shrouded circular path. Following the shouts, I found Abplanalp seated on the ground in a thicket of bougainvillea. He said he was lost. He had been wandering for an hour in Jimmy's man-made rainforest unable to find the main house or his own bungalow. Helping him to his feet, I led him back to the path. As we walked, I asked how he had met Nixon.

Abplanalp told me that he had been a Swiss American engineer with no interest in politics most of his life. He made a fortune designing the shaving cream valve, which he had done in a workshop in his garage in Yonkers in the 1950s. It allowed a small can to release a burst of shaving foam and gas. Gillette and other major companies paid him licensing fees from every can. Through their mutual passion for sportfishing, he then became friends with Rebozo, who arranged for them to buy Walker's Cay, a tiny island off the Florida coast. Rebozo invited Nixon there, which was how Abplanalp met him. He also contributed to Nixon's 1972 reelection campaign. Then came Watergate in 1973, and he found himself under investigation as an associate of Nixon. He told me how Terry Lenzner, the chief investigator of the Senate Committee on Watergate, interrogated him for six hours. During the long intervals between the sessions, he became proficient at completing that day's *New York Times* crossword puzzle.

"There was nothing I could tell him other than about the blue marlin we caught."

When we finally arrived at the palapa at La Loma, the servants instantly brought out breakfast.

Nixon arrived 10 minutes later. He was dressed in a dark blue suit and preparing for the flight back to New York. I realized this could be my last opportunity to ask him about his China initiative. As we left breakfast, I caught up with Nixon in the library. He had paused to look at the shelf of books on politics. Seeing that Jimmy had removed my *Agency of Fear* from it, I breathed a sigh of relief.

With China, Nixon acted contrary to what had been the established policy in the State Department, Pentagon, and CIA since 1948, reestablishing diplomatic relations. He had not only succeeded in defying the prevailing wisdom about China, but he broke ranks with his conservative colleagues. In doing so, he radically changed both the politics and economics of the world. I asked him how he could accomplish this feat.

"The key was secrecy," he answered, not looking away from the bookshelf. He elaborated, as we walked to the front door, that, with the help of Henry Kissinger, his national security advisor, he bypassed the State Department and kept the entire enterprise secret from most government officials.

"Even Richard Helms at the CIA?" I asked.

"Especially Helms," he replied.

I asked why previous presidents had failed to open the door to China.

"They couldn't keep a secret," he said with a quick smile. He obviously did not believe in the merits of transparency.

We reached the front steps and saw that the servants were lined up to wave goodbye. After Nixon spent almost 10 minutes posing for photos with the servants, we got into the waiting SUVs and jeeps and proceeded to the airstrip. Jimmy, Jethro, and I escorted Nixon to the plane. Rebozo, Simon, Abplanalp, and Endicott followed. The twin-engine Otter taxied down the runway between the coconut trees as Nixon waved to us from the window. The Otter would take them to the international airport at Puerto Vallarta, where they would transfer to Jimmy's waiting Gulfstream and fly back to New York.

After they left, Jimmy told me about his private discussion with Abplanalp. Abplanalp told him the Nixon Library was costing him personally $20,000 per month, and unless Jimmy was willing to help with a like amount, Nixon would have to turn the library over to the government.

"Will you give them the money?" I asked.

"That remains to be seen," he answered, which I knew was his polite way of saying no.

So ended my Nixon vacation.

# CHAPTER TWENTY-NINE

# DONALD TRUMP AND THE TOKYO WHALE

In November 1991, Jimmy asked me to an impromptu lunch in the Grill Room of the Four Seasons. It was an unusual invitation since Jimmy usually had his lunch at home. He said he had also invited an "amusing character," identifying him only as the person who had bought Khashoggi's 282-foot yacht *Nabila* and changed its name to *Trump Princess*. "He likes naming things after himself," Jimmy said.

I knew he was talking about Donald Trump, who recently was in the news for the lavish opening of the Trump Taj Mahal, a casino he built on the Atlantic City boardwalk at a cost of over a billion dollars.

Jimmy and I both arrived 15 minutes early, as was our custom, and Julian, the maître d', ushered us to a table at the back of the Grill Room. While we waited, Jimmy said Trump was in serious financial trouble—he had financed the Taj with $675 million of junk bonds on which he had to make annual interest payments of more than $90 million. Jimmy himself owned casinos, including part of Aspinall's in London and the Diamond Beach Casino in Darwin, Australia. He was puzzled by Trump's massive investment in the Taj, saying, "There is no way that casino can earn that much money."

"Does he want you to bail him out?" I asked.

"I am retired," Jimmy said with a playful smile. "Let's order." Jimmy made it a policy not to wait for time-challenged guests. He called the waiter over and ordered four gravlax salmon for us and Trump when he arrived.

Donald Trump, a tall man with a beaming smile, strode into the Grill Room 10 minutes later. He seemed to know half the people in the room, stopping by tables and shaking hands like a movie star. When he finally arrived at our table, he seemed surprised that Jimmy had ordered an appetizer for him but happily ate it.

After some initial chatter, Trump asked Jimmy if he was in contact with Akio Kashiwagi.

Jimmy said with a shrug, "I don't know him."

Trump was taken aback. "You know, he's called the 'Japanese Whale.' He is a Yakuza."

I had heard the name before from Frank Osborne, a half-brother of John Aspinall. Frank, who I got to know on a trip to Mongolia, managed the Darwin casino for Aspinall and Jimmy. He described Kashiwagi as a Yakuza gangster covered in tattoos. According to Osborne, Kashiwagi had won $20 million at baccarat at Jimmy's casino in Darwin in 1990, a loss that nearly broke the bank. Jimmy had to personally fund the loss, which made him furious. He forbade Osborne from ever admitting him or any other Yakuza into the casino. So, despite what Jimmy told Trump, he certainly knew about the Japanese Whale, even if he didn't know him personally. I suspected that Trump also knew the Darwin story since, rather than accepting Jimmy's firm denials, he politely ignored them.

After Jimmy tried to change the subject from the Yakuza to American politics, Trump returned to it. He was nothing if not persistent. He described in a voice that alternated between sadness and fury how the "Tokyo Whale" had taken advantage of him. He said, as if it was an altruistic act, that he had provided

Kashiwagi with a complementary penthouse suite at the Trump Plaza in Atlantic City, free lavish meals, and a private table to play baccarat. He further accommodated him by waiving the house limit of $250,000 a hand. Despite Trump's generosity, Kashiwagi won hand after hand and then abruptly left the table and cashed in his chips. "The Tokyo Whale flew back to Japan with $6 million of my money," Trump griped.

Jimmy, busy eating the remaining gravlax on the table, gave Trump a sympathetic what-can-I-do shrug.

Trump said he had a "favor" to ask. He wanted Jimmy to talk to the Tokyo Whale and persuade him to play again at his casino.

Jimmy again pretended total ignorance of the Yakuza. "The only whale I am familiar with is the one in my movie *When the Whales Came*," Jimmy joked. He was referring to the 1989 film that he had financed, a film based on a children's book about whales that, aside from a trained narwhal, starred Helen Mirren, Paul Scofield, and David Suchet.

Trump, missing Jimmy's pun, thought that Jimmy had misunderstood him. "I am talking Kashiwagi, the guy called the Tokyo Whale."

"I never laid eyes on Kashiwagi," Jimmy replied dismissively.

Trump looked so baffled by Jimmy's feigned ignorance that I tried to ease the tension, reminiscing about the time I had spent in Tokyo with Jimmy in May. I described at length a weird dinner at an unbelievably expensive geisha house in which the geishas fed us noodles with chopsticks, taught us a game that involved holding cards on our heads, and serenaded us with traditional Japanese instruments.

Trump laughed. "I bet they didn't speak English either." He seemed to know Tokyo, saying he had spent part of February there promoting a boxing match with Mike Tyson.

At that point, Marla Maples, Trump's 27-year-old girlfriend and future wife, joined us for dessert. She wore No Excuses jeans, which was her fashion line, and radiated goodwill. Jimmy was so taken with her that he invited the two of them to Mexico.

Trump was, however, not finished with the Tokyo Whale. With an obsessive persistence that matched Captain Ahab's in *Moby-Dick*, he returned yet again to the subject of the Tokyo Whale. "If you run into Kashiwagi," he said in parting, "I'd consider it a great favor if you speak to him about coming back to my casino."

"Let me think about it," Jimmy answered. Once again, Jimmy used his polite turndown.

After Trump and Marla left, Jimmy ordered another double espresso and, shaking his head in disbelief, said, "What kind of idiot would want to get a Yakuza gambler back in his casino?"

"Maybe he doesn't like the idea of losing," I said.

"Kashiwagi would have cleaned him out again."

"I assume he can afford it."

As we got up, Jimmy said, "You know you were the second-richest person at the table today."

"But I don't have any money."

"Neither do they."

Despite Trump's continued efforts with Jimmy, Kashiwagi never returned to his casino. In January 1992, he was found dead in his palatial home near Mount Fuji. He had been stabbed over a hundred times with a samurai sword. Since the murderer was never found, police assumed it was the work of his Yakuza associates.

As Jimmy had foreseen, Trump's casinos went bankrupt. What he had not foreseen was that Donald J. Trump would be sworn in as the 45th president of the United States on January 20, 2017.

# CHAPTER THIRTY

# KISSINGER

Although I had attended a seminar given by Henry Kissinger at Harvard in the mid-1960s, I didn't get to know him, or even to talk to him privately, until May 1978. The occasion was a small dinner party in Georgetown. The host was Richard Helms, the former CIA director, and his wife, Cynthia. Henry and Nancy Kissinger were the guests of honor that night. The other guests were Joe Alsop, the columnist and art collector; his wife, Susan Mary, an author and hostess whose well-attended dinner parties earned her the nickname "the grand dame of Washington society"; and the journalist Arnaud de Borchgrave.

I found Kissinger even more impressive in person than in his classroom lectures. With his deep voice, wry humor, and powerful intellect, he made an unforgettable impression on me. To be sure, Alsop, who I had not met before, was a fascinating raconteur, who described the history of art collecting with much passion, and de Borchgrave, who had just returned from a meeting with the shah of Iran, was a fountain of insider's gossip, but no one at the table even came close to Henry Kissinger in spellbinding insights into past and present events. When he spoke, everyone at the table stopped their conversation to listen. And for good reason. Kissinger had served two successive presidents, Nixon and Ford, as both national security advisor and secretary of state. After dinner, over cigars and brandy, the conversation was mainly about the mistreatment of the shah by the Carter administration. Helms, who had been ambassador to Iran only a year earlier and had been a close friend of the deposed shah, had a great deal to say on that subject. In his view, we had betrayed the shah by failing to act as an ally. As dinners often do in Washington, the evening ended promptly at 10:00, with the guests rushing out.

Since I did not find the opportunity at dinner to ask Kissinger about an idea I had for writing a book about the vulnerability of US intelligence, I wrote him a brief note the next day asking if I could come to his office to discuss this idea. Instead, Kissinger and his wife Nancy invited me to dinner at their cottage on the Rockefeller estate in Pocantico Hills, New York.

It was about a 90-minute drive from New York City through the Hudson Valley to the magnificently landscaped estate belonging to the Rockefeller family. John D. Rockefeller had originally acquired it at a time when he was the richest man in the world. It took 15 minutes more to find the cottage, which Rockefeller's grandson, Nelson, allowed Kissinger to use. Kissinger had not only worked for Nelson since the 1950s, but he had been secretary of state when Nelson served as vice president. Kissinger had also transferred all his files from the State Department and White House here. Even though my driver stopped midway to take photographs of some of the works of art on the property, I arrived nearly half an hour early.

Kissinger was on the porch with a playful golden Labrador—the first of many I would meet with him. He told me he had been working on a book about his White House years. He had read my recently published book, *Legend: The Secret Life of Lee Harvey Oswald*, and my interviews with Angleton intrigued him.

"I never met him myself," he said, "but I heard about his theories when I was in the White House."

At that point, his wife, Nancy, arrived on the porch. She was a strikingly tall, thin, and elegantly dressed woman. She had met Kissinger when she was a political analyst on the staff of Nelson Rockefeller. The other guests, who arrived promptly on time, included William Buckley, the founder of the *National Review* and host of the weekly PBS TV show *Firing Line*; Pat Buckley, his statuesque Canadian-born wife; William D. Rogers, who had served as the undersecretary of state for economic affairs under Kissinger and who was helping Kissinger organize a consulting company to be called Kissinger Associates; and Suki Rogers, William's wife.

At dinner, I asked Buckley about his 1976 spy novel, *Saving the Queen*. How closely had he based its CIA hero, Blackford Oakes, on his own experiences in the CIA? Both Oakes and Buckley were in the CIA in 1952.

"I think of Oakes as my Cold War avatar," he replied. "Unlike le Carré's spies, Oakes has no moral ambiguity about what he is doing."

"But moles must have some ambiguity," Kissinger said in his deep bass voice. "After all, they officially work for one country and steal secrets for another."

"Not mine," Buckley answered.

I brought up Frances Gary Powers, the CIA's U-2 pilot who was shot down in Russia in 1960, put on trial in Moscow, convicted, and then traded by the Russians for an American spy. Since U-2 pilots were given a cyanide suicide pill, there were many people who believed he should have killed himself so he could not divulge secrets.

Buckley was one of them: "He lacked moral fortitude. He was a coward."

"I interviewed Powers shortly before his death," I said.

"I hope you refused to shake his hand," Buckley said. "Why would you want to see him?"

"For my Oswald book." I told him I would have had no

compunctions about shaking Powers's hand because I considered him a victim of the failure of US counterintelligence, which, by not heeding reports of Russian advances in ground-to-air missiles, allowed him to fly into a trap. After all, Oswald, after defecting to Russia in 1959, claimed he had traveled from Minsk to Moscow for the express purpose of attending Powers's trial. One possible reason Russia would allow him to attend it was that Oswald had worked at a U-2 base in Japan before defecting to Russia. I said, "I needed to ascertain if the Russians had brought Oswald to the trial to rattle Powers."

"Did they?" Pat Buckley asked.

"Powers said he did not see him there," I replied, "but he gathered from his interrogation that Russia had a great deal of knowledge about the U-2 flights from some source."

"That detail hardly excuses his cowardice," Buckley said.

"But it suggests that the CIA is also at fault," I answered. "Or badly erred in underestimating Russia's intelligence as well as ground-to-air missile capabilities."

Buckley arched one eyebrow as if I was on *Firing Line*. "Why would the CIA err in such a disastrous way?"

"Perhaps they were misled," I said, attempting to introduce the concept of Russian deception.

Kissinger said, with a smile, "Is that a subject that interests you?"

"What sort of deception?" Buckley asked.

"Not extramarital deception," I joked. "I'm interested in how state actors use deception to undermine intelligence."

Kissinger said nothing further on the subject and I had no answer to my question on deception when the dinner ended.

I did not hear from Kissinger for over a year. Then, in March 1980, I had a call from Kissinger's secretary.

"Are you free for lunch with Dr. Kissinger at 1:00 p.m. next Wednesday at the 21 Club?"

Of course, I accepted the invitation.

I arrived early at the 21 Club, a former Prohibition-era speakeasy occupying two floors in a brownstone sandwiched between skyscrapers on West Fifty-Second Street. Above the entranceway were dozens of statues of jockeys in their stable's racing colors. Its restaurant also served as a prized venue for power lunches. Its regulars, who all received silk scarves stamped "21" at Christmas, included Roy Cohn, Donald Trump, and Rupert Murdoch.

I was shown to a banquette in the Bar Room, whose ceiling was adorned with model cars and other antique toys. Kissinger arrived on time. We sat in a leather booth.

After we ordered, he asked me whether Angleton had ever mentioned to me a spy code-named Colonel Bor.

I replied that Angleton's operations chief, Scotty Miler, had first mentioned the name in the early 1960s. He said that in the early 1950s a Polish defector named Michael Goleniewski had said Colonel Bor was a KGB mole.

"Who is this Goleniewski?"

I not only knew who he was, but I had interviewed him a few months earlier for an article on spies I was writing for the *New York Times Magazine*, published just a month or so earlier under the title "Spy Wars." I wondered if Kissinger had invited me to lunch because he read that article. I told him Goleniewski was a defector who had been deputy chief of Polish military intelligence. He provided the CIA with documents that helped the CIA identify several Russian spies, most notably British intelligence officer George Blake. Another spy he revealed, code-named Colonel Bor, was never identified.

"The reason I am asking is that some nuts are trying to associate Bor with me. Why would he say that?"

I was well versed in this torturous and sad case. Goleniewski told me that he had been put under relentless pressure to name additional people. According to him, CIA officers had attempted to jostle his memory by giving him hallucinogenic drugs. He recalled his CIA case officer taking him to a dentist repeatedly when he had no dental problems. Each time, the dentist injected him with something, and afterward he had hallucinations. It was at this time he said the KGB had recruited a source that worked as a civilian employee for the army with the cryptonym "Bor." Since Kissinger had been a civilian worker for the army in 1946, his name might have come up when Goleniewski was drugged. "Angleton's staff might have given him names of civilian workers and asked him which was Colonel Bor," I said.

"Tens of thousands of civilians were employed by the army," Kissinger said.

I said, "The story gets more bizarre."

In 1964, Goleniewski informed his case officer, Howard Roman (whom I also interviewed for the article), that his real name was not Goleniewski. That surname was just an alias he adopted after fleeing Russia. His real surname was Romanov; he was the Grand Duke Alexei Romanov, the son and heir to Nicholas II, the last czar of Russia. In return for naming moles, he asked the CIA to help him reclaim the czar's overseas fortune. The CIA, concluding he had gone mad, put him "on ice," as his case officer put it.

"So the Bor story comes from a lunatic who thinks he is czar. Did Angleton actually believe it?" Kissinger asked incredulously.

"I doubt it." I explained that Angleton ran his Counterintelligence Staff like a Hollywood studio executive runs brainstorming sessions. His subordinates would pluck out of old files possible clues, which Angleton called "the serials," and pitch possible scenarios, most of which would go no further. I assumed the Colonel Bor story was one of them.

• • •

In the mid-1980s, my friendship with Kissinger deepened when Jimmy Goldsmith, who was mesmerized by Kissinger's view of the world and the keen political insights of his wife Nancy, invited them to his estate in Mexico every February. On each visit, Jimmy also invited me, and it was during these weeks that I further came to appreciate the Kissingers.

At Cuixmala, Kissinger made no pretense of being a nature-lover or having any desire to explore the rainforests and lagoons on the estate. Nor was he interested in riding even a tame horse. When Jimmy proposed we go on a horseback ride on a trail through the surrounding jungle to the ecological station, Kissinger replied, in his German accent, "Thanks, but I don't ride anything that doesn't have brakes."

"We could go on foot," Jimmy continued.

"Unfortunately, I am allergic to mosquitoes," Kissinger answered, and returned to the subject of Russia.

The only time Kissinger visited the lagoons was in February 1993. I brought as my guest Ivana Lowell, the founding editor of Miramax Books, who Kissinger got along with. When I said I was taking Ivana for a sunset boat ride in the lagoons, to my surprise, he decided to come with us. So did Jimmy, who took great pride in spotting large crocodiles. We all got into one of his fleet of electric lagoon boats. It glided silently for about 10 minutes, and then Jimmy pointed to a dark-gray crocodile patiently waiting for prey.

"Looks like a log," Kissinger said and changed the subject back to geopolitics. He feared that President Bill Clinton, who had been sworn in only three weeks earlier, would not continue President George Bush's policies in the Middle East.

Jimmy said he was not a fan of Bush's policy. "We should have invaded Iraq from Kuwait in 1991. We should have removed Saddam Hussein," Jimmy said, speaking loudly enough to cause a siege of herons to fly out of a tree. "When you go after a dictator, you go for the jugular."

Kissinger was too diplomatic to directly disagree with his host. I knew that one of Kissinger's closest associates, Brent Scowcroft, was involved in the decision not to take the war into Iraq. He avoided a conflict with a generalization: "Geopolitical considerations can outweigh removing a dictator."

"Such as?" Jimmy asked.

"Bush may have given too much weight to Saudis' interests."

Ivana whispered in my ear, "If Kissinger doesn't stop talking geopolitics, I am jumping overboard."

Thankfully, Ivana was not driven to such desperate measures. She was spared further of Kissinger's political talks, though I spent many more years in his company. Back in New York, I saw a great deal of Henry and Nancy Kissinger. The Kissingers deeply appreciated dogs, especially their own Golden Labradors, and they often invited me to the table they took at the annual gala held at Cipriani 42nd Street in New York to benefit the Animal Medical Center. I also regularly attended their Christmas and birthday parties. These gatherings included friends at the highest reaches of the political and financial establishment. They usually took place at the Kissinger home on East Fifty-Second Street in Manhattan or the nearby River Club. Unfortunately, the COVID-19 pandemic interrupted these gatherings, as well as most other social activity, and when it forced the cancellation of his birthday party that was to be held on May 23, 2022, he wrote me with his usual consideration:

Dear Ed,

After considering New York's Covid statistics and the Covid experience of too many acquaintances, I have asked Marie-Josée [Kravis] and Eric [Schmidt] to postpone the party they had sensitively prepared to celebrate my upcoming 99th birthday. It would have been a great joy and nostalgic to spend the evening with a group so thoughtfully selected by Nancy from all phases of my life and so central to giving it meaning. Thank you for your warm response and for your friendship. Onward to the 100th.

In this kind note, Kissinger demonstrated, as he had done so many times in his incredible statecraft, that even in the darkest of times, he could see a path to the future.

# CHAPTER THIRTY-ONE

# THE LAST DAYS
# OF JIMMY GOLDSMITH

In November 1994, Jimmy plunged deeply into European politics by creating the Referendum Party. It had only one issue: Requiring Britain to hold a Yes or No referendum on its proposed membership in the European Union.

When I had previously accompanied Jimmy on parts of his successful campaign to be elected a member of the European Parliament, I became uneasy about some of his supporters. In Munich, for example, we were met at the airport by men in black leather coats and blond children carrying bouquets of white roses, all of which reminded me of a bad Nazi movie. In France, he had been supported by right-wing elements that wanted to separate Burgundy from the rest of France. This time his new party, which fielded no fewer than 547 candidates for the 1997 British general election held on May 1, did not win a single seat. It ended his hopes for blocking Britain's entry into the EU but adumbrated, a quarter century later, Brexit.

In late May 1997 came another and more damaging moment of truth. He received a diagnosis of inoperable pancreatic cancer.

When I called him in June to discuss the election, he was busy seeking an experimental treatment and suggested I visit him at his

Montjeu castle in Burgundy. He said he would call as soon as he had got "matters under control."

That call came on July 11.

When I asked about his health, he answered, "It's not a disease I would recommend."

I then asked if I could visit him.

"If you'd like to come to lunch today, my driver will meet you at the station."

It was only an hour on the TGV train from Paris, where I was staying, to Burgundy. A car was waiting. During the half-hour ride to the castle, I made a mental list of the many islands and countries I had visited with him in the past 12 years. I reckoned that I had traveled over 600,000 miles on Jimmy's private planes, a yacht, and cars. I had last stayed at Montjeu for a week in June 1989, when he was planning to stage his largest takeover, the $21 billion acquisition of B.A.T. Industries, which through its British-American tobacco unit was the world's largest cigarette producer. To finance this monumental venture, he had teamed up with Jacob Rothschild and Kerry Packer. Like Rothschild, Packer was a longtime friend and frequent guest at Jimmy's estate in Mexico. Born in 1937 in Sidney, Australia, he was the son of Sir Frank Packer, an Australian media mogul who controlled Australian Consolidated Press as well as the Nine Network. Kerry Packer had a disproportionately large head and toothy smile that reminded me of the head of a crocodile. He was a ruthless and successful businessman who was partners with Jimmy in a gambling casino in Darwin, Australia. He was very guarded about speaking about the deal in my company, as was Jimmy. He told me he was working on the biggest deal of his life and that Packer and Rothschild were his partners, but, since he was concerned (rightly), that I could not keep a secret, he did not tell me his target. Instead, he used a code word when discussing it with them on the phone. But, during these cryptic communications, Gianni Agnelli landed in a helicopter on the lawn. Casually dressed in a rumpled Caraceni jacket, open sport shirt, and unlaced suede shoes, he greeted us with a blinding smile. If charisma could be defined by a single person, he would be that individual. Less visible was his immense power. His companies, including Fiat, accounted for over four percent of Italy's entire economy. After a brief tour of the property, Agnelli and Jimmy closeted themselves in Jimmy's office for over an hour before lunch on the terrace. Looking at the Daytona Rolex he wore on the outside of his sleeve as if he was timing a race car, Agnelli said it was time for his departure. The rotor blades were already whirling when we reached the helicopter. Ducking his head, he ran under them to the stairway and, in his parting words, let the cat out of the proverbial bag, shouting to Jimmy, "As soon as I get back to Torino, I'll have my people see if Farmers works." A moment later, Agnelli was gone.

Clearly, Agnelli wasn't referring to farmers at work. I recalled that Farmers, the giant US insurer, had recently been acquired by B.A.T. as protection against a takeover. Then the pieces fell into place. Jimmy's big deal, which Agnelli had flown here to discuss, was taking over B.A.T. I asked, "Is Agnelli involved in the deal?"

Jimmy's face grew as red as an ostrich's, which I knew from past blunders I made meant I had asked the wrong question. He stared daggers at me for a long moment, then said, "You need to forget ever seeing Agnelli here, forget ever hearing the word 'Farmers,' and not mention a word about it to a living soul."

"It's already forgotten," I said, trying to calm him down.

"There are secrets that can prove fatal."

After this warning, I kept his secret. As it turned out, his B.A.T. takeover failed because of the concern by insurance regulators that Farmers would fall into his hands. It was his last takeover attempt. As we drove back through the gates to his castle, I wondered how many other of his secrets remained within these walls.

Now, back at Montjeu for the first time in three years, Jimmy's driver told me that the staff was very worried. Jimmy had been in great pain, screaming during the night. Seeing the 17th-century chateau brought back a rush of memories. It stands on top of a hill in a 700-hectare park surrounded by stone walls. The last time I was here in 1994, Jimmy had organized a wild boar hunt to reduce the population on the grounds. Many of the boars were blind because of five centuries of inbreeding behind the walls. One of the other palaces housed the stables where Jimmy was breeding champion horses, including Montjeu, who would win the Prix du Jockey Club race in 1999. The gardens around the house, originally built by André Le Nôtre, included magnificent fountains, but no green trees, as green was a color that Jimmy detested.

When I arrived at the house, Jimmy was seated in the library, wearing his usual blue cashmere pullover, tan slacks, and sandals. I could see he was terribly thin, his face so gaunt that he looked like another person. He sounded, though, surprisingly upbeat.

He said that he had learned he had cancer 10 years earlier but kept it secret from everyone except his immediate family. He didn't want his friends feeling sorry for him. I now realized that many of his erratic and seemingly bizarre actions over the past decade—such as his decision to abruptly leave Vietnam and fly to Thailand to get yogurt—had proceeded from his illness. It made sense to me that he would keep it secret: he had always looked at mortality as a weakness rather than as an inevitability.

Only now did I realized what he meant when he told me three years earlier that his new 757 jetliner was "free." Though the plane had a list price of just over $40 million, Jimmy didn't pay a penny in cash for it. Instead, he negotiated a non-recourse loan with a single balloon payment covering the principal and interest that would not come due until 2004. If he was unable to repay it in 2004, the bank would repossess the airliner. Since he knew, in light of his medical prognosis, he would not live to 2004, he considered it a free plane.

At lunch, I asked him about the Referendum Party. "It won't survive without me." That prediction also proved true.

He also feared he would lose his "war with the conifers," which he considered "an invasive alien."

The gardens in front of the house were squares of gravel and box tree that extended to a forest of oaks. "I don't see any pine trees here," I said.

"I had them rooted out with great delight."

Jimmy, despite the circumstances, seemed surprisingly optimistic about the future. He invited me to join him on a yacht cruise to Turkey, adding, "If we can trust the prognosis of Dr. Prakash, we'll set sail in September." He excused himself to take a nap, adding, "It's the doctor's orders."

I then met Dr. Prakash. He told me he dispensed Ayurveda remedies, but he was not a licensed medical doctor. Nor was he a member of any medical institution. Before this assignment, he practiced in rural southern India.

"How did Goldsmith find you?" I asked.

"Through a series of fortuitous events," he answered with a heavy Indian accent.

He had flown from New Delhi, India, to Lahore, Pakistan, six weeks earlier to offer his medical services to a daughter of the former Pakistani foreign minister, Ayub Khan. He read in the newspaper that she was suffering from muscular dystrophy, which he could treat with Ayurvedic herbs. When he presented his credentials to the guards at the gate, he was turned away because he was Hindu. He now had a logistics problem. His return ticket was not valid for two days and he had no money to pay for two nights' stay at a hotel. He needed a free place to stay. He heard that Imran Khan had opened a cancer hospital in Lahore, so he went there hoping to barter his medical services for a bed for two nights. He met with Imran Khan and told him about his Ayurveda skill. Jemima Goldsmith had told Khan about her father's diagnosis. So Kahn asked Prakash if he could cure pancreatic cancer. Prakash answered that he had cured dozens of cases. Khan then told Jemima, who called

Jimmy. As a result, Jimmy sent Prakash a ticket and, the next day, he was on a plane to France.

"What kind of medicine do you use?" I asked.

Prakash was giving Jimmy "an ancient mixture" of roots, flowers, and gold dust. He said he analyzed Jimmy's blood every day and Jimmy's cancer was now nearly in remission. "By September, he will be totally cured."

I asked if Jimmy was taking painkillers, recalling what the driver had reported. "I forbid him to take painkillers," Prakash said. "It interferes with Ayurveda medicine."

Laure told me Jimmy was now sleeping, and I should return to Paris with Jimmy's daughter Alix. On the train, we were surprised to find Prakash with his tattered suitcase. He said he needed to pick up a new shipment of herbs and roots but would go back to Montjeu on the morning train. Alix, always generous, invited him to dine with us in Paris at Laurent, the elegant restaurant that Jimmy owned. Alix also invited her friend Diane de Bellville, a Parisian psychologist. After the appetizer, Prakash became visibly agitated and left the table, saying he needed to pick up his shipment. After he left, Diane told us she had rebuffed persistent advances he had made under the table. Alix was not surprised: she had heard reports that he had attempted to molest a maid at Montjeu. None of these revelations enhanced my confidence in his treatment.

When I returned to my hotel that night, Alix called and said that Prakash had disappeared. He had not returned to Montjeu and had emptied his room. Jimmy now knew he was a charlatan and assumed he fled back to India.

On Thursday, Alix called to say that Jimmy had asked her to say goodbye to me for him. He was at that moment on his 757, headed for Spain. He did not want to die in France because he feared French authorities would levy immense death taxes against his estate. He had left the chateau that morning for the airport, barely alive, in an ambulance. He was then carried aboard his plane, accompanied by a local physician. To alleviate the pain, he had requested a dose of morphine, from which he never awakened. His wife Annabel and the Spanish doctor who issued the death certificate met the plane in Spain. Jimmy's body, according to his wishes, was cremated, and his children scattered the ashes over Cuixmala.

I had lost a friend whose thundering intellect would never be forgotten.

# PART SIX

# ENCOUNTERS ON THE DARK SIDE

# CHAPTER THIRTY-TWO

# DECEPTION

In 1982, I became fascinated with a single question about the intelligence services: Are they deeply vulnerable to deception by their adversaries? Other areas do not face this challenge. Scientists can reasonably assume that the subjects of their observation are not conspiring to fool them. For example, a microbiologist looking through a microscope need not worry that the microbes are willfully putting on a show to deceive him. An astronomer looking through a telescope need not worry that information from a distant galaxy is being purposely faked to dupe him. A marine biologist need not worry that a dolphin being tracked is modifying its behavior to fool him. So scientific observers, except in the exotic fields of quantum physics, can assume that what they see, they can believe. But that assumption cannot be so easily made by case officers in the realm of espionage. As Angleton made clear to me, intelligence services have two functions. The first is to obtain their adversaries' secrets. The second is to deny them their own secrets by, if not blocking their sources, corrupting any information adversaries receive. The latter was achieved by adding deceptive messages. If the CIA was good at it, so was its Russian adversary.

My interest in Russia traces back to a single lecture given by Vladimir Nabokov in 1955 at Cornell. It was on Gogol's novel *Dead*

*Souls.* As he spoke, he drew with squeaky chalk on the blackboard a circle with spokes emanating from its center. At its most superficial level, the center was the wheel of the coach in which the protagonist Chichikov is traveling through Russia. The wheel's spokes represented the various levels of a massive deception scheme using dead serfs as collateral to borrow money. Like a master chef peeling an onion, Nabokov stripped away, one by one, the layers of faked reality. I was so impressed with his analysis of literary deception, I sent him a three-page letter in Montreux, Switzerland, where he moved after the publication of *Lolita*, suggesting that *Dead Souls* could be updated to the Soviet Union. (He never replied.)

The issue of Russian deception came up again when I began interviewing the KGB defector Yuri Nosenko and learned that one part of US intelligence—including the head of the Counterintelligence Staff, the deputy head of the Soviet Russia Division, and the chief of the FBI's counterintelligence division—believed he was a fake defector manufactured by the KGB to dupe the CIA, and the other part, including his interrogators in the Office of Security and the CIA's inspector general, believed he was a true defector. As I got more deeply immersed in the case, I realized the CIA, even after employing its full arsenal of techniques, including lie detectors, hostile interrogation, sleep deprivation, and imprisonment, was not able to settle the issue. Our intelligence services simply did not possess sufficient unambiguous means to differentiate between a real windfall of intelligence and its doppelgänger, a KGB deception.

I therefore decided to embark on an investigation to determine if the CIA was vulnerable to KGB deception. It proved far more difficult than I expected. Times had changed from the mid-1960s, when I could get access, unimpeded by a communications officer, to the members of the Warren Commission and its staff. By 1980, all government agencies employed press communications officers, whose job it was to prevent outsiders from getting anything but approved sound bites. US intelligence services had also become more serious about preventing any leaks of documents. To be sure, a Freedom of Information Act had been passed in 1966, but any classified material or documents deemed of national security concern were excluded. The clearance of any document also often took many years.

The more restrictive rules in the government were not an insurmountable barrier to an investigation. There were still a few people in the intelligence establishment who would be willing to discuss and help me understand the deception problem. Finding them would require time, a commodity I had.

My starting point was Andrew Marshall, who pioneered the study of intelligence vulnerability. He had first worked on the issue as a strategic analyst at the RAND Corporation. When Congress mandated in 1973 that the Pentagon create the Office of Net Assessment to keep track of American power vis-à-vis its adversaries and report to it, Marshall was appointed its first director. In the following decade, he turned it into a highly specialized think tank within the Pentagon with a single product: a continuing hardball assessment of America's ability to defeat Russia and China. To arrive at that calculus, Marshall had to take into account the capability of Russian intelligence to deceive the CIA.

I also had a means of getting to see him. His new deputy was Captain James Roche, who had been a friend of mine since 1972 when he served on the State Department's Policy Planning Staff under Paul Wolfowitz. I invited Roche for a drink at the Jefferson Hotel and told him about the book I wanted to write.

"You need to speak to Andy," he said, and he made an appointment for me to meet with Marshall on August 9, 1982.

The Office of Net Assessment was located in the Pentagon. Marshall, a slight, bald man with a bullet-shaped head, greeted me at the door, Roche standing behind him.

I asked Marshall whether he factored into his net assessments the possibility of strategic deceptions. "What if a nation used deception, for example, to make itself look weaker in the eyes of an adversary?"

"A wolf-in-sheep's-clothes tactic?" he asked.

"That was the deception the Japanese used to hide their torpedo-bombing capabilities before the Pearl Harbor attack," Roche chimed in.

"Or an adversary could use the sheep-in-wolves'-clothes to make itself look stronger, as Hitler did before Munich," I said.

"Of course these deception possibilities need to be factored in." Marshall spoke slowly and precisely. "But it is easier said than done. What is successfully hidden from view, by definition, can never be seen."

I told him that I planned to write my next book on that subject: Can nations be decisively misled by disinformation fed to them through their own intelligence channels? "Has your office done an analysis of deception between nations?"

"I am not sure such a study exists," Marshall replied. "But I can offer you two things that might help you."

The first offering was the four volumes of notes on 3x5 index cards that had been compiled by Herbert Goldhamer, a RAND Corporation social scientist who had worked with Marshall. "Unfortunately, Herb died before he could complete the study."

I quickly leafed through the material, called "Reality and Belief in Military Affairs." I could see it would provide me with an extremely historic overview of possible deceptions.

"What is your second offering?" I asked Marshall.

"The Boyd briefing," he replied. He said it would take only an hour and offered to schedule it the next time I was in Washington, DC.

I was eager to get the briefing on deception that Colonel John Boyd had given to a number of top officials, but as I had already scheduled a trip to Scotland, Austria, and France that fall, and

Boyd also had a busy schedule briefing top generals, the briefing did not take place until 11:00 a.m. on November 4.

I again went to the Pentagon. After I cleared security, Roche escorted me to a sealed-off briefing room, where Colonel John Boyd, a short, compact man, was standing straight as a ramrod. He shook my hand with an iron grip. Roche jokingly said, "Meet Genghis John."

Boyd had been a decorated fighter pilot during the Korean War, then a combat plane instructor and a mathematical analyst of fighter plane tactics at the Pentagon before he developed his deception briefing. He told me he had given it to hundreds of decision-makers, including Dick Cheney when he was the White House chief of staff for President Ford. He turned down the lights and began his 59-minute slide presentation.

It began with the proposition that all intelligent organisms act after a loop of interaction with their immediate environment. The diagram called it the "OODA loop," which stood for "Observation, Orientation, Decision, and Action." Deception, by interfering with the first step, observation, could fatally corrupt the final step, action. For example, if a decoy led a fighter pilot to hesitate for a split second in observing an enemy plane on his radar, he could be shot down.

"Timing is everything," Boyd said. "Deception causes the mis-timing of a move." His point was that deceptions need only to momentarily confound a person's perspective.

When the presentation ended, I asked how the OODA loop applied to national intelligence-gathering systems, such as the CIA, NSA, and FBI. "Wouldn't an intelligence service realize its observations were being corrupted by disinformation?"

"Eventually it might," Boyd answered. "But a great deal of damage could occur in the interim. If its observations were deliberately distorted by an adversary, its orientation would be corrupted, its decisions would be misguided, and it would take the wrong actions."

"This vulnerability would apply in peace as well as war?"

"In wartime, a false observation is easier to recognize. If a source reports a submarine is at location X, for example, and it is not found there, the source is discredited."

"So intelligence services are more vulnerable in peacetime?"

"That is what we are learning in the Cold War."

The lights flickered back on, Colonel Boyd stood up, and the deception briefing was over.

It was not the only deception briefing I received that week. Just two days before meeting Colonel Boyd, I received another briefing on the subject of strategic deception at the Century Club in New York City. My briefer this time was the movie star Douglas Fairbanks Jr. It came about in a most unexpected way. After I told Jones Harris, the leisure-time private investigator who had helped me with my Garrison investigation in New Orleans, that I was planning to write a book on deception, he had arranged the meeting. "You need to talk to Doug Fairbanks," Harris said in a conspiratorial whisper. "He is a close friend and will be happy to see you."

We met at 1:00 p.m. in the library at the Century. Although nearly 73, he looked remarkably youthful as he approached me. His hair, tinged on the edges with gray strands, was still blond. He wore an impeccably tailored charcoal-gray suit with a red carnation in the lapel, a white shirt, and a perfectly knotted Sulka tie. He introduced himself in a crisp, courtly voice.

I of course knew he was even before he spoke. Douglas Fairbanks Jr. came as close to Hollywood royalty as anyone. Indeed, his father (whose mother changed his last name from Ullman to Fairbanks) was called "the king of Hollywood" for good reason. Aside from his swashbuckling roles in silent movies, along with his wife Mary Pickford, Charlie Chaplin, and D.W. Griffith, Fairbanks Sr. created the United Artists studio in 1919. His son followed in his acting tradition, starring in such hits as *Gunga Din*, *The Sun Never Sets*, and *Angels Over Broadway*.

But the career Fairbanks Jr. discussed with me over a three-hour lunch had nothing to do with Hollywood. As he explained, during World War II, he was assigned to Lord Mountbatten's Commando staff in England. Under Mountbatten, he became well schooled in British deception operations and fascinated by these con games. When he returned to America in 1942, he convinced Admiral Ernest King, chief of Naval Operations, that America needed to boost its capacity for deception. Under Fairbanks's tutelage, the navy created a super-secret unit, called the Beach Jumpers, to run these deception operations. Through a bag of tricks, it simulated phantom amphibious landings in Africa, Sicily, and France that succeeded in luring German forces away from the actual US landing locations. For his work in organizing these mass deception, Fairbanks, who held the rank of lieutenant commander, received the navy's Legion of Merit, Italy's War Cross, France's Légion d'honneur, and the British Distinguished Service Cross. Despite his decorations, the navy insisted on keeping his deception work secret even after the war ended.

I asked if his proclivity for deception flowed from his experience in the movie business.

"Strategic deception is as different from Hollywood deception as night is from the day," he answered. He explained that whereas the deceptions used to fake reality in a movie, such as trick photography, stunt doubles substituting for actors, dubbing voices, and inserting additional material at a later date, were known to everyone involved in the production and even the audience understood it was seeing an illusion, strategic deceptions in wartime worked only if the intended enemy believed what they were seeing, and the intelligence that they were gathering, was real. And since there were bound to be leaks and spies, maintaining the illusion required that no one involved in the operation, except the planners themselves, was aware that the operation was a deception.

I wondered how such a complex enterprise as a fake invasion, involving personnel, trucks, and landing ships, could be kept a secret from the thousands of people involved in it. Didn't even the most brilliantly conceived swindle take place in an envelope of reality that spies could discern?

"Not necessarily in time," he replied with his winning smile. "It is an 'as if' deception."

He explained that in an "as if" deception, real orders were issued as if this was a real invasion. The officers and troops would not know that at the last moment the invasion would be aborted. Only he and his deception planners knew that ultimate move. Since the landing force was not aware it was a deception, if enemy spies penetrated it or anyone leaked anything, that information would serve to confirm the operation and further dupe the enemy.

When our lunch ended, Fairbanks gave me his phone number and suggested we meet again after I had learned more about the subject.

I decided the best way to further acquaint myself with such a secretive subject was to join the Consortium for the Study of Intelligence. It met around a rectangular table at the International Club in Washington.

The Consortium included many former CIA intelligence executives, as well as former officials from the State Department, the Arms Control and Disarmament Agency, and the Defense Department. Paul Wolfowitz, then head of policy planning at the State Department, and whom I had known since Cornell, was happy to recommend me. The driving force behind the group was Georgetown professor Roy Godson, who was so erudite about the history of espionage that I recommended him to Jimmy Goldsmith to put together the book collection of the two-story circular library that Jimmy was building at his chateau in Burgundy. As a result, I would also see Godson there.

At the Consortium's monthly meetings, I met many well-placed people who could tell me about deception, including one former and two future CIA directors: William Colby, a dour man, who had fired Angleton in 1974 (and who in 1996 was found dead in a canoe in Rock Point, Maryland); William Casey, a savvy lawyer who told me "everything is politics in the intelligence business"; and Robert Gates, a pragmatic veteran of intelligence wars, who invited me to interview him at the CIA headquarters when he became its director. It was a perfect platform for the networking I needed to do to gain access to the so-called defense intellectual complex.

James Roche, who was also a member of the Consortium, continued to help get me invited to intelligence seminars, conferences, and briefings on deception in the United States, Europe, and Canada. (Roche subsequently became secretary of the air force.)

Throughout my investigation, the American side of the intelligence equation was far easier to understand. It stood to reason that there would be far more deception deniers than deception believers at the highest levels of US intelligence. After all, the American espionage business largely runs on the assumption that its case officer can obtain trustworthy secret information from sources in adversary countries that have access to these secrets. If they believe that the adversaries engage in systematic deception to feed these case officers and their sources misleading information, they are essentially out of business.

The Russian side of the equation was not as easy to read. The only available resource was former intelligence officers who had defected from the Soviet Union and its allies. Finding and interviewing them took seven years.

I also had a personal brush with Britain's obsession with Russian moles burrowing into its intelligence establishment. After British intelligence officers Guy Burgess, Donald Maclean, and Kim Philby had defected to Moscow, media attention turned to the putative fourth and fifth men in the infamous Russian spy ring known as the Cambridge Five. In late November 21, 1979, the British government revealed that the fourth man was British art historian Sir Anthony Blunt. By the spring of 1980, rumors began circulating that the fifth man was Lord Victor Rothschild, a 70-year-old scientist who, along with his wife Teresa, had served with Blunt in MI-5 during World War II and afterward served as a top advisor to both the Edward Heath and Margaret Thatcher governments. In June 1980, at the height of the speculation in the press about whether not Lord Rothschild was the fifth man, I rented a villa just outside St. Tropez in partnership with his youngest daughter, Tory Rothschild. Soon after we arrived at the villa, she told me that she had invited her parents and sister Emma, but I had to keep her father's presence there a secret.

Victor, who enjoyed interrogating me about my study of deception and James Jesus Angleton, refused to go outside or even to the pool, perhaps because he was unnerved by a pair of au pairs from New Zealand, which came with the villa as the condition of the rental. He called them "naked kiwi provocateurs" because they sunbathed topless at the pool. On his first day there, he asked me in a hushed tone if I would do him a favor.

"Anything," I answered.

"One day this week, I am not sure which, I need you to drive me to a bank in St. Tropez."

It seemed a simple enough request. "Is that all?"

"I may also need you to drive me to the airport in Fréjus."

"Does Fréjus have an airport?" I asked.

"I'll give you directions," he replied.

When I told Tory about her father's mission for me, she said, with a nervous laugh, "If Blunt names him, he might be planning to defect."

After I drove him to the bank, he said there was no need to go to the airport. As it turned out, the fifth man was later identified as John Cairncross, not Rothschild.

Finally, in 1989, I finished the book. It argued that US intelligence was vulnerable to Russian deception because of the mindset in the CIA that denied the very existence of such deception.

Jimmy Goldsmith gave two launch parties for the book, neither of which ended well. The first one was in the Salon Elysees banquet room of Laurent on October 30, 1989. When I saw that my close friend Natasha Fraser was missing from the guest list, I called Jimmy's secretary, Edith. She told me Jimmy had ordered her to disinvite Natasha. Jimmy, who could be extremely thin-skinned, was offended by an offhand joke Natasha had made belittling the whales in the movie *When the Whales Came*, which Jimmy had helped produce.

The guests who did attend included the actress Arielle Dombasle and the philosopher-journalist Bernard-Henri Lévy. I had met Arielle at, of all places, the Drexel Burnham junk bond conference, also known as the "Predator's Ball." I had attended it to write about Drexel Burnham; she had attended it to raise money for her film *The Blue Pyramid*. Lévy, called in France by his initials, BHL, was her husband. Jimmy also invited Alain Gomez, the French industrialist; Clementine Gustin, Laure's writing partner; Joseph Fitchett, a Paris-based journalist; Marty Peretz, the editor of the *New Republic*; and his wife, Ann Peretz. Just as I was giving a short speech about my book, Marty Peretz collapsed to the floor, unconscious. His wife tried to revive him without success. Jimmy called an ambulance. That abruptly ended the book party. I followed the ambulance to the nearest hospital in a taxi with Ann. When doctors there failed to revive him, another ambulance with an ICU team aboard it brought him to a medieval-looking neurological hospital. We waited there till 2:00 a.m. to find out from a doctor that Marty was in a coma. I had to leave for my flight back to New York, but Marty awoke two days later and fully recovered.

The second party, two weeks later in New York, was in the ballroom of the Pierre Hotel in New York. Guests included George Tenet, the future director of the CIA; Vernon Walters, the deputy director the CIA; Eli Jacobs, a member of the president's Foreign Intelligence Advisory Board; Senator Wyche Fowler, who would become the US ambassador to Saudi Arabia; the Shahbanu Farah Pahlavi, the former empress of Iran; James Roche; and Henry Kissinger. But my speech about the Soviet threat was overtaken by other events. That very evening, the Berlin Wall, which symbolized the Soviet threat to Europe, was being torn down as I spoke, signaling the unraveling of the Soviet Union. The scores of intelligence executives I interviewed, while battling each other over concepts of espionage, had all missed the single most important piece of intelligence: the imminent collapse of the Soviet Union. So had I.

I had spent the better part of a decade trying to unravel the deception of the Kremlin, but those intelligence games did not save the Soviet Union. It collapsed and, in doing so, made the threat of Russian deception that I was warning against seem irrelevant. It also doomed my book to, if not the ashcan of history, the remainder piles of bookstores. The only tangible good that came out of the evening was that Kissinger brought with him the Swedish publisher Peter Wallenberg, who bought the Swedish rights to *Deception*.

Thirteen years later, perhaps due to the cunning of history, a Beijing publisher owned by the People's Liberation Army offered to buy the Chinese rights to *Deception*. Since the Cold War had been over for more than a decade, I asked him why he thought my book would be of interest in China.

"James Jesus Angleton," he replied. "There is great interest in him in China."

"Angleton has been dead 15 years," I said.

"But not his ideas on deception," he answered.

# CHAPTER THIRTY-THREE

# THE HAMMER TAPES

My fascination with Armand Hammer, an entrepreneur who had gone to Russia, met with Lenin and other top Communist Party leaders, and became a world-class oil tycoon, began in September 1980 on a remote island in the Java Sea on which the apex predators were eight-foot-long Komodo dragons. The guesthouse where I was staying belonged to Natomas, a San Francisco–based petroleum company with offshore oil concessions in the Java Sea. The two other guests were Dorman Commons, chairman of Natomas, and Clay Felker.

Just months earlier, Commons had met Clay at investment banker Felix Rohatyn's dinner party in New York and invited him to see Natomas's oil operations in Indonesia. Clay asked me to accompany him since I had written a two-part article on the history of the global oil cartel. After dinner at the guesthouse, the conversation turned to Armand Hammer for two reasons. First, he was in the news. Reuters was reporting that Hammer, now 82, was a leading candidate to win the 1989 Nobel Peace Prize because of the good relations he had fostered between President Ronald Reagan and Mikhail Gorbachev, the dictator of the Soviet Union. And second, before joining Natomas, Commons had worked for Hammer as the chief financial officer of Occidental Petroleum, the oil company that Hammer had built from a tiny Californian one-rig driller into an international behemoth in the 1960s and 1970s. When Commons scoffed at the idea of Hammer succeeding at bringing about peace, I asked him how he had succeeded so spectacularly in the oil business.

Commons leaned forward in his bamboo chair, hesitated till he had our full attention, and answered, "Bribes. With Hammer, it is high art. From what I saw in Libya, he is the true Nijinsky of bribery."

As Clay and I listened raptly, Commons laid out the entire scheme by which Hammer corrupted the entire entourage of King Idris of Libya and got a major oil concession in the Libyan desert. Commons, as the CFO, saw the cash flowing out, which was one reason he left Occidental in 1975. (It was only in 1977 that the anti-bribery provisions of the Foreign Corrupt Practices Act applied to all US executives.)

Clay asked a very pointed question. Since Occidental still had those concessions, how did Hammer keep them after Muammar Gaddafi overthrew King Idris in 1969?

Commons answered that the Russians, who supported Gaddafi's revolution, helped Hammer after Gaddafi took over.

"Did Hammer also bribe the Russians?" I asked.

Commons shrugged, showing the palms of his hands, and said he was not privy to Hammer's relationship with the Russians.

Why would the Soviet Union help Hammer in Libya? It was a relationship worth looking into. Soon after I returned to New York, I proposed a profile of Hammer to the *New York Times Magazine*. Clifford May, an editor at the magazine, approved the idea if I could get Hammer's cooperation. He pointed out that the *Times* would need photos for the profile and I would need to accompany him on his global trips for "color." So began my travels with Armand Hammer.

On February 21, 1981, after meeting in his office on the top floor of the Occidental Petroleum Company headquarters in Los Angeles, we left for the airport to board his private Boeing 737, OXY 1. It had been specially designed for intercontinental flights, with a 100-foot-long cabin configured as a personal salon with twin beds and a shower. Jim Pugash, Hammer's new personal assistant, was waiting on the tarmac with Hammer's two pieces of luggage. Pugash, a 31-year-old graduate of Harvard Law School and a concert pianist, had been an aide to Senator Henry "Scoop" Jackson (D-WA) up until only one week before. Hammer, looking annoyed at Pugash, without saying a word, grabbed his two suitcases from just behind Pugash and strode toward OXY 1. Pugash ran after him.

On the flight, Hammer was very keen on the profile, which he envisioned would be on the cover of the *New York Times Magazine*. He told me he was just beginning his new campaign to win the 1982 Nobel Peace Prize. He also was fully confident that my profile would present him favorably since he was on friendly terms with Arthur "Punch" Sulzberger, the chairman and publisher of the *Times*. He asked me if I knew Punch. I said I did not. "I'll take you to dinner with him," he replied. He clearly wanted me to know he could go over my head at the *New York Times Magazine*.

True to his word, when we got back to New York, he invited me and Laurie Frank, my girlfriend, to an extraordinary dinner party he was hosting at Lincoln Center. The other guests were Sulzberger (who Hammer sat me next to), Nancy Reagan, who was then First Lady, and Charles, the Prince of Wales. Hammer seemed in complete control of his guests, tugging the prince around the room by the arm to make introductions. When he introduced me to Sulzberger, he told him he wanted my story about him to be featured on the cover of the magazine. At the time, I did nothing to disabuse him of the idea that my article would be a puff piece.

Despite his affinity for powerful people, I found Hammer personally to be a modest and even affable man. He far more closely resembled a country doctor than a corporate magnate. Since the thick glasses he wore did not entirely correct his severe myopia, at times he reminded me of the Mr. Magoo cartoon character.

He had bought Leonardo da Vinci's codex at auction in London in 1980 and renamed it the Hammer Codex but had not yet taken possession of it. He suggested I accompany him back to London for the handover.

In London, he stayed at Claridge's and suggested Pugash and I join him in the dining room, but, since he was not wearing a tie, the headwaiter refused to seat him. Infuriated, Hammer booked a suite just for us to eat in and ordered from room service. The next morning he used a news conference to commemorate his purchase of the Da Vinci Codex. To call attention to its value, he arranged for four Chinese guards trained in kung fu to surround it. The codex was then put into an armored car, which followed Hammer's Rolls-Royce to OXY 1 at the airport.

With the codex in tow, we flew to Paris, where Hammer had a meeting at the Plaza Athénée. He left the codex aboard the plane, telling me, with a chuckle, that the kung fu guards were "just for show." The next morning, when we checked out, the Plaza Athénée refused to accept Pugash's credit card. Hammer did not himself carry credit cards. That was the job of his assistants. Hammer flew into a rage when the hotel held up the delivery of baggage to his waiting limousine.

During the trip to New York, we spent hours discussing his life, achievements, and business strategies. It was not always easy. He was slightly hard of hearing, and he used this infirmity to great effect when he did not want to discuss an issue. When I asked Hammer questions he did not expect or want to answer, he simply ignored them. When he crossed time zones in OXY 1, I noticed that he had little respect for other people's off-hours. He had no inhibitions about calling subordinates at home in the middle of the night. He meanwhile kept his own schedule, napping or working to suit his convenience. When the plane landed in New York, a public relations man, two security men, and his personal photographer met him. His entourage, which often strained to keep up with him as he spryly walked from the plane, gave him more the appearance of a visiting head of state than a corporate executive.

While I was writing the article, Hammer took me to a constant stream of events at which he was the center of attention. I went with him to diplomatic receptions, award ceremonies, museum openings, private parties, press conferences, and charity events. He introduced me to a dazzling array of celebrities and politicians, including Bob Hope, Louis Nizer, Senator Charles Percy, Edgar Faure, Sir John Foster, Al Gore, Prince Bandar bin Sultan of Saudi Arabia, and Pierre Trudeau. I realized that his purpose was to provide me with colorful material for a story in which, as he conceived it, he would be a central actor in a rarefied universe of money, altruism, and power. When I still had not completed the story by summer, Hammer grew so impatient that he offered to help me write it.

The delay proceeded from unresolved questions about his dealings in Russia in the 1920s. Angleton had told me there was "another side" to Hammer's activities that could be found in the Soviet trade mission documents seized by British intelligence agents in 1927. But how to unearth half-century-old intelligence records in Britain? Fortunately, my research assistant, Rebecca Fraser, was not only brilliantly resourceful but also remarkably well connected in Britain. Her father, Sir Hugh Fraser, was a former member of Parliament, cabinet minister, and member of the Privy Council of the United Kingdom, and her mother, the author Lady Antonia Fraser, after divorcing Fraser, was now married to the playwright Harold Pinter. Indeed, on my research trip to London, Rebecca recruited me, since she knew I was a bridge aficionado, as a fourth in a game at her mother's Holland Park home. The other players were her mother, Pinter, and Ruth Jackson, a BBC documentarian. We rotated partners. When Pinter became my partner, I found that the future Nobel laureate was not above informing my bids with eyebrow lifts and other facial gestures, a more subtle form of cheating than kicking under the table. While this helped with my much-needed social education, it was Rebecca's father who helped me with Hammer. As a former MP, he had access to archival intelligence records, which he shared with me. They confirmed that Hammer's past was darker than he had described. He had been acting, according to these records, as a front for the Soviet government in evading the US embargo and selling art of questionable provenance in the 1920s and 1930s. The US complaint also should have been in the National Archives, but I discovered that Hammer's well-connected lawyer, Arthur Groman, had them expunged.

I thought it might help if I had the exact dates that Hammer entered and left the Soviet Union. So I asked him if I could look at his passports, which in those days were issued every 10 years. When I told him that it would speed up the publication of the *New York Times Magazine* cover story if I could pinpoint a few dates in his past, he looked at me suspiciously and said that these passports were historic documents that belonged in a museum.

"I would only need then for a few days," I said.

He growled simply, "No."

Three days later, one of Hammer's assistants appeared at my door with an attaché case handcuffed to his wrist. He asked if I had a safe.

I nodded affirmatively even though I did not even have a locked drawer in my apartment.

He opened the attaché case and took from it six passports held together with two rubber bands. "Keep these in your safe," he said, handing them to me.

I leafed through them and saw Hammer's face age, in 10-year intervals, from a 20-year-old youth to an old man. Giving them to Rebecca, I asked her to go through them and copy all the dates of Russian entry and exit stamps. As I watched her work, I got an idea of how the passports might be used as an illustration by the *Times* magazine. My mother, an accomplished artist and sculptor, had recently completed and shown in the National Arts Club her collage work. She also had a flatbed Xerox machine in her studio. My idea was for my mother to make copies of the passports and use the images of his passport stamps to make a collage of a man resembling Hammer. I explained my concept to Rebecca and asked her to take them to my mother's studio. Meanwhile, I went to Paris to work on another story.

I returned home a week later and called my mother to see how the collage was progressing. She told me she was finished, having cut pieces out of all the passports to build the assemblage. Thinking that she had misspoken, I said, "You mean that you cut up the Xeroxes of the passports?"

But she had not misspoken. She said Rebecca had instructed her to cut up the actual passports, and I realized, to my horror, that I had inadvertently omitted telling Rebecca the key step of making copies.

It was all my fault. While I was pondering how I would tell Hammer that I had destroyed his historical passports, my mother called back to tell me that she could put his passports back together, filling in any destroyed bits from her own old passports.

Rebecca picked up the reconstructed passports, and, lo and behold, except for her additions such as passport stamps from my mother's honeymoon in 1934 in Bermuda, they looked untampered with. After putting the rubber bands back on the pack of them, I asked Rebecca to call the man with the attaché case to pick them up.

"If he looks at them, wouldn't he know he's never been to some of these places?" Rebecca asked.

It was a good question. I said that he probably would never look at them, and, if he did, he would not be able to conceive of any plausible scenario to explain why his passports had been cut apart and reassembled. Hammer's man arrived that afternoon. He put the passports in his attaché case, and I never heard again from Hammer about the passports.

I did have two later reminders of this unfortunate miscommunication. First, my mother's copy of the passport collage hangs in my hallway. Second, in 1987, Hammer published his own autobiography, entitled *Hammer*. In it, I spotted photographs of some of his passport pages with my mother's entry stamps.

However, even with the data gleaned from his passports, I could not prove Hammer was a front for the Russians. But my profile still took a different direction than he had anticipated.

It appeared in the *New York Times Magazine* in November 1981 under the title "The Riddle of Armand Hammer." Hammer was infuriated by it. He wrote a 25-page letter to the editor of the *Times* describing himself in the way that he wanted to be described in the article. He demanded that the editors publish it in full, but instead they ran a one-page excerpt in the "Letters to the Editor" section.

After Hammer died on December 10, 1990, I decided to write a book about him. One obvious advantage of writing a biography of a dead person is that it has a logical beginning (birth) and end (death). But I also had another reason. With the collapse of the Soviet Union in 1989, the KGB archives on Hammer's activities in Russia became available to researchers. When I had written the magazine profile of him, I had no way of pursuing his Russian connection in Moscow. Now I did.

To find these archives, I went to Moscow in 1991 on a trip sponsored by the *Nation* and organized and led by Victor Navasky, the magazine's owner. The other invitees included Katrina vanden Heuvel, the *Nation*'s managing director; Hamilton Fish, the head of the Nation Institute; Faye Wattleton, the head of Planned Parenthood; and Carl Bernstein, coauthor of *All the President's Men*. Since I had challenged Bernstein about his "Deep Throat" source in a *Commentary* article entitled "Did the Press Uncover Watergate?" I thought there might be tension between us. But Bernstein was, among his other virtues, a forgiving journalist, and we spent much time together discussing our common interest in high-end stereo. The group had dinners in Armenian, Georgian, and Kazak restaurants, all serving remarkably similar cuisine, with many entrepreneurial Russian journalists, who had plans to use their newly gained freedom to launch investigative journals. Learning about the new Russia was a high priority for me, but I also had another agenda. I needed to find someone who could get me the KGB documents on Hammer. The morass of red tape at the KGB archives would make digging out documents on Hammer a long, arduous, and uncertain enterprise. I needed a shortcut. So I hired Kent Lee of East View Publications, a company that specializes in obtaining documents from Russian archives, to get the documents about Armand Hammer for me. It wound up costing about $30,000, but it was well worth the price. The East View research team in Moscow found 3,000 pages of classified Soviet documents in the KGB archive that described in considerable detail Hammer's relations with the Soviet authorities in the 1920s and 1930s.

The basic outline was that Hammer had been a medical student at Columbia in 1920 when his father, Dr. Julius Hammer, who was one of the founders of a political group that became the US Communist Party, was sentenced to three and a half years in prison for performing an illegal abortion. At the time of his arrest, he had important business connections with the Communists who had taken over Russia. Since he was now headed to prison, he sent Armand to Moscow in his place. Armand spent most of the next 10 years in Moscow tending the family business. He returned to the US with a vast trove of Russian art, which he continued to receive, and sell, throughout the 1930s.

When it came to his art of bribery, I chanced on the potential smoking gun I had missed in the magazine article. Like Richard Nixon had famously done in the Oval Office, Hammer secretly taped many of his conversations, including those dealing with bribery and other murky activities. I obtained the Hammer tapes in 1996 from a family member to whom I promised anonymity.

The Hammer tapes came in formats including reels, cassettes, and microcassettes, which reflected the changes in recording technology from 1963 to 1981. They had been made in hotels, restaurants, cars, offices, and unknown venues. The unwitting participants included everyone from lowly employees of Occidental Petroleum to a sitting president of the United States, John F. Kennedy. Hammer taped his directors, executives, lawyers, consultants, and go-betweens. He also taped himself describing his meetings with foreign leaders. In all, they contained some 60 hours of his recorded conversations.

I found one intriguing lead: a typed note stapled to one micro-cassette made in July 1979 that read,

> Enclosed are (1) the original micro-cassette of the recording made in your office on July 23 and (2) an insurance copy of the same recording on a standard cassette (which I used to make the verbatim transcript I gave you.) In keeping with the confidential nature of the recording, the labels are written in Russian. There are no other copies of either of the recordings or the transcript.

It was signed simply "JH."

The obvious candidate for "JH" was Julian Hammer, who spoke Russian. He was Armand Hammer's only progeny. Julian, who I saw at his home in Bel Air, in a ritzy residential enclave of Los Angeles in the foothills of the Santa Monica Mountains.

Julian admitted that he was "JH" and that he had helped his father make the tapes. The story he told me was a sad one. Julian was born in Moscow in 1929 to Olga Vadina, a Russian singer whom Hammer had married shortly before he was born. Her pregnancy had been so unexpected that Hammer suspected he was not the biological father—and he continued to harbor these dark suspicions until 1988, when, through a DNA sample secretly tested at UCLA Medical Center, he finally determined that Julian was indeed his son.

Armand Hammer introduced me to a different mode of doing business: bribery. Almost immediately after the Hammer family returned to New York in 1931, Hammer began distancing himself from Olga and Julian. Julian's mother believed Hammer was embarrassed by his Russian connection. When Julian was six, his father told Olga that it was better if they lived apart. He sent her and Julian first to Upstate New York and then to Los Angeles. In growing up, Julian said he rarely saw his father—not even on Christmas holidays. His father did not attend his wedding in 1954 or even send his congratulations.

On the night of Julian's 26th birthday, an event happened that reunited them. Julian had invited a soldier over to his apartment that night, and after they both drank heavily, the soldier made advances toward his wife. Julian, getting his pistol from a drawer, shot the soldier to death. After the police arrested Julian for the shooting, the *Los Angeles Times* headline, above the story about the killing, read "Millionaire's Son Kills GI."

Whether he liked it or not, Hammer was again linked to his son. The publicity could not have come at a worse time for Hammer. He had just divorced his second wife, Angela, and was having financial problems with his art business, the Hammer Galleries. He wanted to avoid a trial that could further embarrass him. He borrowed $50,000 in cash from Frances Barrett Tolman, who would become the third Mrs. Armand Hammer the following year. According to Julian, he had a woman friend deliver the bribe to a lawyer in Los Angeles. As a result, Julian was released from jail after the state's attorney accepted his explanation that he had shot his guest in self-defense.

All charges against Julian were dismissed. He said he was free in the eyes of the law but not in those of his father. Hammer would not let him forget his $50,000 bribe. He wanted his son to repay his debt to him by disappearing from public sight so that he caused him no further embarrassment. He would provide him with a cash remittance each month. He also asked Julian to help him with a "discreet task" that he did not trust his regular employees to perform. Armand Hammer called it "James Bond stuff." Taking advantage of Julian's technical skills with electronics—skills he had developed initially as a hobby—Hammer had his son install a sophisticated recording system in his home and office. Then he had him devise a microcassette recorder that he could conceal on his person. Its miniature microphone was concealed in one of Hammer's gold cuff links. On several occasions, he would have Julian come to his private office to tape the recorder to his body and run the wires to the cuff link while he stood there shirtless. As Julian rigged him up, he could also sense the power his father derived from being able to secretly tape the words of people close to him. Julian would watch him put on his shirt, tie, and jacket and, with the confidence this concealed weapon gave him, go to his appointed meeting. He would then bring the cassette back to Julian, who would return to him a copy on a conventional cassette along with a transcript.

Although Julian did not always know the identities of the voices on the tapes, he realized through the conversations that his father was trying to build a major oil company and that cash payments were meant to advance this enterprise. His father was paying individuals emoluments off the books and then secretly taping their acknowledgment of the bribes. His father also taped conversations with executives he was about to fire and explained to Julian he always "needed an edge." He told Julian he employed only undocumented servants so he could fire them without fear they would complain to the authorities. Hammer gradually extended the James Bond operations by having Julian plant hidden surveillance devices in other people's homes and offices. Julian knew much of what he was doing for his father was illegal, but he saw he had little choice. It was the only service he could perform to repay his debt.

One tape that Julian made in November 1971 was of particular interest. Julian said he concealed a microphone in a desk in his father's home in Los Angeles. It provided possible blackmail material for Hammer because, Hammer confided in Julian, it concerned an ongoing crime: the bribing of high officials in Venezuela.

Hammer began: "You talked to the minister, didn't you?"

"Yes, sir," answered John D. Askew in a deep southern accent. He was, as I learned, Hammer's "conduit and agent." A native of Arkansas, Askew had been doing business in Venezuela since 1946. In 1968, he told Hammer that Venezuela was going to invite foreign oil companies to bid on developing five large tracts near Lake Maracaibo that contained an estimated three billion barrels of oil. These concessions were to take the form of "service contracts" that guaranteed the foreign companies a substantial proportion of the oil revenue for seven years. Up until then, two international oil companies, Exxon (then Esso) and Shell had a near-monopoly on oil production in Venezuela. Askew had told Hammer that he could win three of the five tracts for Occidental if he paid $3 million in cash under the table, or as Hammer said, "outside the money that is paid under the contract."

"He's getting paid, isn't he?" Hammer continued. He had routed the $3 million to Askew from the Worldwide Trading Corporation, Occidental's Liberian subsidiary. Hammer then transferred the money through a shell corporation called Noark International to two Panamanian shell corporations. Presumably, the Venezuelan recipients withdrew it.

"You betcha," Askew answered.

"Well, then why in the hell won't he deliver?" Hammer said, since the tracts had not yet been awarded to his company, Occidental. "This isn't such a big thing."

"Yes, it is to them. It's beyond their powers. It's strictly political.

I hate discussing this but maybe you're not paying this minister enough."

"How much are we paying? The total amount of money."

"We've paid $3 million," responded Askew.

"How is that $3 million divided?" Hammer asked. "Who gets what?"

Askew answered, "It's beyond their powers. It is strictly political."

"Money talks." Hammer tells Askew to "take a quarter of a million or even a half million of that money away from other people" and use an intermediary to "go to [Rafael] Caldera," the president of Venezuela.

Hammer was relentless in pressing Askew for names. Askew gradually named a dozen recipients. They were his partners in the service contract that Askew had earned through the consulting work he performed for Occidental.

Since I could not identify many of the names in the chain of recipients, I brought the tapes to William Luers, who was now the president of the Metropolitan Museum of Art and had been the US ambassador to Venezuela in the 1970s. Before that, he had served in the CIA. I met him at his office at the Met.

When I began playing the tape, his demeanor changed. He took notes and he seemed particularly interested in a portion that concerned the then minister of finance, Pedro Tinoco. In it, Hammer asked who is being paid off.

"One million is divided to Pedro and his bunch," Askew responded.

"That's Tinoco? He gets a million?"

"Yeah," Askew said.

Luers explained that Tinoco had been, before his death in 1992, one of the most powerful men in Caracas. His father had served as minister of the Interior in a dictatorship. A heavy man with a square face and a bald head, he had his law firm, which specialized in international business, and owned one of Venezuela's leading banks, the Banco Latino. He spoke calculatingly and tended to impress people, as Hammer described him on the tape: "a tough guy [who] could go in and see the president." After serving as finance minister, he went on to become head of Venezuela's central bank. In this latter role, the US supported his policies on controlling inflation and considered him "America's man in Caracas."

"My guess is that when this becomes public, they will try to hang the whole thing on Tinoco since he is dead," Luers said. "Do you really want to open this Pandora's box?"

I next went to see the Venezuelan ambassador to the United Nations, Enrique Tejera. I understood that Ambassador Tejera, who had served as foreign minister, was a close friend of President Caldera. As I prepared to play the tape in his office, he joked, "I hope I'm not on the tape."

He told me on his first meeting with Hammer in Caracas in 1969, Hammer had insisted on showing him a videotape of a ceremony in which he stood with King Idris of Libya. Tejera assumed it was Hammer's way of making the point that he had obtained his oil concession in Libya through his connections to the king. Hammer had also, as I knew, delivered a multimillion-dollar payoff to one of Idris's inner circle.

"Venezuela is not Libya," Tejera said. "We take corruption very seriously. We have had strictly enforced anti-bribery laws since 1936, and we have put two presidents in prison for it."

I then played the tape. It took about 20 minutes. When it concluded, he walked to his desk and placed a call to President Caldera. A few moments later, Caldera called him back and, in my presence, Tejera described in Spanish the contents of the tape. Caldera then asked for a transcript, which I agreed to supply.

After the president hung up, Ambassador Tejera placed a call to Maurice Valery, who, in 1971, had headed the Venezuelan

National Petroleum Company (CVP), which had awarded Occidental the three service contracts. He reached Valery in Caracas on his cell phone and, after summarizing the situation, handed me the telephone.

I told him Askew said on the tape: "Then I come back and had to give to Valery. I swung him a half a million dollars. I gave him $250,000 and he said, 'Now I'm going to work this out.' I said OK. He said he got some other people in with him … " And Hammer answered, "You gave Valery a half million."

"Voices from the grave," Valery said. He seemed shocked and dismayed that Hammer could have talked about him in this way. "I had little to do with Hammer. I saw him at the ceremony in which the contracts were signed, and I had dinner with him once and he told me about his meeting with Lenin. The only thing he ever gave me was a catalog for his art collection." As for Askew, he recalled meeting him only once at a large social function.

I asked about the putative half-million-dollar payoff. "That's pure invention," he answered. "Probably Askew cheated Hammer out of the money."

I doubted that, since Dorman Commons described Hammer as the Nijinsky of bribery. After Hammer's death, John Tigrett, who had been Hammer's bagman since the 1970s, confirmed that skill. He described to me how he had personally delivered attaché cases full of $100 bills to a Russian minister in Moscow for Hammer. He also said that he had given cash in envelopes to a dozen Norwegian parliamentarians in an attempt by Hammer to win the Nobel Peace Prize (which is awarded in Oslo).

My book *Dossier: The Secret History of Armand Hammer* was published in 1996 with a picture of one of the microcassettes on the cover and was excerpted in the *New Yorker*. It also won the $60,000 Booz Allen–Financial Times award for both best biography and business book. I used the prize money to convert a room in my rent-stabilized apartment into a dedicated screening room with a state-of-the-art projector in the ceiling, a 10-foot screen on the wall, six hi-fi speakers around the room, blackout shades on all the windows, and two tiers of stadium seating. I decided to show Russian operas, including ones by Mussorgsky, Borodin, Tchaikovsky, Prokofiev, and Shostakovich, that were available with English subtitles on laser discs. I was greatly educated and assisted in this enterprise by Sasha Lazard, a young opera singer with a magical bel canto voice, who had a very knowledgeable Russian voice coach. Before each opera night, Sasha and I would go to the "Little Odessa" section in Brooklyn's Brighton Beach and bring back enough Russian food and vodka for dinner, which was served after Act I. Sasha also invited friends who were opera singers, who would sing arias during the dinner. Aside from Sasha, the regulars for my opera nights included Susana Duncan, who had by now become a doctor; the food critic Jeffrey Steingarten; the *New York Times* book reviewer Richard Bernstein; Cristina Cuomo, the editor of *Gotham*; the financier Frederick Iseman; and the Italian journalist Mario Platero and his wife Ariadne.

I also invited guests who had special connections to Russia. For example, I asked Olga Rostropovich, the daughter of the cellist Mstislav Rostropovich and the celebrated Russian soprano Galina Vishnevskaya, to see Prokofiev's eight-hour-long *War and Peace* (which I showed on two consecutive nights). Armand Hammer bragged that he had used his contacts in the Kremlin to help Olga, who was then 18, escape the Soviet Union in 1974. When we broke that first night for the first course of the Russian dinner on my terrace, I gingerly asked her about Hammer. She painted a picture of an immensely kind, considerate, and generous man, who had spared no effort to help her and her family re-establish itself in the West. Needless to say, the Hammer she described, as we consumed cold borscht from Brighton Beach, could not have been more different from the heartless, manipulative, and devious Armand Hammer in my book, a difference that made me realize that biography, like any other artful pursuit, depends on the perspective adopted by the biographer.

# CHAPTER THIRTY-FOUR

# THE CURIOUS CASE
# OF JEFFREY EPSTEIN

In Joel and Ethan Coen's 1991 movie, *Barton Fink*, a writer in pursuit of the big story accidently winds up befriending a serial murderer who lives next door. That dark comedy's ironic juxtaposition did not escape me in August 2019 when Jeffrey Epstein was found hanged in the Metropolitan Correctional Center in New York and the mushrooming scandal involving him threatened to engulf three of the wealthiest men in America, two former presidents of the United States and the second son of the queen of England. For me, his sad saga began unfolding some 33 years earlier when I was still investigating a world-class financial mystery in Europe that began with the hanging of the Italian banker Roberto Calvi, known as "God's banker," under Blackfriars Bridge in London on June 18, 1982. It involved an even more sinister financial scandal that threatened to bring down the Vatican Bank and cause what Pope John Paul warned would be "a catastrophe of unimaginable proportions in which the Church will suffer the gravest damage." Archbishop Paul Marcinkus, the Vatican Bank's head and a principal player in the scandal, had guided me through some of the inner sanctums of the Vatican, but, even with his help, the missing $1.5 billion funds remained a mystery. I was still trying to unravel the financial threads of the missing money when I encountered Jeffrey Epstein on October 31, 1987.

I had gone that evening with Jimmy Goldsmith and his 35-year-old daughter Isabel to a Halloween party at the Upper East Side home in Manhattan of Coco Brown, a movie producer who rarely, if ever, made a movie. Soon after our arrival, a young man in his mid-30s with a big, toothy smile sauntered up to us, hugged Isabel, and introduced himself as Jeffrey Epstein. He was with his brother Mark Epstein. "A surfeit of Epsteins," remarked Isabel, who knew Jeffrey Epstein from London.

The next day Epstein called me and said there was something he would like to talk to me about. We met for tea at the Mayfair Hotel on Sixty-Fifth Street the following Thursday. He told me at the outset he had information that I might be interested in for my Wall Street Babylon column in *Manhattan Inc.* He said he had learned it in the course of his business dealings.

"What is your business?" I asked him.

"I'm sort of a financial bounty hunter," he said, with an I-know-more-than-you grin that rarely left his face throughout our tea. He explained that he hunted down hidden money for a fee. He described the convoluted network of hiding money in Andorra, Fiji, Gibraltar, and the Cayman Islands in such vivid detail that it sounded like he might be in the business of hiding as well as finding it. He dropped many legendary names in the realm of money machinations—such as Adnan Khashoggi, Aristotle Onassis, and Sheikh Zayed bin Sultan Al Nahyan—but his tales, though intriguing, didn't quite add up. For one thing, I knew Khashoggi well enough through Jimmy Goldsmith to doubt that he needed help from Epstein in either hiding or finding hiding places for money. I asked him about the only hidden money of interest to me, which was the $1.5 billion from the Vatican Bank that vanished into shell companies in Panama. Epstein knew nothing about those funds. As we finished the tea, I mentioned I was leaving for Spain on Monday.

"How do you go?" he asked.

"Iberia Airlines." I added that I always flew coach.

"If you like, I can upgrade you to first class. Much better food."

"How?"

"Drop your ticket off with my doorman tomorrow morning. It won't cost you a penny."

Jeffrey lived in a one-bedroom apartment at Solow Tower at 265 East Sixty-Sixth Street. As instructed, I brought my ticket to the doorman on Friday morning, and Friday evening I picked it up with a first-class sticker and a first-class seat assignment. I flew to Malaga, Spain, and back in great style and comfort.

When I mentioned Epstein's ticket trick to Jimmy Goldsmith, he warned me to be careful with him. It was good advice I stupidly did not immediately heed.

In December 1988, I needed to go to Los Angeles to interview associates, and possibly victims, of the so-called Junk Bond King Mike Milken, now involved in a growing scandal. When I told Epstein about it, he not only converted my coach tickets to first class, but he also insisted that I stay at his house in Santa Monica. He had rented the two-bedroom house near the pier for his girlfriend Eva Andersson, a former Miss Sweden in her third year of medical school at UCLA. Since I needed to be in Los Angeles for weeks for my interviews, I happily stayed at Eva's house. She couldn't have been a better host.

Epstein had another surprise for me in L.A. It came in the form of a call from the actress Morgan Fairchild. At his behest, she met me for lunch at the Polo Lounge at the Beverly Hills Hotel. She was preparing for her role in the upcoming *Murphy Brown* TV series, and Epstein had told her I could tell her all she needed to know about investigative journalism. It was a subject that typically made people's eyes glaze over, but Fairchild seemed keenly interested. I dined with her many times in L.A.

Back in New York, Epstein introduced me to a diverse group

of his acquaintances. We had lunch with Leslie Orgel, a Salk Institute theoretical chemist who, over lunch at the Italian Pavilion, said that human life might have been seeded on earth by a higher intelligence in the universe, a theory that greatly interested Epstein; Vera Wang, a former *Vogue* editor, who had just opened a bridal-dress store on Madison Avenue; Evangeline Carey, the wife of former governor Hugh Carey, who shared an office with Epstein at Villard House; and Stuart Pivar, a Brooklyn-born scientist who made a fortune in plastic containers and helped endow the New York Academy of Art. Epstein also took me to several events at the Academy of Art, including his former girlfriend Paula Fisher's wedding celebration (which ended in a food fight between Pivar and Barbara Guggenheim).

It was all dazzling fun, but in late 1988 a dark cloud began to overshadow the festivities. It began when I tried to board an ANA flight to Jakarta that Epstein had upgraded to first class. The ANA representative told me it could not be a first-class ticket, which cost $6,000, because I had only paid $655. When I pointed to the first-class sticker, she said anyone could steal one and paste it in. I was unceremoniously moved to coach.

I later asked one of his girlfriends about the upgrade. She told me it only works about one in three times, and that Epstein would send her to the airline counter to check to spare himself the potential embarrassment. She explained he had obtained the stickers from a friend and, after pasting them on, entered the airline's computer to make the seat assignments. I suspected Epstein had obtained the first-class stickers from Pan Am Airlines, of which he was working with Steven Hoffenberg in a failed attempt to get control. I had met Hoffenberg with Epstein at the Regency Deli in New York. Epstein told me he owned a bill-collection agency. Hoffenberg was a tall man with dark sinister eyes who looked the part of a tough repo collector.

The cloud darkened further when I got a frantic call from Dick

Snyder, the CEO of Simon & Schuster, the publisher of my book *Deception: The Invisible War Between the KGB and the CIA*. Snyder had met Epstein at a dinner at my house. He told me he had given Epstein $70,000 to invest in a deal to take over the chemical company Pennwalt. He told me that after sending the money, he had not received the necessary papers and that Epstein was not returning his calls. He called one of the principals in the deal, who said he had never heard of Snyder. I told him I would look into it.

Epstein was in Palm Beach at the time, but he had given me a computer program called Carbon Copy so I could get real-time quotes on the stocks I was interested in. It was another way of showing off his technological prowess. The program allowed me to remotely access his computer via my telephone modem. I decided to use it to find out what was going on with my publisher's investment in Pennwalt. Remotely, I clicked on "home" on Epstein's computer and went to the archive, where I found a file of recent transactions. In it were dozens of letters from people demanding the return of their investments, including Vera Wang's father, C.C. Wang, the owner of a pharmaceutical company. Another was from a financier involved in the takeover deal of Pennwalt who reported that a check from Epstein for $83,000 had bounced a second time. The sums were considerable, but from the one-way correspondence, I could not determine if they were repaid. One set of transactions involved Steven Hoffenberg, the person who may have indirectly provided my first-class stickers. Rather than demanding repayment, he wanted to transfer large sums to Epstein from Associated Life and United Fire, two small insurance companies that Hoffenberg controlled. As I read through this material, I found nothing about Snyder's money, but I grew increasingly queasy about Epstein.

In early 1989, I wrote my Wall Street Babylon column about a small-time grifter trying to pass as a big-time financier. Although this character was modeled on Epstein, I didn't identify him by name. The point of the column was that the takeover game had become so lucrative that even operators without money—who had their power breakfasts in the Regency Deli instead of the Regency Hotel—could play in it. All that was needed was enough charm to convince investors they too could score like the big corporate raiders. It was titled "The Win-Win Game." After it was published, Epstein stopped speaking to me.

Epstein, meanwhile, had reportedly scored well in the win-win game. I heard of his success from Eva, who had married Glenn Dubin, a financier with whom I invested. Epstein had moved from his one-bedroom apartment in the Solow Tower, first to a townhouse that had belonged to the Iranian government before it had been seized by the US government in 1977, and then to a mansion on Seventy-First Street. That mansion had previously belonged to Les Wexner, the billionaire chairman of L Brands, which owned Victoria's Secret, The Limited, and other retail chains, and who Epstein bragged he was advising. According to other mutual friends, I learned that he acquired a large ranch in New Mexico, a mansion in Paris with a stuffed baby elephant in the living room, and a private airliner. I was puzzled as to how Epstein, who only a few years earlier had bounced checks, had come into this windfall. Were his apparent newfound riches the product of his own financial skills? Or, in light of his reported association with politicians, power brokers, and financiers, was he a larger-than-life version of F. Scott Fitzgerald's Jay Gatsby?

These doubts escalated when I had lunch in 1994 with Alfred Taubman, who, among other things, owned Sotheby's. Taubman, who I had met at Jimmy Goldsmith's home in Mexico in 1989, told me over a long lunch at San Pietro on Fifty-Fourth Street of his discovery that Epstein had extorted a kickback of $65,000 from the commission due to Sotheby's real estate brokerage arm from Wexner's original purchase of the mansion on Seventy-First Street. According to Taubman, Epstein, to whom Wexner had given a power of attorney, threatened to block the deal unless he got his kickback, which he called a "finder's fee." Even though it was possibly illegal to pay a share of the commission to someone who was not a registered real estate broker, Sotheby's paid him. When he found out, Taubman demanded Epstein repay Sotheby's, but Epstein coldly refused. Taubman went directly to Wexner, with whom he had served on several boards. But Wexner laughed off the kickback, saying Epstein had extracted it simply to demonstrate that he could reduce Sotheby's commission, and, just that week, he had given it back to Wexner as a "present."

So I was not surprised in 1996 when the corporate detective Jules Kroll told me he was conducting a discreet investigation into Epstein's background. I owed Kroll a favor since he had helped me in my Vatican Bank investigation by providing me a videotape of a reconstruction of the hanging of Roberto Calvi that proved that "God's banker," rather than committing suicide, had been murdered. Kroll sent one of his top investigators, Thomas Helsby, to interview me about Epstein. Over our lunch at Petaluma, Helsby told me that a board member of Wexner's company, concerned about Epstein's influence over Wexner, had personally hired the Kroll agency to find out about Epstein's past. Its investigators had already determined that Epstein had not been truthful in his claims that he had academic credentials. In fact, he had dropped out of college, worked as a roofer in Brooklyn, and faked his résumé to get a teaching job at Dalton, the private school on New York's Upper East Side. This did not come as a total shock. Even though Epstein told me he had a degree in nuclear science, I had always assumed that, like Jay Gatsby, he had invented his credentials as well as himself.

The real shock came 10 years later when I read that Epstein had been arrested in Palm Beach for soliciting underage women to perform sexual acts. I knew he liked the company of highly attractive women but not underage ones. The women he had introduced me to all had substantial careers: doctors, actresses, art dealers, theater producers, academics, money managers, and filmmakers. It didn't occur to me that he would consider having sex with underage girls. Such ugly perversity was not only criminal, but it also made him vulnerable to blackmail. Evidently, he had fallen prey to the "master of the universe" complex in thinking he was immune from federal law and the rules of civil decency. In true master of the universe style, he made a deal with the Department of Justice, pleaded guilty to two charges of soliciting and underage prostitute, and went to prison in Florida for 13 months.

After a hiatus of some 24 years, I heard from Epstein in April 2013. He said he had read an article I had written in the *New York Review of Books* on Nabokov, and he would love to discuss it with me. He invited me for tea the next afternoon at his home.

I went because I wanted to see this mansion he acquired from Wexner. On the outside of his house on East Seventy-First Street, just off Fifth Avenue, was a plaque with the initials "JE." A tall, striking woman in her late 20s answered the door with a friendly smile. She introduced herself as Jennifer and showed me to the anteroom. The walls contained photographs of rich and powerful men posed with Epstein. There were three photos of him with Bill Clinton. (As I would later learn, the visitor logs at the White House showed that Epstein visited Clinton there no fewer than 17 times.) When Jennifer reappeared, she asked if I would like an omelet or anything else to eat and led me to a long rectangular table in the dining room.

"Just tea," I replied.

A few minutes later, Epstein came in accompanied by Svetlana, another of Jeffrey's assistants. She was almost as tall as Jennifer. Then a third assistant came in the room, named Leslie, who served us tea and left with Jennifer.

Epstein, wearing a tracksuit, sat at the head of the table. Except for his gray hair, he looked very much the same as the last time I saw him, in 1989. His glistening know-it-all smile had not changed. He began the conversation by saying that Nabokov was his favorite writer and he kept a copy of *Lolita* next to his bed and on his plane. He wanted to know what the author was like. The last time I had spoken to Nabokov and his wife, Vera, had been more than a half century before, and my memory of him was dim, but I recounted a few vivid impressions. I then asked Epstein what he was working on.

He told me his main interest was cutting-edge artificial intelligence. He was funding a group in Hong Kong to produce "the world's smartest robot," which would have "more empathy than a woman." He said one problem his robot team had was simulating the feel of human skin. As he discussed the progress on the prototype robot, I couldn't help thinking of George Bernard Shaw's play *Pygmalion*. In it, a phonetics professor, Henry Higgins, attempts to implant his intelligence in a young flower girl and winds up enthralled with his own creation. I asked, "What would the robot be used for?"

"The elderly," he answered. His theory was that advances in medicine and biotechnology would result in an increasingly large population of centenarians, many of whom would need 24-hour assistance. Empathetic robots would provide it.

I changed the subject. "How do you make money these days?"

"I manage money for a few select clients," he replied.

I knew that his guilty plea to felony charges in Florida in 2008, including soliciting sex from a minor, would have made it difficult, if not impossible, to get a license to manage other people's money in the US. So how was he making his money? "Do you have an offshore hedge fund?" I asked.

His smile broadened. "Hedge funds are a thing of the past. But there are wealthy individuals in various parts of the world who need help protecting their assets. I help them."

In the anteroom, along with the Clinton photos were photos of Epstein with Saudi prince Mohammed bin Salman and Emirate prince Mohammed bin Zayed, some in beachwear and with snorkel gear. I asked, "Are these clients in the Middle East?"

He answered that some were and that he was planning to buy a house in Riyadh since that was becoming the new center of international finance.

"What about Russia? Any clients there?" I asked.

He shrugged and said he often flew to Moscow to see Vladimir Putin.

I found this hard to swallow. He was, after all, a fabulist, as I learned from the Kroll report. Nor did it make any sense to me that powerful financiers would trust someone like Epstein to secure or hide their money. After all, they knew that he had made a deal with the Department of Justice to avoid federal charges. How could they be sure he wouldn't make another deal to reveal their secret funds?

When I asked him further about the service he performed for these men, he called it jokingly a "reverse Ponzi scheme," explaining that instead of making it appear there was money when there was none, which is the essence of a real Ponzi scheme, he made it appear there was no money when actually there was money.

I understood that a wolf-in-sheep's-clothing strategy might be useful in warfare, but why would a wealthy person want to seem poorer than he was? Who would pay him for such a service?

He said there was no shortage of rich spouses, without a prenuptial agreement, seeking a divorce. By reducing their apparent assets, he would save them a small fortune.

I was unsure whether or not he was speaking hypothetically. But if he found potential clients for his reverse Ponzi strategy among people interested in minimizing alimony, he could likely also find them among individuals wanting to minimize their tax liability and the exposure of ill-gotten gains. Before I had the chance to ask him more about his business, Leslie opened the door a crack and announced, "Leon is here."

Svetlana rose to her feet. I assumed it was my signal to leave, but Epstein seemed in no rush to end our chat. He went on for another 15 minutes discussing his curious enterprise.

Then, walking me out, he introduced me to a man patiently waiting in the anteroom with Jennifer. It was Leon Black, who I had met once before during my investigation of the junk bond world, where he worked for Mike Milken. He was now head of Apollo Global Management, a private equity fund with over $300 billion in assets, and had a reported personal net worth of $10 billion. He was also one of the most important collectors of modern art in the world. I wondered what was he doing patiently waiting in the anteroom of Epstein's home. His very presence there made me realize that I had underestimated Epstein's continued connections with the rich and powerful.

I saw Epstein only occasionally over the next six years. Almost all our meetings were in that same room in his house for afternoon tea. New pictures were on his walls that showed him with unlikely acquaintances. Indeed, at one point, he talked about putting together a dinner at his home with the linguist Noam Chomsky, the movie director Woody Allen, former president Bill Clinton, and the living God, the Dalai Lama. If it occurred, I was not invited.

Only once did we go out for lunch. In May 2014, we went on a walk into Central Park to a hot dog stand with two of his friends. He called its fare "the best hot dog outside of Coney Island" while passing one to each of us.

Four of his female assistants, including Jennifer and Svetlana, accompanied us. They walked at a discreet distance, two on either side of our group, keeping pace in a way that caused Epstein to jokingly call them "my Russian wolfhounds." They were more functional than that, since they carried, in case Epstein needed them, Fiji water, cash, and cell phones.

I got the opportunity to find out more about Epstein's female staff through a chance meeting. A week after our walk in Central Park, I ran into Jennifer in Maison Kayser, a café on Third Avenue and Seventy-Fourth Street. She said she was buying croissants for a trip she was taking to Little St. James, Epstein's private island in the Caribbean, that afternoon. Over coffee, I asked how she had met him.

She had come to New York from Minnesota to be a model and wound up in a difficult relationship with a man. Enter Epstein, who rescued her from it and gave her a job as an assistant. He also gave her free use of an apartment on East Sixty-Sixth (near where he had lived in 1989). When she told him that she dreamed of being a chef, he paid for her to take courses at the Culinary Institute of America, arranged a part-time internship for her at a steak house, and found her a full-time position in the food industry.

I next asked her about Svetlana, the assistant who had sat across from me at my first tea with Epstein. She told me Svetlana was now studying dentistry at NYU at Epstein's expense. At that point, I recalled that Eva Andersson, his former girlfriend, had, with Epstein's help, become a doctor. She became the chief doctor for NBC News and founded with her husband the Dubin Breast Cancer Center at Mount Sinai Hospital. A chef, a dentist, a doctor, an empathetic robot? I wondered after speaking to Jennifer how far Epstein's Pygmalion ambitions went.

I spoke to Epstein on February 25, 2019, just after Robert Kraft, the wealthy owner of the New England Patriots, was charged with two counts of soliciting sex in a massage parlor in Jupiter, Florida. The police claimed his arrest was part of an investigation into suspected human trafficking. Epstein had pleaded guilty to two counts of soliciting sex in Florida and said the difference was that Kraft went to a massage parlor while Epstein had hired women from massage parlors to come to his house. Both cases involved long-term police surveillance. Epstein pointed out, "In my case, the police had gone through my garbage for months and had my house under surveillance according to the report. No one had asked the question how they could allow young women to go in and out, and not protect them and question them if they truly believed they were underage." His outrage, if I understood him correctly, was that if the local police had acted sooner and prevented underage girls from coming to his house, he would have been spared the need to make the deal with the federal government.

After the *Miami Herald* published an exposé of his exploitation of women in November 2018, Epstein sought help, as I learned from one of his close friends, Steve Bannon, Trump's former strategic advisor. Epstein befriended Bannon after Trump fired him in 2017 and even planned a trip with him on his plane to the United Arab Emirates and Saudi Arabia. Now he sought Bannon's help restoring his public image. Bannon suggested Epstein should go public by giving an exclusive interview on CBS's *60 Minutes* or another high-profile TV show. Bannon then became his media coach and schooled him on how to take control of a television interview. To this end, in March 2019, Bannon prepared him through a sham *60 Minutes* interview in the living room of Epstein's mansion with a TV camera crew and indoor lighting. Playing the role of a *60 Minutes* interviewer, Bannon fired questions at Epstein about the source of his money, his guilty plea, and his relations with women. Although Epstein thought he did well in this trial run, according to a person who attended this mock interview, he decided against having Bannon try to arrange a real *60 Minutes* interview.

The ax finally came down on Epstein on July 6, 2019. After flying back from Paris, he was arrested at Teterboro Airport by an FBI SWAT team. He was hauled off to the Metropolitan Correctional Center (MCC), the federal detention center in Manhattan. The indictment charged that Epstein had recruited women under the legal age for sex between 2002 and 2005 and engaged in sex trafficking. He would not be a free man ever again.

Epstein was found dead on the floor of a jail cell at the MCC on 6:30 a.m. on August 11, 2019. How did he die in a locked cell just

15 feet away from two guards? Barbara Sampson, the chief medical examiner in New York City, determined the cause of death was suicide by hanging—a finding she said was based on a "careful review of all investigative information." The presumed motive was that he could not face remaining in prison.

Martin Weinberg and other of Epstein's defense lawyers expressed to me doubts about this finding. Unlike the coroner, they had direct knowledge of Epstein's state of mind less than eight hours prior to his death, since they had met with him in the MCC. Telling Epstein that they were about to file an appeal for bail with additional security measures designed to meet the judge's stated concerns, in addition, Weinberg told him there was a high-level Department of Justice witness who had agreed to swear that the prosecutors in Florida had illicitly transferred material about Epstein to prosecutors in New York, an error that provided grounds for Epstein's indictment to be quashed. Since when they left Epstein seemed buoyed over these developments, and expressed hope about being released on bail, his lawyers could not see any clear motive for him killing himself a few hours later.

In any case, his sudden demise added to the mystery of the source of Epstein's wealth. According to the court filings released after his death, he had $577,672,654 in cash, bank deposits, and property. This meant in the 30 years since I first met him, he had gone from being a small-time grifter, who faked airplane upgrades and bounced checks, to a tycoon who had amassed over a half-billion-dollar fortune, even after he had paid out tens of millions of dollars to settle lawsuits by his "Jane Doe" victims, as was required by his plea agreement, and vast legal fees. He had also given over $100 million for scientific research at Harvard, MIT, and other universities. He told me in 2013 that he was working with Bill Gates to create a multi-trillion-dollar philanthropic fund, a claim that I did not believe. Yet the New York Times, partly confirmed, reported after his death that Epstein told Gates he had "access to trillions of dollars of his clients' money that he could put in the proposed charitable fund."

But how could he have clients since he could not legally manage other people's money after his felony conviction? He also had no known business enterprises other than shell companies registered in the Virgin Islands.

The first postmortem question that arose involved the origin of Epstein's money. How did he go from bouncing checks in the late 1980s to having private planes in the early 1990s? The person in a position to answer it was Steven Hoffenberg. When Epstein introduced me to Hoffenberg in 1988, he had an armed bodyguard and struck me as an odd business associate of Epstein's. Seven years later, I discovered Hoffenberg was a major-league swindler. In 1994, he was charged with running a massive Ponzi scheme during the time he was involved with Epstein, in which some $475 million was stolen from clients and banks. He pleaded guilty and was sentenced to 20 years in prison. But a large part of the missing funds was not recovered.

When Hoffenberg got out of prison in 2013, he went, uninvited, to Epstein's home to demand money that he claimed Epstein owed him. According to Epstein's version of the confrontation, Epstein told Hoffenberg that he was crazy and threw him out. But Hoffenberg told a different story. In a recorded interview in September 2019, Hoffenberg said that Douglas Leese, a London financier, had introduced him to Epstein in 1987 as someone who could help him in his criminal enterprise. Leese, who had employed Epstein to do money laundering for his clients, recommended Epstein, according to Hoffenberg, because Epstein had a "criminal mindset." So Hoffenberg hired him to help in the Ponzi scheme for part of the loot. If true, it could go some way to explaining how Epstein got his windfall. But the problem with Hoffenberg's story was that Epstein was never implicated by either the state or federal prosecutors of the Ponzi scheme, not even after Hoffenberg and his associates at

Towers Financial cooperated with the investigations. Why didn't Hoffenberg name Epstein as a participant in the swindle? Was Hoffenberg counting on Epstein to hide part of his money since he had often bragged about his ability to hide money? What Hoffenberg claimed after getting out of prison, though Epstein denied it, was that some of Epstein's money belonged to him.

Wherever Epstein's original windfall came from, it was established after his death that at least two billionaires paid him hundreds of millions of dollars long after Hoffenberg was arrested. Presumably, he provided for them a benefit. And from everything he and others told me, it was financial in nature.

One of them was Les Wexner. Born in 1937 in Dayton, Ohio, to parents of Russian Jewish origins, he made a multibillion-dollar fortune with his retail chains well before he befriended Epstein in the late 1980. My friend Alfred Taubman, who was Wexner's close friend and mentor, told me that Wexner granted Epstein power of attorney over his personal finances, made him a trustee on the board of the Wexner Foundation, and permitted him to choose models for Victoria's Secret fashion shows. By 1994 Epstein had so involved himself in Wexner's finances that Taubman pointedly asked Wexner about allowing Epstein such latitude. Wexner replied, "If you knew how much money he has made me, you wouldn't ask." As far as Wexner was concerned, his relationship with Epstein was all about money, but in July 2008, he discovered that Epstein had misappropriated millions off him by taking excessive fees and other means. He revealed after Epstein's death that Epstein repaid his foundation $46 million but claimed that was only part of the missing funds. It becomes a criminal matter when someone with a power of attorney misappropriates funds. The fact that Wexner never pursued the matter by informing the authorities raises a question about the nature of the services that Epstein was providing.

Leon Black was the second multibillionaire who paid large sums to Epstein for his services. Born in July 1951 in New York City, Black was the son of Eli Black, who headed United Brands Company. After becoming a top deputy to Michael Milken at Drexel Burnham Lambert, Leon Black cofounded Apollo Global Management, which became one of the largest private equity firms in America. He became friends with Epstein in the mid-1990s at a time when Epstein, nearing the peak of his political influence, was a frequent visitor at the Clinton White House. Soon afterward, they entered into a business relationship that lasted to 2017, and Epstein was made a trustee of the Debra and Leon Black Family Foundation.

According to a close associate of Jeffrey Epstein, Black broke off both the personal and the business relationship in 2018. After Epstein's death, Black said in a press release that he had paid Epstein for his advice on "tax strategy, estate planning and philanthropy." Although tax avoidance schemes could fall in a gray area, it was not unusual for wealthy men to pay brokers a fee of 5 to 10 percent of the money saved if they found a loophole in the tax code. According to Dechert LLP, a law firm hired at Black's request by Apollo's board, Black paid Epstein around $158 million from 2012 through 2017 for financial services, suggesting that Epstein had saved him at least $1.3 billion. But the means Epstein used became murkier when the *New York Times* revealed that, according to documents it reviewed, Black had paid Epstein at least $50 million in suspicious wire transfers that drew scrutiny of the Deutsche Bank, which handled them. And Black transferred money to other entities controlled by Epstein, supposedly as an investment. According to a lawsuit brought against Epstein's estate by the attorney general of the US Virgin Islands, Black, along with his personal holding companies, invested possibly as much as $154 million in the Southern Trust Company, a corporation that Epstein created in the Virgin Islands in 2013 to do DNA data research, but it produced no profits. Black, as was his right, did not explain the rationale for these investments.

I discussed Epstein's activities in 2020 with a financier who had known Epstein since the late 1990s. Like Wexner and Black, he was also a philanthropist and art collector. "Why did anyone give Epstein money?" I asked.

The financier told me about a proposition Epstein had once made him. Epstein told him that he could save him over $40 million in US taxes if he gave him $100 million to put through a maze of offshore nonprofit companies that he controlled, and the funds would wind up, free of taxes, in the financier's foundation. When the financier told Epstein that the scheme could amount to fraudulent tax evasion, Epstein replied that it was highly unlikely the IRS would unravel it, and if it did, he could protect the financier from any criminal exposure if he gave him total power of attorney over the funds, as if this ploy would provide an alibi for him to the IRS. Shaken by the criminal nature of the offer, the financier turned down Epstein's proposition. It is possible that other, less prudent investors entered into Epstein's reverse Ponzi scheme.

# EPILOGUE

# HALL OF MIRRORS

On September 25, 2017, *Hall of Mirrors* was featured in the 55th New York Film Festival at Lincoln Center. Directed by two talented sisters, Ines and Ena Talakic, the film centered on my investigative career, and I was the leading actor in it. How I became the focus of a biographic documentary is a story that originated some four years earlier.

Like many New York stories, it began with a party. On July 6, 2013, I went to a large gathering on the terrace of the economist Nouriel Roubini, who became known as "Dr. Doom" after he correctly predicted the financial meltdown in 2008. His terrace parties, not unlike my own, usually had a diverse mix of people. While wandering among the guests, I met Ines and Ena Talakic, who looked so much alike I initially mistook the sisters for twins. But they weren't. The older sister, Ena, was 27; Ines, the younger sister, was 26. They had been born in the former Yugoslavia. The Talakics left as children during the civil war, literally walking through a mine field to escape the civil war with their parents. They went first to Munich, Germany, and then to Milan, Italy. Ena went to film school in the Czech Republic; Ines, a concert pianist who had won the Amadeus piano competition for Mozart for all of Europe at the age of 14, went to music school in Italy. They then came to New York in 2011 to become documentary filmmakers. Even though they had only been in America for two years when we met, they spoke near-perfect English, as well as Italian, German, Serbian, and Spanish.

Initially, when they proposed making a full-length documentary about me, I was reluctant. I knew well from my experience of following news crews for my book *News from Nowhere* that a camera, or even a tape recorder, tends to unnerve interviewees. My experience as an actor was limited to two cameos. The first was a *Saturday Night Live* skit called "Prose and Cons" on October 2, 1981. I played the literary agent for a prisoner portrayed by 19-year-old Eddie Murphy, his first appearance on *Saturday Night Live*, in which he read a poem entitled "Kill My Landlord." The second cameo was in the movie *Wall Street 2: Money Never Sleeps* in November 2009. Oliver Stone gave me the silent role of the chairman of the New York Federal Reserve Bank in that film so I could have an inside perspective of moviemaking for a book I was writing. Neither cameo suggested I have a talent for acting, but the sisters were as persistent as they were charming. After the documentary filmmaker Eric Nadler told me, "Everyone needs a documentary to complete his career," I agreed to participate in their documentary.

Ena and Ines were extremely creative in their approach. They constructed a tent out of black material in the screening room of my apartment. They called it the black cocoon. I would sit in it in total darkness, and they would poke a camera through, turn on their filtered lights, and ask me questions about my interest in such subjects as deception, the CIA, Nixon's drug war, the JFK assassination, and other parts of my past. The first question was why I became a detective of international intrigue, whereas my sister Linda Nessel, who grew up with me, became a social worker who dedicated herself to helping people in need. Why had we chosen such different paths? It was not easy to answer. Linda, just two years younger, shared the same childhood homes as me, spent the same weekends at the country club, Cold Spring Harbor, went to the same public school, high school, and even college (although she always achieved higher grades than me). She also took many of the courses I took at Cornell, including those given by Andrew Hacker and Vladimir Nabokov. But we somehow turned out different. Unlike me, she had a clear vision of her future even in high school. She wanted to do social work and acted on it. She became a social worker, a career she pursued and succeeded in her entire life. In the movie *Match Point* directed by Woody Allen, the hero, who might have had a career as a tennis professional if the ball had dropped on the other side of the net in a match, said that it was luck, not genes, that determined a career. My career as a journalist also had an element of luck. After failing at an absurd attempt to produce *The Iliad*, I stumbled into an investigation of the Warren Commission by pure chance. The day I arrived back at Cornell happened to be November 22, 1963, the day JFK was shot, and speaking about the traumatic event to Professor Hacker that night at dinner set me on a path that led me to interview the commission's members and staff. It was that unique experience that taught me my talent lay in finding missing pieces in a mystery, but it might never have been published as a book if not for the accidental intervention of Hannah Arendt. Luck, of course, needs to be taken advantage of. By doing so, I had found a career as an investigator.

In another of these black cocoon interviews, they asked me why I had chosen to investigate conspiracies. "Why are you called a conspiracist?" Ena asked.

"It traces back to the JFK assassination," I answered, trying to reconstruct what had happened. Although my 1966 book *Inquest*, as well as everything I wrote on the subject, concluded that a lone gunman, Lee Harvey Oswald, had assassinated President Kennedy, by also showing that the Warren Commission had done an incomplete investigation, it opened up a Pandora's box of conspiracy theories that fueled a sizable enterprise for publishers, talk show hosts, and magazines.

In October 1966, John Berendt, the features editor at *Esquire*, asked me to write an article on the theories about who killed JFK.

"But there are dozens of theories," I replied.

"Great," he said. "Flesh them all out and list them. Include their selling points and drawbacks. We'll do one of our *Esquire* charts."

The *Esquire* article published in December 1966, and though it ridiculed all the theories I had collected, it further associated my name with conspiracy theories.

And, of course, conspiracies furnish many of the most enduring mysteries, including political cover-ups such as Watergate, financial scandals such as the Vatican machinations in the 1980s, and terrorist activities, such as the 9/11 attack. Indeed, over 90 percent of federal indictments against alleged terrorists since 1993 contain at least one conspiracy charge. So I saw my calling to investigate crimes without preemptively excluding the possibility that they might involve more than one perpetrator. For those who equated the questioning of received wisdom with conspiracy thinking, I was deemed a conspiracist.

Ena and Ines were also enterprising at reconstructing my visual past. They even discovered an 8-mm Kodachrome film reel from my childhood I had inherited from my mother, footage from my disastrous 1960 movie of *The Iliad*, and photographs from Jean Pigozzi's archives taken on yacht and plane trips with Jimmy Goldsmith.

Privacy, alas, is the first casualty of a documentary. Ines often rigged me up with a tiny wireless microphone at my Sunday terrace lunches, opera evenings, and other gatherings in my screening room. They had me wear spy glasses to record what I was seeing when I hung out in the lobby of the Bowery Hotel.

It was a curious experience being an actor in one's own life, an experience that made me realize how thin the line is dividing performance from ordinary behavior. As they unearthed forgotten parts of my life, I felt like I had entered a time machine. I re-experienced distant memories, some of which were not pleasant, that now became part of my life.

Ena and Ines had a wealthy friend, Chinh Chu, a partner at Blackstone, who allowed them to use his yacht and Gulfstream G4 for their film. The yacht, the SS *Libertas*, which was 129 feet long and had a crew of eight, took us to the Bahamas several times where they filmed me at such new pursuits as jet skiing through sandbars in the Exuma islands and trying to snorkel in an underwater Bahamian cave used to film a James Bond movie.

The high point for me was being taken by the sisters on a memory-jogging trip around the world. They wanted to film me reconstructing some of my global investigations for their camera, saying they needed action as well as "talking head" interviews. We left on April 6, 2015. Our first stop was the Beverly Hills Hotel in L.A., where I had stayed during my investigations of the Hollywood studios. It was a logical stopover since I had spent nearly 10 years on this investigation. It began in January 1997, when my friend Tina Brown, now the editor of the *New Yorker*, offered me an assignment writing about the financial underpinnings of movie-making. I was eager to accept it, if only to take a vacation from writing about the espionage machinations of the once and future Cold War, but quickly realized that getting information from studio executives was no easy task. Those I called had PR teams dedicated to protecting them against any unauthorized leak of studio secrets. My plan to sidestep these PR gatekeepers was to attend the coming ShoWest, a four-day movie industry event in Las Vegas in which studio executives meet directly with multiplex theater owners to pitch their studio's strategy for upcoming films. The problem was that ShoWest did not admit journalists, and, it turned out, the only way I could attend the event was to find a multiplex owner willing to accredit me as part of his team.

I turned to my friend Frederick Iseman for help. Born in

1952 in New York, Fred ran a boutique private equities company, Caxton-Iseman, which specialized in financing leveraged buyouts for medium-sized companies, including theater chains. I had helped launch his career in private equity 13 years earlier by introducing him to Jimmy Goldsmith, who immediately saw his uncanny talent for finding solutions to tricky problems. Could he find me a multiplex owner?

"I have just the person," Fred said. "He was just in my office." Fred's candidate was Thomas W. Stephenson Jr., who headed a medium-sized Dallas-based chain called Hollywood Theaters. "He has ambitions to become well-known," Fred said, "and would do anything to be part of a *New Yorker* story."

With a phone call from Fred, Stephenson agreed to accredit me to ShoWest and let me tag along with him and his team to meetings with Hollywood executives in Las Vegas.

For four days that March, I accompanied Stephenson to one after another of the studios' hospitality suites at Bally's Hotel. The meetings were relaxed. After offering us soft drinks, studio executives discussed their strategy for making money in the coming summer season. After each meeting, I collected the executives' business cards, which would become the prime sources for my future investigation of Hollywood that resulted, aside from the *New Yorker* piece, in two books on Hollywood—*The Big Picture* and *The Hollywood Economist*—and a lucrative gig as an expert witness in two endless Hollywood lawsuits.

Our next stop was Honolulu. I first had been there nearly a half century ago. That was also an eye-opening trip that came about unexpectedly on September 14, 1970. At that time, I was working on my PhD in the government department at Harvard, and Larry Schiller, an extremely enterprising photographer, called out of the blue and offered me $400 a day to work as a speechwriter on a Democratic senatorial campaign in Hawaii that he told me he was managing. His candidate was Cecil Heftel, a television magnate in Hawaii. Not only was the fee vastly more than I would be paid as a course assistant that term, but I had always wanted to see a political campaign from the inside. One problem, alas, was that I had no idea how to write a political speech. When I told Larry, he said, "You're a quick learner."

I accepted on condition I could have an assistant to make up for my deficiency. He agreed and I hired Terry Malick, who I had met at Harvard. I knew him to be a brilliant film writer and highly perceptive about politics. Unfortunately, that gig lasted less than a week. At our first staff meeting in Honolulu, Heftel's top honcho at the broadcasting network gave Larry two options.

"Choice number 1," he said in a steely but quiet voice, "I know how Hawaii works and I can give you input."

"And what is choice 2?" Larry asked.

"We can shut up and leave you alone."

To my shock, Larry answered, "Choice 2. Bye."

The executive left the room. Three hours later, Larry was fired. Terry and I meanwhile took the opportunity to travel around Hawaii. A week later, when the new campaign manager arrived, I returned to my teaching duties at Harvard and Terry went on to become a successful film director. His first film, *Badlands*, was released in 1973.

Now, for this second trip, my task was retracing the Hawaiian part of my investigation of Edward Snowden's defection in 2013. They planned to film the NSA base in Oahu, Hawaii, since it was the actual crime scene in the theft of 1.5 million files by Snowden. Considering the NSA's secrecy, that would not be easy. I had been advised that if any unauthorized persons drove into the base, they would be detained and individually questioned, but Ines and Ena said they needed the scene for their movie, so we drove in.

The security guards barely let us drive past the gate before stopping us. We remained there for over an hour to wait for the interrogation team to complete their work. When they asked me for my ID, I realized that I had left my passport in the hotel. "All I have is my Amex card," I said.

"That will do," the NSA security officer said.

At that point, I realized that the NSA had the capability of learning a great deal about my life from my Amex account. They called us out of the car and questioned us individually. Ines had a miniature spy camera mounted in the buttonhole of her dress that recorded sound and hi-fi video. It filmed her entire interrogation.

From the vantage point of where they were questioning me, I could see the so-called "tunnel" where Snowden worked and stole the NSA's secrets. I asked the woman questioning me about it.

"Everything on this base is secret," she answered politely. She asked me about the thesis of my book.

I told her it was about the failure of security procedures that allowed Snowden to compromise so many top-secret files.

She nodded to show she understood. She asked in a matter-of-fact voice, "Have you taken any pictures?"

I handed her my Samsung Galaxy phone, and she scrolled through all the photos I took in Hawaii and Beverly Hills. What I didn't tell her was that the two filmmakers were surreptitiously recording the entire scene, including her, for the opening scene of their documentary.

The next day we went to the teahouse in downtown Honolulu that Snowden had used for his anti-surveillance "crypto party" in December 2012. I wanted to better visualize this extraordinary event: Snowden, an NSA worker with top-secret clearance, invited others at the NSA to hear his rant against surveillance.

That night we hung out, as they say in Hawaii, with the performers of the same acrobatic troupe that had employed Snowden's girlfriend Lindsay Mills in 2013. This allowed me to meet and be filmed with acrobats who knew her and Snowden. Ena and Ines bonded with the troupe by going on a strenuous hike with them to the top of Diamondhead Mountain.

Our next stop was Japan, a country that has always fascinated me. Aside from dining with my friends in Tokyo, I went to the US Yokota Air Base, where Snowden had worked in 2009 and 2010. At the base, Ena and Ines filmed me interviewing, among others, the registrar of the school at which Snowden claimed to have taken graduate computer courses.

From Tokyo, we flew to Hong Kong, a city that evoked very powerful memories for me. I had gone in May 2014 to investigate Snowden's activities there prior to his defection to Moscow. My main contact was Sir David Tang, who I had been friends with since our trip to Vietnam in 1991. David, born in 1954, was in all but name the uncrowned prince of Hong Kong. His grandfather, Tang Shiu Kin, had made a fortune founding the Kowloon Motor Bus Company in 1933. David, after graduating King's College in London, went on to build his own fortune, creating the China Club in Hong Kong, Shanghai Tang, and the Pacific Cigar Company. He was also a concert pianist, author, and columnist for the Financial Times and had close connections in the Hong Kong government that could be helpful in my Snowden investigation. I was horrified to learn after I arrived that he had received a diagnosis of terminal cancer, which he called "the big C." He immediately needed a liver transplant and, given the long queue for organs in most of the world, his only hope of getting one was through his connections in mainland China. As the grim search went on, he, an inveterate believer in luck, invited me to the horse races at Happy Valley (the only legal gambling in Hong Kong), where he had a box in the clubhouse so he and his guests could watch the races on closed-circuit television while enjoying a continuous feast of Chinese food. When I arrived, he was seated with Sarah Ferguson, the Duchess of York. She had come to Hong Kong to accompany David and his wife Lucy to China when, and if, a liver was obtained.

Fergy proved to be not only a very kind and thoughtful person but also extremely skilled at picking winning horses for me. At the table, women in silk robes served us Peking duck and other delicacies as they took our bets. Afterward, we boarded David's yacht for a late-night cruise. On deck, David kept checking his phone, waiting for a text about the availability of a liver. When Fergy, as she liked to be called, asked him about his exercise regimen, he said that his only exercises were "jogging his memory, stretching his imagination, jumping to conclusions, and running for cover."

David insisted we come to his house in the New Territories the next day for lunch, Ping-Pong, and a swim and sent his Rolls-Royce to pick us up. His other guests that Sunday afternoon were Tony Leung, the Hong Kong movie star, and Will Topley, a British portrait artist. David had brought Topley to Hong Kong to give painting lessons to Leung, who was to be cast as an artist in the next James Bond movie. We played Ping-Pong, with David serving robotically. In the midst of lunch, David received a text that a liver had been found for him in Tientsin, China. That ended our stay at David's remarkable house in the New Territories. While David, Fergy, and Lucy prepared to immediately leave for China, Leung, Topley, and I returned by car to Hong Kong Island. It was the last I was to see of him. He survived the transplant but never fully recovered and died on August 29, 2017, in London.

On this trip, just one year after my time spent with David, Ena and Ines wanted to film me retracing Snowden's footsteps in Hong Kong two years earlier, including his alleged visit to the Russian consulate. To go to the consulate I needed a new suit, so we went to Sam's Tailor store that morning in Kowloon, and the sisters filmed Sam fitting it and me wearing it out of the store that afternoon. They also filmed me on the ferry between Kowloon and Hong Kong, on Victoria Peak overlooking the city, and on a giant Ferris wheel, where, trying to replicate a scene in Orson Welles's *Third Man*, Ena asked me if I had ever worked as a spy. I answered that a journalist by profession is a spy.

After four days in Hong Kong, we flew to Moscow on the same

Aeroflot flight that Snowden took in 2013. In Moscow, we stayed at the National Hotel, a czarist-era hotel where I had stayed on all my trips to Moscow since 1960 because it overlooked the Kremlin.

In Moscow, I arranged filmed interviews with a number of former Russian intelligence officers I had long wanted to meet. One was Oleg Nechiporenko, the former KGB officer who, more than a half century earlier, had been in contact with Lee Harvey Oswald in Mexico less than two months before Kennedy was assassinated in Dallas, making him the last known intelligence officer to deal with Oswald. Nechiporenko now explained to me that in September 1963 he had been posted to the KGB station in Mexico City in the guise of a consular officer. His real job was assessing would-be defectors who walked into the Soviet embassy to sell secrets or otherwise offer their services to Russia. On September 30, 1963, just as tensions between the Kennedy administration and Fidel Castro were reaching the boiling point, he assessed two American candidates who walked in of their own volition to the Soviet embassy within hours of each other. The first one, a tough crew-cut man with a square jaw, was a US Air Force enlisted man who wanted to sell military secrets to Moscow. The second one was an ex-Marine who identified himself as Lee Harvey Oswald. According to Nechiporenko, Oswald said he had lived in Russia from 1959 to 1962 and, after he returned to the US, became dissatisfied with the Kennedy administration's policies and had been arrested for protesting US actions against Cuba.

He asked Oswald, "Why have you come to the embassy?"

Oswald answered that he needed the Russian embassy to back up his request for a Cuban visa. Nechiporenko saw potential in Oswald but needed to check his story with KGB headquarters in Moscow. He therefore told Oswald to return in a day.

"Did you ever see him again?" I asked.

"No, he never returned."

"What about the other walk-in that day, the air force man?"

The KGB knew the CIA had been photographing everyone who entered the Soviet embassy in 1963, and therefore he assumed it must have taken photographs that day of both the air force man and Oswald. His real surprise came seven weeks later. After Oswald was arrested for the assassination, a photo of the air force walk-in was sent by the CIA to the FBI and labeled "Oswald." He wondered why the CIA would misinform the FBI. This photograph also misled the public and led to 50 years of speculation about the so-called "Second Oswald."

"Did you think it was an innocent mix-up?" I asked Nechiporenko.

He shrugged with a complicit smile on his face. "We never assume the CIA is innocent."

I smiled to myself thinking how, after more than a half century, I was still trying to find missing pieces in the JFK assassination puzzle.

Nechiporenko left the room, still wearing his wireless microphone. Ena needed to retrieve it for the next interview and ran after him. When she finally caught up to him in the hotel lobby, she could hear on her earpiece him speaking in Russian on his cell phone. The CIA says there is no such thing as an ex-KGB officer. If that is true, Nechiporenko was presumably reporting to his KGB control officer on his interview with me.

That evening we went to a performance of the *Le Corsair* ballet at the Bolshoi. Ena and Ines hoped they might run into Snowden there since he had been seen there before. He was not in attendance, but we enjoyed the performance all the same.

Our last Moscow breakfast took place at Dr. Zhivago, my favorite restaurant in Moscow. Afterward, we flew back to New York, completing the nearly month-long global loop. Upon our return, Ena and Ines filmed interviews with many people who were part of my professional life, including my longtime agent, Mort Janklow, and my Knopf editor, Jonathan Segal. They also filmed the publication party given by Dan and Joanna Rose for my book on Snowden. Unfortunately, during that party, Ena, strained from carrying the heavy camera, dramatically fainted just as Henry Kissinger walked in the door. Ines screamed in panic. Kissinger, who was used to being the focus when he entered a room, was confused, he told me later, to see that the center of attention was a girl on the floor.

After filming me for nearly three years, Ena and Ines culled the hundreds of hours of footage into the 90-minute-long documentary *Hall of Mirrors*. I first saw it on July 29, 2017, in the Soho loft of film director Bennett Miller. This screening came about because of a serendipitous encounter I had with Bennett four nights earlier on Bleeker and Lafayette Streets. He was in the midst of a lively conversation about the just-released *Mueller Report* with a man and woman who I didn't immediately recognize. When Bennett called the man "Warren" and referred to his movie *Reds*, I realized his friends were Warren Beatty and Annette Benning. At Warren's invitation, we went back to their rented apartment on Bond Street, where Annette made popcorn for us. When Bennett, who was a friend of Ena and Ines, asked me about the progress of their documentary, Warren expressed an interest in seeing the film. So Bennett arranged to screen it that Saturday night in his home.

After Ena and Ines hooked up their digital device, the lights went out, and the film began with Michael Mukasey, a former attorney general of the United States, introducing me at a lunch at the Harvard Club: "Edward Jay Epstein's writing stands in relation to what passes today as investigative journalism as a Vermeer stands in relation to a paint-by-numbers creator. Vermeer was a genius with light; Edward Jay Epstein is a genius with shining light on his subjects." For the next 90 minutes, the Talakic sisters' interviewees talked about me as at a memorial, making me feel like the ghost of the deceased grandfather in Woody Allen's movie *Everyone Says I Love You*, watching testimonials about him at his funeral as he danced a jig to the song "Enjoy Yourself, It's Later Than You Think."

When the lights came back on, Annette told Ena and Ines that she loved their work, while Warren, more reserved, asked if they could screen it again for him in a regular theater with a big screen and an audience. Elated by his reaction, they were on the verge of renting the Walter Reade Theater in Lincoln Center when, by sheer coincidence, the New York Film Festival accepted *Hall of Mirrors* as one of its feature-length documentaries to be shown at the same Walter Reade Theater.

In the Q&A that followed the film, the moderator asked me if investigative journalism is on the decline. My reply was not overly optimistic. "If investigative reporting is indeed on the wane, the fault lies not in a lack of diligence, enterprise, or intelligence by younger journalists but in the changing world. A half century ago it was possible for someone like me to walk in and see, without the disintermediation of a PR team, members of a presidential commission that just had investigated the assassination of a president. Today access to sensitive information is so tightly protected by communications officers, litigious lawyers, nondisclosure agreements, and PR teams that investigative journalists face a truly daunting barrier." Time changes everything.

# ACKNOWLEDGMENTS

Many of the investigations I did had their origins in the *New Yorker*, the *Atlantic*, *New York* magazine, *Vanity Fair*, *The Public Interest*, and the *New York Review of Books*. I am deeply indebted to their editors, including William Shawn, William Whitworth, Clay Felker, Tina Brown, Harry Evans, and Irving Kristol, for providing the resources, time, and insights needed for these deep dives. In my seven decades of writing, I have reaped the bounty of perceptive and often brilliant editing.

I also benefited enormously from the efforts of wise teachers to educate me. I especially want to pay tribute to Allan Bloom, Andrew Hacker, and Vladimir Nabokov at Cornell and Edward Banfield, Daniel Patrick Moynihan, and James Q. Wilson at Harvard. I also appreciate the intellectual guidance I received from my fellow graduate student Bruce Kovner.

I am also grateful to the friends who read and made suggestions about the material in this book, including Renata Adler, Richard Bernstein, Howard Blum, Sid Blumenthal, David Braunschvig, Tina Brown, Kelly Burdick, Howard Dickman, Susana Duncan, Jeffrey Frank, Ben Gerson, Morton Janklow, Anne Jolis, Roger Kimball, Jonathan Leaf, Peter Pringle, Joe Rose, Michael Wolff, and Daniel Yergin.

I am indebted to Jean Pigozzi for providing me with photographs of our global trips with James Goldsmith and to Michael Endicott for providing photographs of my vacation with Richard Nixon.

The manuscript was greatly improved by the meticulous copy-editing and suggestions of Barbie Halaby. I am also grateful to

Amanda DeMatto at Encounter Books for the magnificent job she did in the production of this book.

Finally, I need to thank the filmmakers Ena and Ines Talakic for their documentary *Hall of Mirrors*. Its reconstruction of my investigations, including those in Moscow, Hong Kong, and Japan, helped awaken many of the memories in this book.

# INDEX